주한미군지위협정(SOFA)

군민관계
임시분과위원회 4

주한미군지위협정(SOFA)

군민관계 임시분과위원회 4

한국학술정보

| 머리말

미국은 오래전부터 우리나라 외교에 있어서 가장 긴밀하고 실질적인 우호 · 협력관계를 맺어 온 나라다. 6 · 25전쟁 정전 협정이 체결된 후 북한의 재침을 막기 위한 대책으로서 1953년 11월 한미 상호방위조약이 체결되었다. 이는 미군이 한국에 주둔하는 법적 근거였고, 그렇게 주둔하게 된 미군의 시설, 구역, 사업, 용역, 출입국, 통관과 관세, 재판권 등 포괄적인 법적 지위를 규정하는 것이 바로 주한미군지위협정(SOFA)이다. 그러나 이와 관련한 협상은 계속된 난항을 겪으며 한미 상호방위조약이 체결로부터 10년이 훌쩍 넘은 1967년이 돼서야 정식 발효에 이를 수 있었다. 그럼에도 당시 미군 범죄에 대한 한국의 재판권은 심한 제약을 받았으며, 1980년대 후반 민주화 운동과 함께 미군 범죄 문제가 사회적 이슈로 떠오르자 협정을 개정해야 한다는 목소리가 커지게 되었다. 이에 1991년 2월 주한미군지위협정 1차 개정이 진행되었고, 이후에도 여러 사건이 발생하며 2001년 4월 2차 개정이 진행되어 현재에 이르고 있다.

본 총서는 외교부에서 작성하여 최근 공개한 주한미군지위협정(SOFA) 관련 자료를 담고 있다. 1953년 한미 상호방위조약 체결 이후부터 1967년 발효가 이뤄지기까지의 자료와 더불어, 이후 한미 합동위원회을 비롯해 민 · 형사재판권, 시설, 노무, 교통 등 각 분과위원회의 회의록과 운영 자료, 한국인 고용인 문제와 관련한 자료, 기타 관련 분쟁 자료 등을 포함해 총 42권으로 구성되었다. 전체 분량은 약 2만 2천여 쪽에 이른다.

2024년 3월

한국학술정보(주)

| 일러두기

· 본 총서에 실린 자료는 2022년 4월과 2023년 4월에 각각 공개한 외교문서 4,827권, 76만 여 쪽 가운데 일부를 발췌한 것이다.

· 각 권의 제목과 순서는 공개된 원본을 최대한 반영하였으나, 주제에 따라 일부는 적절히 변경하였다.

· 원본 자료는 A4 판형에 맞게 축소하거나 원본 비율을 유지한 채 A4 페이지 안에 삽입하였다. 또한 현재 시점에선 공개되지 않아 '공란'이란 표기만 있는 페이지 역시 그대로 실었다.

· 외교부가 공개한 문서 각 권의 첫 페이지에는 '정리 보존 문서 목록'이란 이름으로 기록물 종류, 일자, 명칭, 간단한 내용 등의 정보가 수록되어 있으며, 이를 기준으로 0001번부터 번호가 매겨져 있다. 이는 삭제하지 않고 총서에 그대로 수록하였다.

· 보고서 내용에 관한 더 자세한 정보가 필요하다면, 외교부가 온라인상에 제공하는 『대한민국 외교사료요약집』 1991년과 1992년 자료를 참조할 수 있다.

| 차례

정/리/보/존/문/서/목/록					
기록물종류	문서-일반공문서철	등록번호	17780 11245	등록일자	2001-06-13
분류번호	729.419	국가코드		주제	
문서철명	SOFA 한·미국 합동위원회 군민관계 임시분과위원회 - 주한미군 군수품 도난 및 암거래 방지, 1971-73				
생산과	북미2과	생산년도	1971 - 1973	보존기간	영구
담당과(그룹)	미주	안보	서가번호	--	
참조분류					
권차명					
내용목차	1. 1971 - 10.18 제3차 회의 개최 2. 1972 3. 1973 * "729.419 SOFA 한 · 미국 합동위원회 군민관계 임시분과위원회," 도 보시오 1971 제1-5차, 1971				

마/이/크/로/필/름/사/항				
촬영연도	*롤 번호	화일 번호	후레임 번호	보관함 번호
	2007-9/Re-07-10	11	1-148	

1~2

결 번

넘버링 오류

1. 1971

- 10.18 제7차 회의 개최

3

증 천 ... 건 설

재 무 부

감사 821-2782 (7내 221) 1970. 12. 11

수신 외무부장관

참조 북미국장

제목 부정유출 양담배 단속을 위한협조 의뢰

1. 70.5.16 외무부 미이 723-9726 의 관련임

2. 우리나라는 연초의 제조 및 판매가 전매제도로 되어 있음으로 국내에서는 외국연초의 판매.양도.양수 및 소지가 법에 의하여 금지되고 있읍니다.

3. 그러나 한미군대지위협정 체결이후 주한 미군의 P.X 및 제기관에서 판매한 면세연초가 계속 다량으로 국내시장에 횡류되고 있어 양담배 근절을 위한 대통령 각하의 특별지시 이후 감시력을 총동원 하여 감시공무원으로 하여금 집중단속을 하고 있읍니다마는 제한된 감시공무원으로는 근절 시키기는 어려운 실정인바 이는 근본적인 대책이 시급하다고 사료되며 이는 공급량의 제한 입니다.

4. 당청 감시공무원에 의하여 적발 검거된 수량만 하더라도 상당한 량에 달하고 있어 우리나라 전매권의 침해는 물론 이로 인한 전매사업 수입에 막대한 지장을 초래하고 있읍니다(별표 2.3 참조)(70. 10월 현재)

5. 또한 미군 P.X 에서 통보된 70.1월-10월(10 개월) 양담배 판매실적과 P.X 이용권자 수를 감안할때 부정유출 양담배 추정량은 1일 1갑 조비로 보면 년간 4,447만갑이며 1일 2갑 조비로 계산해도 1,893만갑에 달하고 있읍니다 (별표 1 참조)

6. 따라서 국가재정 확보와 전매권의 옹호를 위하여 한미군대지위협정 계통을 통하여 미군측의 이해와 자발적인 협조가 이루어 지도록 적극 시정토록 협조하여 주시기 바랍니다.

71.3.10 (K)

4

12 DEC '70 11:48

5362

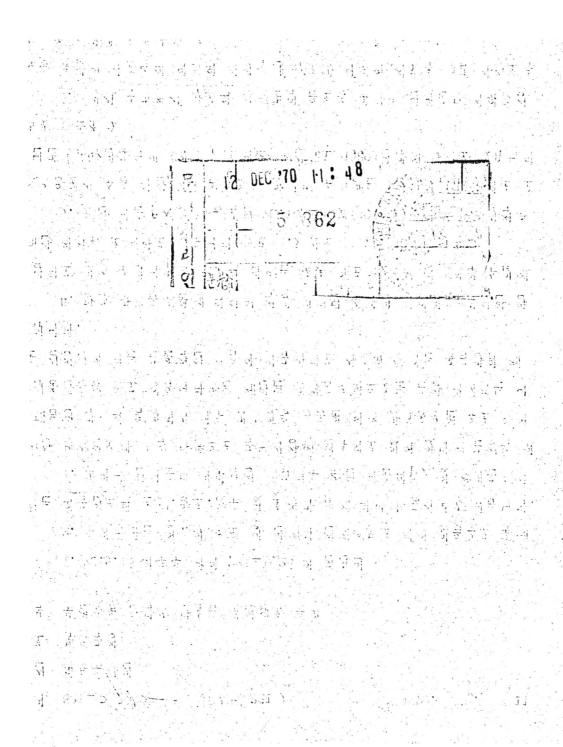

감시 821-　　　　　　　　　　　　　　　　　　　　1970. 12. 11

첨부 : 1. 양담배 부정유출 추정량 산출

2. 특수사건(월별)실적(10 말현재)

3. 양담배 검거실적(10말현재)및 69:70 10말 대비표. 끝

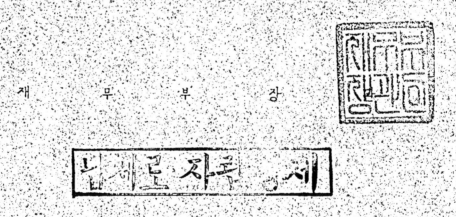

재 무 부 장

5

(별표 1)

양담배 부정유출 추정량 산출

18
25
53

1. 양담배 판매실적(미군측에서 통보)

월별	판매수량	금액	비고
1	6,912,130 갑	1,036,820 $	갑당 15 ¢
2	6,383,430 갑	957,515 $	"
3	6,084,902 갑	933,568 $	"
4	5,976,272 갑	896,440 $	"
5	5,747,235 갑	882,760 $	"
6	5,604,116 갑	860,383 $	"
7	5,506,231 갑	845,714 $	"
8	5,352,600 갑	822,133 $	"
9	5,246,240 갑	910,438 $	"
10	5,065,800 갑	884,908 $	"
평균	5,835,676 갑	903,062 $	15 ¢

2. 년간 판매 추정량

수량 5,835,676 갑 × 12월 = 70,028,112 갑

3. PX 이용권자수(외무부 북미 2과 통보자료)

(가) 미군인 및 군속과 그의 가족수 약 70,000명 7万名

4. PX 이용권자의 년간 소비 추정량

(가) 1인 1일 1갑의 경우

70,000명 × 1갑 × 365일 = 25,550,000 갑 2500万

(나) 1인 1일 2갑의 경우

70,000명 × 2갑 ×365일 =51,100,000 갑 5100万

6

5. 년간 과다 유출 추정량

(가) 1인 1일 1갈의 경우

70,028,112 갈 – 25,550,000 갈 = 44,478,112 갈 440万갈 초과

(나) 1인 1일 2갈의 경우

70,028,112 갈 – 51,100,000 갈 = 18,928,112 갈 180万갈 초과

6. 월평균 유출량

(가) 1인 1일 1갈의 경우

44,478,112 갈 ÷ 12월 = 3,706,509 갈 370万

(나) 1인 1일 2갈의 경우

18,928,112 갈 ÷ 12월 = 1,577,342 갈 150万

※ 특수사건은 200갑 이상
※ 70.10말까지의 통계임.

(별표 2)

특수사건(양담배) 월별실적

구분 \ 관서별	1월		2월		3월		4월		5월		6월		7월		8월		9월		10월		관서별 계	
	건수	물량	건수	물량	건수	물량	건수	물량	건수	물량	건수	물량	건수	물량	건수	물량	건수	물량	건수	물량	건수	물량
서울	2건	927			1	690	1	1,023	2	793	1	466					3	944			10건	4,792갑
인천											1	350									1건	350갑
수원							1	600											1	660	2건	1,150갑
청주															1	460					1건	460갑
대전							1	607													1건	507갑
목포													1	213	1	481					2건	694갑
광주							1	660					3	1,930							4건	2,480갑
대구													1	202							1건	202갑
김천									1	229											1건	229갑
부산											1	[illegible]			1	400					2건	400갑
당월분계	2건	927갑			1건	690갑	4건	2,686갑	3건	1,022갑	3건	816갑	6건	2,366갑	3건	1,341갑	3건	944갑	1건	660갑	24건	11,214갑 (224,280원)

8

(별표 3)

감시단속 실적표 및 69:70.10 말 대비표

구분 / 년도별	총 건 수	양 담 배		벌 과 금
		건 수	물 량	
69.10월말	4,592 건	3,963 건	1,365,032 본 (68,251 갑)	33,901,963 원
70.10월말	3,843 건	3,565 건	1,590,971 본 (79,548 갑)	63,099,063 원
69:70 대비	84 %	90 %	117 %	186 %

9

법 무 부

검찰 821 2216 73-7942 1971. 2. 3

수신 외무부 장관

참조 구미국장

제목 주한미군등의 관세법위반 사건의 방지

주한미군 및 군속과 그들의 가족등에 의한 A.P.O 를 통한 밀수행위 및 P.X 물품 유출행위등 관세법위반 피의사건은 별첨 통계표와 같이 상당한 수에 달하고 있는바, 이와같은 관세법위반자에 대하여는 한국정부 당국에서도 엄격히 단속하고 있으나, 이들의 범법행위를 방지하기 위하여는 주한 미군당국의 협조와 강력한 대책이 보다 효과적이라고 생각되므로 행정협정 제 28조에 의한 한미합동 위원회를 통하여 주한미군 당국이 이에 대한 유효 적절한 대책을 강구하도록 조치하여 주시기 바랍니다.

별첨: 미군인등 관세법위반 사건 년도별 발생 상황표 1부.

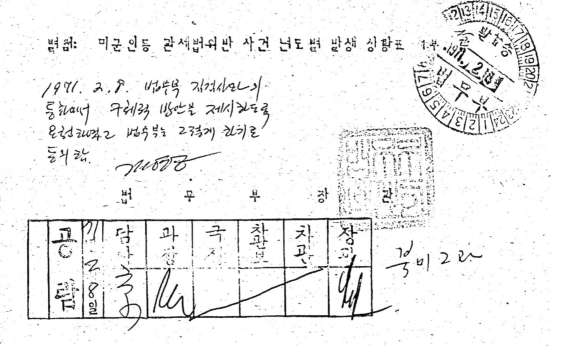

1971. 2. 8. 법무부 지검사와의 통화에서 구체적 방안을 제시하도록 요청하였고 법무부는 그렇게 하기로 동의함.

법 무 부 장 관

공람	71. 2. 8일	담당	과장	국장	차관보	차관	장관

구미2과

10

담당자		
위원회		처리할것

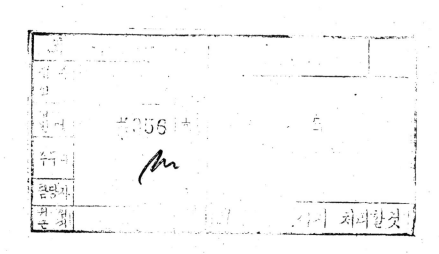

미군인등 관세법위반사건 년도별 발생 상황표

구분 / 년도별	총 발생	일과적	전속적
67년도	20	20	
68년도	41	34	7
69년도	28	18	10
70년도	53	40	13
총 계	142	112	30

※ 단위는 인원임.

.11

SOFA: GI Prison, Death Sentences Noted

SEOUL (AP)—Four American soldiers are serving terms in South Korean prisons and two others, sentenced to death, are awaiting a new trial as the fourth anniversary of the Korean-American Status of Forces Agreement approaches.

The agreement's anniversary comes Tuesday, and under it South Korea has assumed jurisdiction over 133 of 5,580 offenses involving U.S. military personnel in the past four years, a review by the U.S. military shows.

The Korean Justice Ministry dropped 10 of the 133 cases after taking jurisdiction, and 12 other cases are pending, the review shows.

The death sentences were the first two given to U.S. military personnel by South Korean courts. Sgt. John W. Blount Jr., 21, of San Francisco, and Spec. 4 James E. Walters, 22, of Detroit, were sentenced to death by the Seoul District Court last Dec. 4 after conviction on charges of robbing and killing a Korean couple who refused to sell them drugs on credit. Both men have appealed.

A U.S. military spokesman, commenting on the death sentences in view of the generally lenient treatment known to have been given U.S. servicemen in foreign courts, said, "Death sentences in Status of Forces Agreement (SOFA) cases are rare but not unheard of."

The spokesman said SOFA trials in Korea are not hurting or affecting the traditionally friendly Korean-American relations. "SOFA trials are an example of effective Korean-American relations. They are conducted on both sides in accordance with the spirit and letter of the Status of Forces Agreement," he said.

He said he has no complaints or suggestions concerning the conduct of the trials.

One of the four men serving in a Korean prison, the Suwon Correctional Institute near Seoul, is Pfc. Eugene D. Taylor, 24, of Hawkinsville, Ga., convicted of killing a Korean woman. He is serving a four-year prison term.

Two others are serving three-to four-year terms after conviction for rape. Another soldier is serving three and one half years for robbery.

Convicted U.S. military personnel in Korea are all sent to the Suwon Correctional Institute. They are housed in separate facilities for Americans which are better than those for Koreans.

12

증산 수출 건설

관 세 청

심티 1245-177 1971. 3. 5

수신 수신처 참조 (외무부)

제목 회의자료 송부

1. 외무부 미이 723-3326 호 (71. 2. 23) 에 관련 하여 주한 미군인에 의한 밀수사범 방지를 위한 회의를 개최 하였던바,

2. 당청에서 작성한 회의 자료를 송부하오니 업무에 참작하시기 바랍니다.

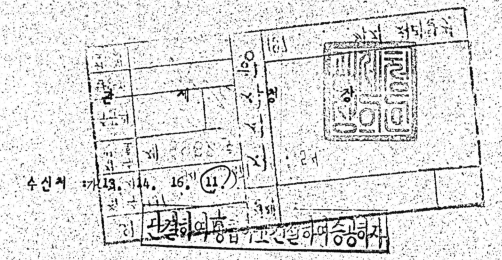

첨부 : 회의자료 1부. 끝.

발송 No. 1971. 3. 5 관세청

관세청장

수신처 : 가13. 14. 16. 11.

단결하여 총화 건설하여 승공하자

저축의 날 따로 없다 날마다 저축하자

밀수신고는 서울 28-0123 인천 3-0123 부산 4-0123

13

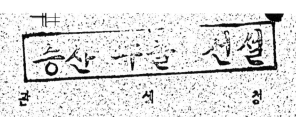

외 무 부		결재	
접수 일시	197 . . . 9시 MAR 1971	지시사항	: 54
접수 번호	제 8962 호		
주무과			
담당자			
위임 구분			197 . . 까지 처리할 것

발송
1971. 2. 5

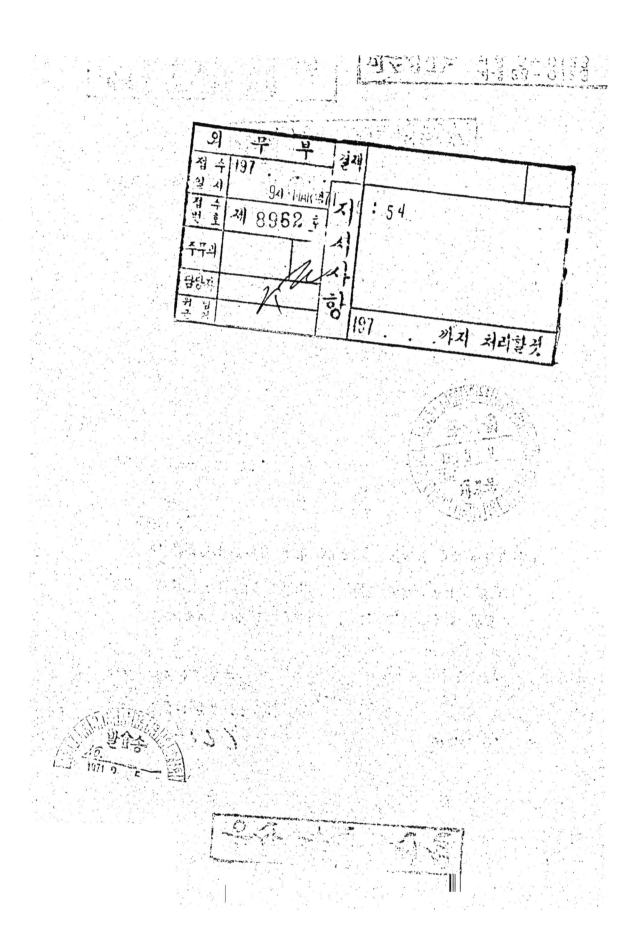

1971. 3. 3

회 의 자 료

(주한 미군인에 의한 밀수방지를 위한)

관 세 청

14

현　　　　황

1. 한미합동 단속반 활동 현황

가. 한미합동 단속반의 편성 근거

본 단속반은 1967. 12. 21 제 19차 한미군대지위 협정에 의한 합동 위원회에서 합의하여 1968. 11. 1 자로 서울, 부산, 대구, 평택, 부평, 의정부, 동두천, 파주 등 8개 지역에 최초로 편성 설치케 되었으며 1970. 10. 12일자 한미합동 단속반 운영에 관한 회의에서 한미합동 단속본부반을 관세청에 신설 하였음.

나. 조　직

한미합동 단속반의 편성은 세관요원 2명 미 CID 또는 수사관 1명, 미헌병 1명이

서울 특별시	
경기도	의정부
"	동두천
"	파주군
"	평　택
"	부　평
경상북도	대구시

부산 직할시등 8개 지구에 각각 조직토록 되 있으며 관세청에 본부반을 두고 있음.

15

다. 검거 실적

년도별 / 구분	1968			1969			1970			계		
	건수	인원	금액	건수	인원	금액	건수	인원	금액	건수	인원	금액
APO	32	29	13,160,250	18	22	12,731,636	26	54	17,867,800	76	105	43,759,686
PX	1791	2040	55,818,894	702	801	56,871,808	1687	1920	199,498,481	4180	4761	312,189,183
계	1823	2069	68,979,144	720	823	69,603,444	1713	1974	217,366,281	4256	4866	355,948,869

라. 관세청 발족이후 검거실적 (70. 9. — 71. 1)

구분 / 월별	APO			PX			계		
	건수	인원	금액	건수	인원	금액	건수	인원	금액
70. 9월	0	0	0	44	44	13,188,533	44	44	13,188,533
10월	3	22	7,912,000	200	283	32,612,585	203	305	40,524,585
11월	1	4	1,200,000	333	363	40,190,241	334	367	41,390,241
12월	6	11	4,660,800	339	350	53,044,609	345	361	57,705,409
71. 1월	5	11	7,490,930	402	448	60,889,751	407	459	68,380,681
계	15	48	21,263,730	1318	1488	199,925,719	1333	1536	221,189,449

2. 문제점 및 건의사항

문 제 점	건 의 사 항
가. APO	
1) APO우편물의 검사량의 확대. APO우편물은 한미행정 협정의 규정에 의거 5% 범위내에서 개장 검사를 실시하여 상품화 물품에 대한 통관 억제와 귀금속류의 은익 밀수를 적발하고 있으나 검사수량의 과소로 실효를 거두지 못하고 있으며 금괴,녹용,밍크목도리,귀금속류,전기용품 등이 밀수입 되고 있음 (주둔군 지위 협정 제 9조 에 따른 합의 양해사항 1— 4 에서 규정한 미군사 우체국을 통한 우편소포에 대한 한국세관 절차)	표본 검사 수량인 5%에 대한 합의 양해 사항 규정의 개정.
2) 금수품이나 불합리한량의 소포에 대한 처리. 현재 시행하고 있는 규정에 의하면 한국세관 관리와 미군우편관계 대표자간에 합의에 의하여 금수품으로 인정되는 물품이 있는 소포는 한미관계당국의 처리 결정이 있을 때까지 미군 우편당국의 관리하에 두고 아울러 그자체가 불합리한 량으로 인정되는 물품의 소포는 한미관계 당국의 처리 결정이 있을 때까지 미군 우편당국의 관리하여	금수품 및 불합리한 수량에 대한 소포의 처리 결정은 적어도 한미 양국의 관계관에 의하여 신속히 결정 하도록 규정의 개정이 요망됨.

17

문 제 점	건 의 사 항
두며 합리 불합리의 결정은 수화주의 사명 가족사항, 수입경위 기타 적절하다고 사료되는 것등을 고려하여 미군 관계관에 의하여 결정 된다고한 규정에 있어서, 첫째, 합리,불합리의 결정은 수화주의 신분 및 수입 경위에 대한 제반사항을 미군 관계관에 의하여 일방적인 조사로서 처리하므로 기인하여 한국 세관으로서는 수입경위 및 범칙 혐의등이 있더라도 이에대한 조사가 불가능 하고, 둘째, APO 의 세관 검사과정에서 밀수품으로 인정되어 적발이 되더라도 화주가 수취 거절 또는 반송처리하므로서 검거 할수 없음.	No. 1971. 3. 5 관세청
나. PX 1) PX물품 판매량의 통보 미군 PX에서 반입하는 물품에 대하여 한국지역 PX 본부에서 재고량은 통보받고 있으나 지역별 PX 별로 내역을 파악할수 없을뿐더러 통보내용의 누락 통보일시의 지연등으로 단속자료로서 활용되지 못하고 있음.	PX 별, 지역별 중요품목의 매상고에 대한 신속한 통보가 요망됨.

18

문 제 점	건 의 사 항
2) PX 물품의 과다 수입의 조정. PX 이용권자의 수와 PX 물품의 수입량을 대비하여 볼때 과다수입되어 시중에 유출되고 있음.	PX 물품의 합리적인 수량을 수입토록 조치 요망.
다. 형사재판권 결정기간에 대한 일자계산의 변경. 종래에는 미군인등 범죄에 대하여는 범죄통고를 받거나 알게된후로부터 15일 이내에 재판권행사의 여부를 결정하도록 되어 있으므로, 첫째, 당해사건을 인지또는 통보를 받아 조치하는 과정에서 본 혐의자의 인근 헌병대장을 통하여 소환코저 했을때 공무, 질병 또는 여하한 재난으로 인하여 한국측이 지정한 일시와 장소에 출두치 못하므로서 한국측이 재판권을 행사할수 없는 거일에 차질을 초래하고, 둘째, 당해사건에 대한 한미양국관계관의 충분한 조사와 검토를 할수 없음.	당해사건을 한국 검찰이 고발을 받은날로부터 15일을 계산하도록 개정 요망. 관세청
라. 합중국 대표의 임명 대한민국과 아메리카 합중국간의 상호방위조약 제 4조에 의한 시설과 구역 및 대한민국에서의 합중국군대의 지위에 관한 협정의 합의 의사록의 제 22조 제 9항 (사) 에 관한 규정에 의거	한국측이 당해사건을 인지 하였을 경우에는 피의자의 소속부대 책임장교가 미국측 대표로서 조사중 참여함이 가하다고 사료되나 미국측으로부터 통고받은 경우에

19

문 제 점	건 의 사 항
피의자 또는 피고인이 미합중국 대표가 참여하지 아니한 조서는 유죄의 증거로서 채택되지 아니한다고 함에 따라 미합중국 대표가 참석한 가운데·조사를 받고 있는바. 당해사건을 인지 또는 미군으로부터 통고받아 조사에 착수코저 하여 해당 피의(고) 자등을 소환하였을때 공무, 질병 또는 천재지변등의 사유로 소환에 대한 출석을 지연시킬 경우에 증거인멸의 우려가 있고 한국측 관계관의 수사에 차질을 초래하고 있음.	는 당해사건을 인지 또는 조사한 당해 수사관이 미국측 정부대표로서 서명함이 족하다고 사료되므로 이에 개정이 요망됨.
마. 한미합동 단속반의 증설.	
기존 한미합동 단속반 이외에도 주한 미군 주둔지역인 김포, 대전, 군산, 광주등 4개지역에서 PX 및 APO를 이용한 밀수의 단속 기관이 없어 한미간의 관세법 위반과 피의사건을 전담하지 못하고 있음.	김포, 군산, 대전, 광주의 4개지역에 대한 한미합동 단속반 증설 요망.

3. 조 치 사 항

본건 문제점 및 건의사항의 가. 나. 마 항은 재무부를 통하여 한미합동 위원회 재무분과 위원회에 안건으로 상정 협의하고 다, 라, 항은 법무부에서 한미합동 위원회 형사 재판권분과 위원회에 상정하여 협의하여 주시기 바랍니다.

재 무 부

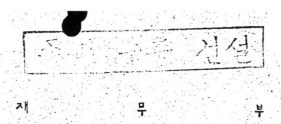

협 력 1245 - 235 1971. 3. 11.

수 신 외무부장관

제 목 주한 미군에 의한 밀수 방지

한미 행정협정 발표 이후 주한 미군의 A.P.O 및 P.X. 이용권자에 의한 밀수가 증가 되고 있으므로 밀수 방지를 위한 개선책으로 별첨과 같이 문제점을 제기하오니 미측에 과제부여함과 동시 필요한 조치를 취하여 주시기 바랍니다.

첨부 : 1. 문제점및 건의사항 1부.

2. 연도별 밀수검거 현황 1부. 끝.

재 무 부 장 관

발송 No. 1971. 3. 12 재무부

21

외 무 부		결재	
접수	197 . . .		
일시	시 분		
번호	12 9542		34
처리			
담당자			
위임근거			197 . . 일 까지 처리할것

[illegible]

[illegible]

[illegible]

[illegible]

[illegible]

[illegible]

[illegible]

[illegible]

[illegible]

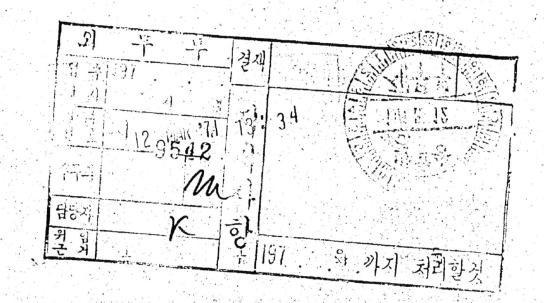

1. 문제점 및 건의사항

문제의 구분	문제점	건의사항	관계규정
1. APO 우편물 검사량제한	현행규정에 의거 비공용(小包) 소포량의 5% 이내의 범위내에서 개장검사를 실시하고 있으나 검사수량의 과소로 실효를 거두지 못하고 있음.	5% 이내로 제한되어 있는 검사량을 한,미 양측의 합의에의거 합리적인양으로 개정함이 요망됨.	S O F A 제9조에 따르는 합의양해사항 1-4의 규정중 제3항. 다.
2. 금수품의 처리및 불합리한 수량의 결정	1. 금수품으로 인정되어 적발하며도 한미관계당국에 의하여 합의 처리될때까지 미군 우편당국의 관리하에 두고있기 때문에 화주가 수취거절또는 반송 처리하므로서 계속적인 검거가 불가한 실정이며 2. 합리 불합리한 수량의 결정이 미군 관계관에 일방적으로 일임되어 있으므로 한국 세관으로서는 수입경위및 범칙혐의 등이 있더라도 이에 대한 조사가 불가능함.	금수품의 처리 및 합리 불합리한 수량의 결정은 적어도 한,미 양측의 관계관에 의하여 신속히 결정하도록 관계규정의 개정이 요망됨.	S O F A 제9조에 따르는 합의양해사항 1-4의 규정중 제5항. 나및 다.
3. P. X. 물품 판매량의 통보	P. X. 본부에서는 반입되는 물품의 재고량 만을 통보하고 있으므로 지역별 및 P. X별로의 내역 파악이 불가할 뿐더러 통보내용의 누락 및 통보시기의 지연등으로 단속자료로서의 가치가 없음.	지역별P.X 별 주요물품의 반입현황및 매장 현황에 대한 신속한 통보가 요망됨.	S O FA 제9조 합의 의사록 3 항.
4. P.X.물품의 수입량	P. X. 물품의 수입량이 P.X 이용권자의 수에 비하여 과다히 수입되고 있으므로 시중에 유출되고 있음.	P.X물품의 합리적인 수량 수입이 요망됨	
5. 한,미 합동 단속반의 증설	현존 한미 합동 단속반 이외에도 주한 미군 주둔지역인 김포, 대전 군산, 광주등 4개 지역에는 P. X및 APC 를 이용한 밀수단속반이 없어 한,미간의 관세법 위한과 피의사건을 전담하지 못하고 있는 실정임	김포, 군산, 대전, 광주등 4개 지역에도 한미 합동 단속반의 설치가 요망됨.	

재무부 관세국

2. 연도별 검거 실적

년도별 / 구분	1968			1969			1970			계		
	건수	인원	금액	건수	인원	금액	건수	인원	금액	건수	인원	금액
APO	32	29	13,160,250	18	22	12,731,636	26	54	17,867,800	76	105	43,759,686
PX	1,791	2040	55,818,894	702	801	56,871,808	1687	1920	199,498,48[illegible]	4180	4,761	312,189,183
계	1,823	2069	68,979,144	720	823	69,603,444	1,713	1974	217,366,28[illegible]	4,256	4,866	355,948,869

중산 수출 건설

재 무 부

협 력 1245-362 1971. 4. 7.

수 신 외무부장관

제 목 SOFA 과제부여 추가

1. 협력 1245-235(71. 3. 12)의 관련입니다.

2. 주한 미군에 의한 밀수 방지를 위하여 과제부여 의뢰한 사항중 한미합동 단속반 증설에 관하여 김포, 군산, 대전 광주등 4개 지역외에 인천, 오산, 왜관의 3개지역을 추가 하여 주시기 바랍니다.

끝.

발송 No. 1971. 4. 7 재무부

재 무 부 장 관

단결하여 일하고 건설하여 승공하자

24

외 무 부		
접수 일시	1971 APR 7 10 : 23	
접수 번호	제 12883	
주무과		
담당자		
처리		

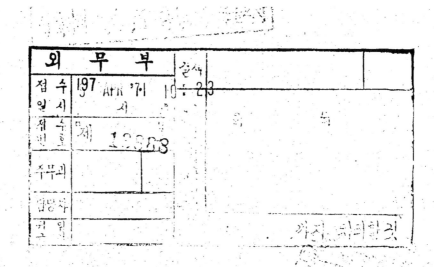

기 안 용 지

분류기호 문서번호	미이 723 -	(전화번호)	전결규정 조 항 국장 전결사항
처리기간			
시행일자	71. 10. 25.		
보존년한		국 장	

보조기관	북미 2과장	협조	
기안책임자	권 찬	북미 2과 (71.10.25.)	

경 유		발신 No 23590 1971.10.25 외무부
수 신	재무부장관	통제 1971.10.25
참 조	관세청장	
제 목	SOFA 합동위 군,민관계 임시분과위원회 Panel 위원 위촉.	

9. 2. SOFA 한.미 합동위원회의 특별의제 채택으로 창설된 군,민관계 임시분과위원회는 10. 18. 제 3차 회의를 개최하고 7개 Panel 에 위원을 위촉[하였는]바, [redacted] 도난 및 암거래 조사반 (Panel on Larceny & Black Marketing)에 재무부 [관세청] 대표를 위촉코저 하오니 ~~양지하시고 재무부 관세청~~ 관지과장을 ~~위촉~~ [추천] 하여 주시기 바랍니다. 끝.

정서
관인
발송

25

공통서식 1-2(갑) 1967. 4. 4 승인

190mm×268mm 중질지 70g/m² 조달청 1,000,000매 인쇄

외 무 부

미이 723 - (74 - 3073) 71. 10. 25.

수신 : 재무부장관

참조 : 관세청장

제목 : SOFA 합동위 군,민관계 임시 분과위원회 Panel 위원 위촉.

9. 2. SOFA 한.미 합동위원회의 특별의제 채택으로 창설된 군,민관계 임시 분과위원회는 10. 18. 제3차 회의를 개최하고 7개 Panel 에 위원을 위촉하였는 바, 도난 및 암거래 조사반 (Panel on Larceny and Black Marketing)에 재무부 관세청 대표를 위촉코저 하오니 관기과장을 추천하여 주시기 바랍니다. 끝.

외 무 부 장 관

26

공한 수출 건설 -

관 세 청

* Kenney에게 通報 11-4. 15:00. 講읍

심리 1245-1006 71. 11. 2.

수신 외무부 장관

제목 SOFA합동위 군.민관계 임시분과 위원회PANEL위원 위촉

1. 미이 723-23590 (71. 10. 25)과 관련된사항입니다.

2. 군.민 관계 임시분과 위원회 도난 및 암거래 조사반의 분과 의원을 다음가 같이 추천합니다.

다 음

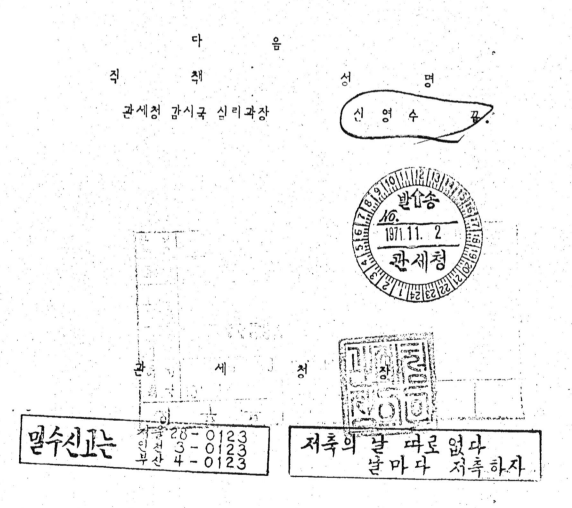

직 책	성 명
관세청 감시국 심리과장	신 영 수

발송 No. 1971. 11. 2 관세청

관 세 청

밀수신고는 서울 28-0123 인천 3-0123 부산 4-0123

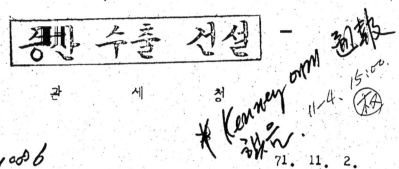

저축의 날 따로 없다 날마다 저축하자

외 무 부	공람	
접수일시	197 . . . 3	NOV '71 13 : 03
접수번호	제 44667	
주무과		
담당자		
처리근거		

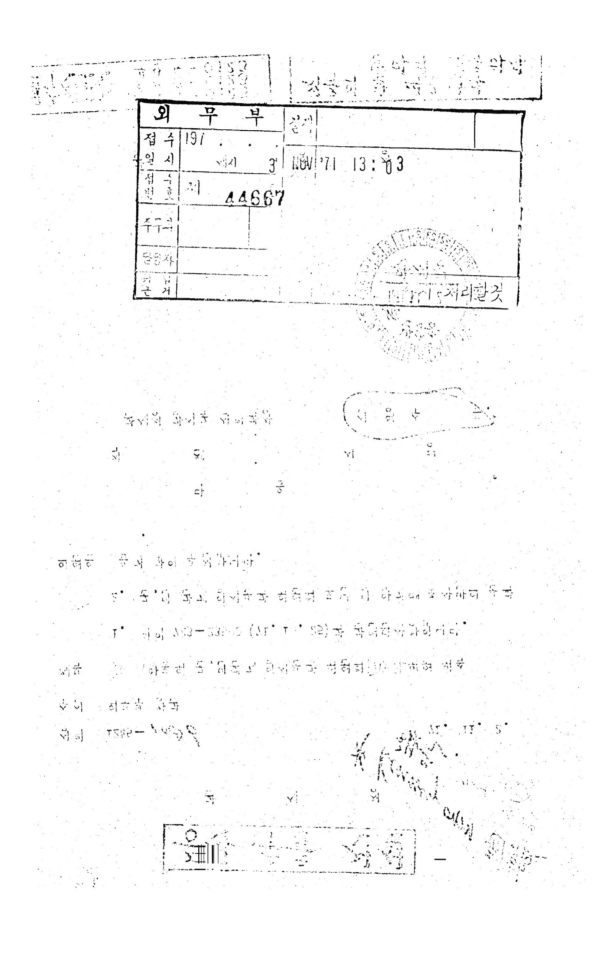

기일내 처리할것

공 란

공 란

공 란

2. 1972

기

공 란

공 란

공 란

공 란

공 란

[1972. 3. 1]

SOFA 한.미 합동위가 채택한 합의사항 (69, 70차)

5. 도난 및 암시장 문제 (Panel on Larceny and Black Marketing)

건의제목 : 미 정부 소유차량의 도난 및 면세차량의 불법처리로 인한 국고손실 방지책

내 용 : (1) 주한미군의 효과적인 작전에 차질을 가져올 정도로 미국정부 소유차량의 도난이 빈번함에 비추어서 대한민국 정부의 관계기관 및 주한미군의 집행기관이 한.미 상호협력의 기존절차에 따라서 도난된 미 정부 소유차량의 소유 및 운용을 검사하도록 할것.

(2) 면세차량의 부정처리가 한국경제에 악영향을 끼치고 한국의 세관수입에 큰 손실을 가져옴에 비추어 기존 한.미 합동조사 "팀" 의 활동을 더욱 강화하고 증강 할것.

37

SOFA 한.미 합동위가 채택한 합의사항 (7기차)

5. 도난 및 암시장문제 (Panel on Larceny and Black Marketing)

1) 건의제목 : 도난 및 암거래문제 방지책

내 용 : 주한미군 당국은 미군장비를 훔쳐서 한국인에게 판매하는 미군인에 대한 처벌결과를 요약형식으로 한국정부에 통보할것.

2) 건의제목 : 도난 및 암거래문제 방지책

내 용 : 주한미군 당국은 한국관계 당국과 협조하여 P.X. 및 코미써리 (Commissary)의 제한품목을 더욱 추가할것이며, 군인 사병이 필요한 적정량 이상의 물품이 흘러나오지 않도록 감시하는 방지책을 더욱 보강할것.

38

한미 협정에 따른 도난 및 암거래 조사반 회의 개최

1. 일 시

72. 7. 27. 15:00

2. 장 소

법 무 부 614 호실

3. 회의 안건

별 첨

4. 참석 범위

한국측

내무부	치안국	총경	송 형 식
법무부		검사	정 구 영
"		"	현 홍 주
외무부		사무관	권 찬
관세청		~~사무관~~ 서기관	신 영 수

미군측

미 8군사 중령 참므스 에이 하이네 외 5명

29

공 란

공　　　란

공 란

공 란

공　　　란

공 란

공 란

공 란

공 란

공 란

공 란

도난 및 암거래 조사반 회의록 요지

1. 일시 : 72. 8. 9. 14:00 - 16:00

2. 장소 : 외무부 회의실

3. 참석자 : 별첨 참조

4. 안건 및 토의내용 : 별첨 참조

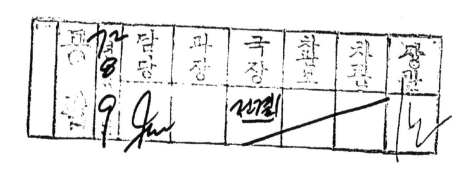

	72. 8. 9.	담당	과장	국장	차관보	차관	장관

51

1. 미측 건의

미 정부 재산 도난예방책

가. 재산 하역장인 각 항구

나. 목적지까지의 운반도중

다. 특히 통신장비, 의약품, 기타 장비의 우선적 보호를 위한 한.미 합동 법률집행 당국의 조치 강화

2. 의 견

가. 관계 규정 — SOFA 2조 1항(가) : 시설구역 부여
SOFA 22조 10항 : 시설과 구역내외에서의 경찰권 행사
SOFA 25조 : 보안조치

나. SOFA 2조 1항에 규정한 시설구역 이외의 여하한 경찰권 행사에 대해서는 대한민국 당국의 약정에 따라야 함. 단, 약정은,

(1) 대한민국 당국과의 연락하에 행사되어야 하고,

(2) 합중국 군대의 구성원간의 규율과 질서유지에 관계되어야 하며,

(3) 그들의 안전보장을 위하여 필요한 범위내에서 해야 함.

고로 동 건의는 상기에 해당되지 않음으로 수락할수 없음.

62

도난 및 암거래 조사반

1. 미측 건의

도난된 미 정부 재산 회수 대책 :

(1) 도난재산에 대한 한.미 합동검사,확인 및 즉각 반환
(2) 장물 발견시, 즉각 통보 및 반송
(3) 통신장비, 의약품 및 기타장비에 대한 우선적 보호

2. 의 견

전 페이지와 동일.

53

1. 미측 건의

미 정부 재산도난 예방을 위한 한.미 친선협의회 활용

(1) 도난 범위

(2) 도난품 및 장비의 모형

(3) 도난 발생장소

(4) 예방을 위한 최선의 방안

등에 대해 토의하므로써 도난예방에 기여할수 있다.

2. 의 견

SOFA 22조 6항 및 25조에 의하여 동 건의를 수락함.

54

1. 미측 건의

미 정부 재산 도난품목의 보고 절차 개선 :

가. 미 법률 집행당국은 모든 도난범죄를 한국 관할경찰에 긴급 위탁 통보

나. 한.미 법률 집행당국은 도난된 정부 재산회수를 미 관계당국에 지급 통보

2. 의 견

가. 관계규정 : SOFA 22조 6항(가) : 수사의 실시 및 증거의 수집과 제출에 대한 상호 협력

SOFA 25조 : 재산 보장에 대한 필요한 조치

나. 상기 규정에 명문화되어 있음으로써, 상기 건의는 중복이 됨.

55

Maj Courtney R Fritts, US Chairman
Lt Cmdr Spydell, J1 Div
Maj Martell D. Fritz, J1 (observes)
Cpt Michael J. Wentink, SAJ
Francis K Cook, J5

ROK SIDE

외무부	정찬 사무관		70-2324
내무부	이해구 총경		70-2622
법무부	현홍주 검사		70-2807
재무부	조영길 사무관		75-3786

0551

회의 참석 보고

1. 회 의 명 : 도난 및 암거래 조사반 회의 (Larceny & Blackmarketing Panel)

2. 일 시 : 72. 8. 9. 14:00 - 16:30

3. 장 소 : 외무부 회의실

4. 참석예정자 : 북미 2과 권 찬 (동 조사반 한국측 위원)

상기 회의의 참석을 재가하여 주시기 바랍니다.

56

공 란

공 란

공 란

공 란

공 란

공 란

공 란

도난 및 암거래 조사반 합의사항

미 정부 재산 도난 예방을 위한 한.미 친선협의회 활용

(1) 도난 범위

(2) 도난품 및 장비의 모형

(3) 도난 발생 장소

(4) 예방을 위한 최선의 방안

등에 대해 토의하므로써 도난 예방에 기여할수 있다.

64

공 란

공 란

북미2과 2626

Korea Tourist Recreation
Service Association
Inchon Branch
#15-5th St. Hang-Dong, Chung-Ku, Inchon, Korea.

October 19, 1972

General W. H. Blakefield
Major General
Headquarters, Eighth U.S. Army
APO San Francisco 96301

Subject: SEAMANS CLUB, PORT OF INCHON, KOREA.

Dear General:

This letter is to express our keen complaints regarding the subject club.

The Seamans Club is granted of the previliege to purchase Tax Free supplies from the U.S. Army sources to serve only to the limited number of U.S.S. and M. S. T.S. personnel.

However, the fact is that this club purchases a very large quantities of club supplies from the U.S. Eighth Army, Commisary and other free tax sources and most part of them are either sold to the black market hr consumed by the unauthorized people.

We must point out that this is a serious matter which will jeopardize both the reputation of U.S. Army and the economy of this country.

We would, therefore, appreciate it very much if you will kindly take up this matter for your adequate action.

Thanking you for your kind cooperation.

Very truly yours,

Kuan, Yong Un
Chairman

cc; 1. Commanding General, Eighth U.S.Army
2. Secretary of Army, U. S. A.
3. Secretary of Navy, U. S. A.

67

Korea Tourist Recreation
Service Association
Inchon Branch
#15-5th St. Hang-Dong, Chung-Ku, Inchon, Korea.

October 19, 1972

General W. H. Blakefield
Major General
Headquarters, Eighth U.S. Army
APO San Francisco 96301

Subject: SEAMANS CLUB, PORT OF INCHON, KOREA.

Dear General:

This letter is to express our keen complaints regarding the subject club.

The Seamans Club is granted of the ~~previliege to~~ purchase Tax Free supplies from the U.S. Army sources to serve only to the limited number of U.S.S. and M. S. T.S. personnel.

However, the fact is that this club purchases a very large quantities of club supplies from the U.S. Eighth Army, Commisary and other free tax sources and most part of them are either sold to the black market or consumed by the unauthorized people. no.

We must point out that this is a serious matter which will jeopardize both the reputation of U.S. Army and the economy of this country.

We would, therefore, appreciate it very much if you will kindly take up this matter for your adequate action.

Thanking you for your kind cooperation.

Very truly yours,

Kuan, Yong Jin
Chairman

cc; 1. Commanding General, Eighth U.S.Army
2. Secretary of Army, U. S. A.
3. Secretary of Navy, U. S. A.

2 jars of orange juice

68

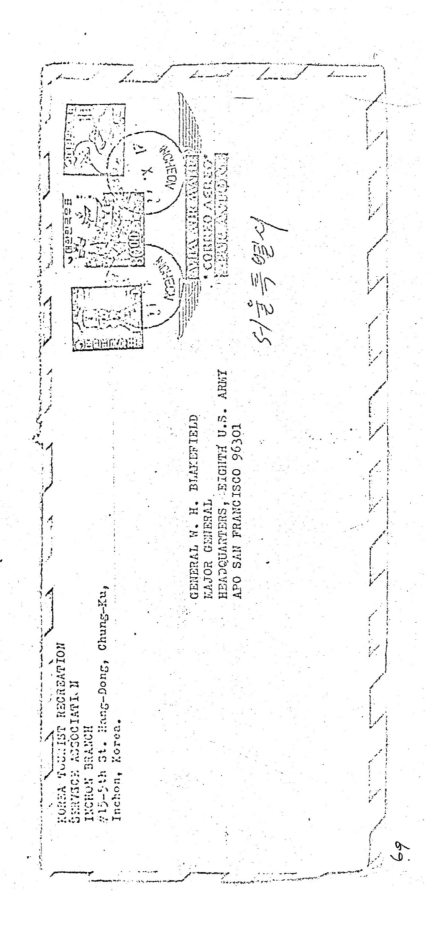

KOREA TOURIST RECREATION
SERVICE ASSOCIATION
INCHON BRANCH
#15-5th St. Hang-Dong, Chung-Ku,
Inchon, Korea.

INCHEON

VIA AIR MAIL
CORREO AEREO
PAR AVION

GENERAL W. H. BLAKEFIELD
MAJOR GENERAL
HEADQUARTERS, EIGHTH U.S. ARMY
APO SAN FRANCISCO 96301

서울특별시

69

기 안 용 지

분류기호 문서번호	미이700-	(전화번호)	전결규정 조 항 국 장 전결사항
처리기간			
시행일자			
보존년한			국 장
보조기관	과 장		협
기안책임자	권 찬	북미2과(72.10.28)	
경유 수신 참조	권영진 한국관광협회회장 귀하 (경기도 인천시 중구합동 5가1 15번지)	발송 No 3410 1972.10.30 외무부	검열 통제관
제 목	인천소재 SEAMANS CLUB 의 PX 물품 부정유출에 관한 조회		

1. 미측이 알려온바에 의하면 귀 관광협회에서 10. 19. 미 8군 당국에 서한을 발송하여, 인천소재 SEAMANS CLUB 이 미 8군 PX 의 면세물품을 대량으로 구입, 이를 암시장에 매각하는 사례가 있음을 지적하고 이의 시정을 요구하였다는 바,

2. 당부는 ~~귀 봉사회의 요구 대로 미 8군 당국에 대하여 이의 시정을 촉구하고자 하오나~~, 귀 봉사회에서 주장하는바의 물적 증거및 근거를 조속히 제시하시기 바랍니다.

3. ~~추후~~ 그러한 사례가 ~~발생할때는~~ 사실인 경우 한.미행정협정에 의한 한.미 합동위원회(한국측 대표: 외무부 김동휘 구미국장)의 공식 ~~"잔넬"을~~ 경로를 통해서 문제를 ~~신속 해결하도록 주장~~ 제기하시기 바랍니다.

끝.

정서 / 관인 / 발송

공통서식1-2(갑) 1967. 4. 4. 승인 — 190mm×268mm(1급인쇄용지70g/㎡) 조달청 (500,000매인쇄)

70

외 무 부

미이 700 - 72. 10. 30.

수신 : 권영진 한국 관광협회 회장 귀하
(경기도 인천시 중구 답동 5가 15번지)

제목 : 인천소재 Seamans Club 의 PX 물품 부정유출에 관한 조회

1. 미측이 알려온 바에 의하면, 귀 관광협회에서 10. 19. 미 8군 당국에 서한을 발송하여, 인천소재 Seamans Club 이 미 8군 PX 의 면세물품을 대량으로 구입, 이를 암시장에 매각하는 사태가 있음을 지적하고 이의 시정을 요구하였다는 바,

2. 당부의 본건 검토에 참고코저 하오니, 귀 봉사회에서 주장하는 바의 물적증거 및 근거를 조속히 제시하시기 바랍니다.

3. 그러한 사례가 사실인 경우, 한.미 행정협정에 의한 한.미 합동위원회 (한국측 대표 : 외무부 김동휘 구미국장)의 공식경로를 통해서 문제를 다루게 되어있음을 유념하시기 바랍니다. 끝.

외 무 부 장 관

71

외 무 부

정세보고처리전
(   )

1972. 11. 10.

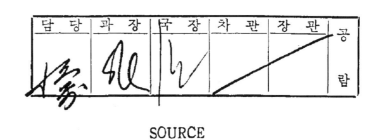

담 당	과 장	국 장	차 관	장 관	공람

발 신 인 SOURCE

요 약 및 비 고

관광 휴양협회가 회시한 물적증거 및 근거(부정유출)

1. 인천 Seamens Club 은 영내 미 해군 전용 클럽인바, 매월 매상고를 7-8천불 이상의 실적을 올리며(원화로 환산하면 약 320만원, 매상고로서 Seamens Club 의 규모와 고객에 비해서 엄청난 실적임.),

2. Seamens Club 의 고객인 미 해군 선원은 월 1척정도 인천항에 입항하여 2-3일간 체류함에 불과함으로, 월 7,000-8,000 불의 매상고를 올린다는것은 놀라운 사실이며, 정상적인 방법으로는 거의 불가능함.

3. 미 군표를 사용하여야 함에도 불구하고 원화 및 불화를 사용하고 있으며, 환율도 정부환율액 보다 인상, 교환하고 있는 실정임.

0072

0001

한국관광유양업협회인천지부

관유협인제제 호 1972. 11. 6

수 신 외무부 장관

참 조 구미 국장

제 목 인천소재 씨멘스 크럽의 PX 물품 부정유출에 관한 조회

1. 미이 700-34104(72.10.30)에 의거 조회하신 사항에 관하여 다음과 같이 회신 합니다.

다 음

가. 인천 씨멘스 크럽은 설립의 목적인 영내크럽으로 미해군 소속 선원전용으로 미 8군 PX 면세물품을 월 약 4천내지 5천 딸라분을 구입하여 매상고 약 7천내지 8천 딸라 이상의 실적을 갖는바

나. 미해군 소속선은 월 1척정도로 인천항에 입항 체류기간 2.3일에 불과함으로서 이 면세 물품소비의 위법성을 입증하는 것이며

다. 일반선의 선원 및 타국선(영국, 카나다, 일본, 그리스등등)의 선원과 또한 내국인에게 회원권을 발행하여 무단출입으로 영내크럽내에 설치되어 있는 특정외래품 매점을 이용케하여 외래품 매매등의 상행위를 하고 있으며

라. 미군표로 거래하게 되어있는 사항조차 위반 한화 및 외화로 거래하며 외화도 정부 환율액보다 인상지급 교환하여 외화를 다액 매입하여 이를 매상액인양 가장 경리하여 면세물품 판매로 간주 내국세는 일체 납세치 않고 영업을 공공연히 계속 하고 있는 것입니다.

73

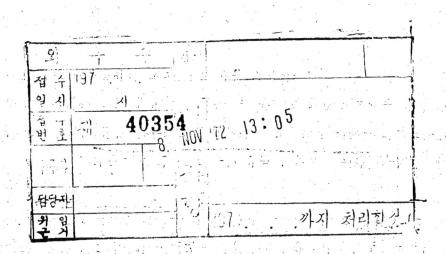

외 무 부			
접수 일시	197 . . . 시		
접수 번호	제 40354 호 8 NOV '72 13:05		
담당자			
위임 근거			197 . . .까지 처리할것

2. 상기와 같은 사항으로 인하여 본 협회 산하 관광휴양업소의 선의적인 영업에 막심한 지장을 초래하여 미8군 및 관계부처에 이의 시정을 요청한 것이오니 적절한 조치 있으시길 간망하나이다. 끝.

한국관광휴양업 협회 인천지부

지부장 권 영 인

74

공 란

공 란

공 란

공 란

The Korean Tourist Recreation Service Association
Inchon Branch

November 16, 1972

To : Minister of Foreign Affairs
Attention: Director of European and American Affairs

Subject: Illegal Flow of PX Merchandises
from Seamans Club at Inchon

1. In response to the official letter No. Mi-2 700-34104 dated October 30, 1972, I would like to inform you as follow:

a. The Seamans Club at Inchon was established to serve only the limitted number of the US Navy seamen. And the said club used to purchase monthly $4,000-5,000 worth tax-free merchandises from the US Eighth Army PX, and to make monthly sales in an amount of roughly $7,000 up to $8,000..

b. The fact that only one US Navy ship per month used to call on Inchon port and to stay two or three days at the port can prove the irregularities of consumption of the tax-free merchandises at the said club.

99

c. The said club has issued membership cards to those seamen belonging to ordinary ships or foreign ships (England, Canada, Japan, Greece, etc.) and to the Korean nationals, and has given them free pass into the special foreign commisary of the club established within the military post and has engaged in such commercial business as the transactions of foreign made tax-free commodities.

d. The Seamans Club often makes transactions, even in violation of authorization to only use the US MPC, in Korean currency or US dollars, and practices the money exchanges at higher rates than the official exchange rate. Thus, the said club purchases good many extra foreign currencies at such a higher rate and put them into its sales account just as they accrue from the sales of tax-free merchandises for the purpose of dodging all the Korean taxes and charges.

2. In view of the fact that such irregularities being made by the said club have brought serious adverse effects on the bona fide business of the Korean Tourist Recreation Service Association, this Association has requested the US Eighth Army and the appropriate authorities concerned to rectify the above elaborated situations.

80

It would be greatly appreciated if you would take appropriate measures in the matter.

(Individual seal)
KWON Yong Un
Chairman
Inchon Branch
Korean Tourist Recreation
Service Association
(Official seal)

위

한국적 민주주의 우리땅에 뿌리박자

내 무 부

수 사 821-10231 1972. 11. 24.

수 신 외무부 장관

제 목 한미 행협에 따른 도난 및 암거래 조사반 위원장 교체에 관한건

한미 행협에 따른 도난 및 암거래 조사반소 위원회의 신구 위원장을 다음과 같이 교체하여 주심을 바랍니다.

다 음

전 위원장

치안국 수사 지도 2계장 총경 송 형 식

신 위원장

치안국 수사 지도 2계장 총경 박

첨 부 : 신 위원장 이력서 1부. 끝.

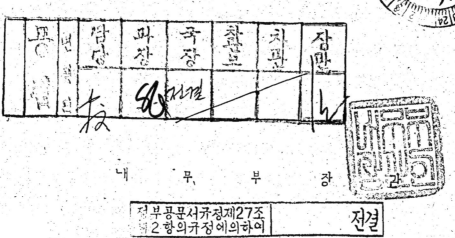

발송 No. 1972 11.24 내무부

기안	보존	담당	과장	국장	차관보	차관	장관
			전결				

내 무 부 장 관

정부공문서규정제27조 제2항의규정에의하여 | 전결

82

인적 사항

본적: 서울 특별시 중구 인현동 2가 181 - 20

주소: 서울 특별시 서대문구 북아현동 192 - 1

치안국 수사 지도과 수사 지도 담당

총경 박 보 영 (1923. 8. 3 생)

학 력

1936. 4. 10 - 41. 3. 30. 동경 대성 중학교 졸업

56. 4. 1 - 60. 3. 10. 단국 대학 법정학부 졸업(정치학사)

경 력

1945. 10. 1. 임 순경

47. 6. 6. 임경사 수도 특별 경비대 외근 감독

49. 12. 9. 임 경위 서울 시경 수사과 형사 주임

56. 9. 27 - 59. 12. 8. 임 경감 서울 시경 수사과 강력 및 형사 계장

67. 10. 28. 내무부 치안국 수사지도과 수사 2계장 서리

67. 11. 15. 임 총경 내무부 치안국 수사지도과 수사 2계장

69. 8. 5. 경기도 경찰국 수사 과장

70. 7. 20. 부산 경찰국 수사 과장

71. 8. 18. 경찰 대학 서무 과장

72. 10. 25. 명 치안국 수사지도과 수사 지도 담당

83

회의 참석 보고

1972. 11. 30.

1. 회의명 : SOFA 합동위 군민관계 분과위 암거래 조사반 회의

2. 일 시 : 72. 11. 30. (목) 14:00 - 16:30

3. 장 소 : 외무부 회의실

별첨 내용으로 한.미 합동회의에 권찬사무관을 참석케 하고저 하오니 재가하여 주시기 바랍니다.

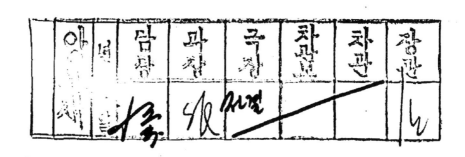

북미 2 과장 김 기 조

안		담당	과장	국장	차관보	차관	장관

84

관리번호
일반문서

AGENDA

FOR

PANEL ON LARCENY AND BLACKMARKETING

30 November 1972

ITEM	TOPIC
1	INTRODUCTION OF NEW MEMBERS (ROK AND US PRESENTATION)
2	INTRODUCTION OF US PROPOSALS (US PRESENTATION)
3	GENERAL DISCUSSION OF ROK/US COOPERATION FOR PREVENTION OF LARCENY AND BLACKMARKETING (ROK PRESENTATION)
4	DISCUSSION OF NEW BUSINESS
5	PROPOSAL FOR NEXT MEETING
6	ADJOURNMENT

85

PANEL ON LARCENY AND BLACK MARKETING

30 November 1972

MEMORANDUM FOR: Ad Hoc Subcommittee on Civil-Military Relations

1. Panel Members:

US	ROK
MAJ Curtney R. Fritts, Chairman	Mr. PARK Bo Young, Chairman
COL Joseph T. Fordham, J1	Mr. KWON Chan, MOFA
MR. Francis K. Cook, J5	Mr. HYUN Hong Joo, MOJ
LTC Calvin C. Quenstedt, USAF-K	Mr. CHUNG Ku Young, MOJ
LTC C. J. Baldree, JAJ	Mr. SHIN Yung Su, MOF
MR. John Nowell	

(3)

2. Subject of Recommendation: Measures to Prevent the Theft of US Government Property at ports of entry into Korea and during Transit to Destination.

3. Recommendation: That US and ROK law enforcement authorities meet before 15 January 73 and monthly thereafter to discuss measures to improve the prevention of theft of US Government Property at ports of entry into the ROK and during Transit to the final Destination.

4. Security Classification: Unclassified.

PARK BO YOUNG
Chairman, ROK Component
Panel on Larceny and Black Marketing

COURTNEY R. FRITTS, MAJ, USA
Chairman, US Component
Panel on Larceny and Black Marketing

86

3. 1973

87

갖보처회답는바, 미측에 통보.

기 안 용 지

분류기호 문서번호	미이 723 -	(전화번호)	전결규정 조 항 국장 전결사항
처리기간			
시행일자	1973. 1. 25.		
보존년한		국 장	
보조기관	과 장		협조
기안책임자	권 찬	북미 제2과	
경유 수신 참조	수신처 참조	발신	발송 1973. 1. 26 외무부
제 목	미 정부 재산 도난에 관한 조치 의뢰		

1. 한.미 군대지위협정에 의한 한.미 합동위 미측대표 "스미스" 장군은 한국측 대표 (외무부 구미국장 김동휘) 에게 보낸 공한에서 주한미군의 면세도입된 개인용품이 계속적으로 암시장에 흘러나오고, 또한 많은 미국정부 재산이 한국내에서 도난, 처분되고 있음을 통보하고, 이러한 도난사건의 빈번한 발생은 한국경제에 악영향을 미칠뿐만아니라 한국의 국가위신에 큰 손실을 가져오며, 주한미군의 군사 작전에도 지대한 영향이 있음을 강조하였음.

2. 상기의 빈번한 도난사건 발생과 관련하여 미측대표는 동 공한에서,

가. 한.미 합동조사반 (SOFA 합동위 제 19차 및 제 20차회의에서 합의함.) 으로 하여금 도난품 및 부정거래의 혐의가 있는 각 구역의 소매상 및 도매상의 판로 (outlets)를 수사할것.

나. 부정거래로 이득을 보고있는 암거래 소매상인들의

정서
관인
발송

공통서식1-2(갑)
1967. 4. 4. 승인

190mm ×268mm (1급인쇄용지70g /m²)
조달청 (500.000매인쇄)

88

영업허가를 취소할뿐 아니라 형사적인 조치를 취할것.

다. SOFA 합동위 양측 간사로 하여금 합동조사반 기능에 관한 제 19차 및 20차 합의사항을 재검토케 하여 필요하다면 동 조사반의 기능을 강화 및 촉진시킬것을 제의해 왔음.

3. 귀부에서는 미 정부 재산의 도난 및 면세도입된 주한미군 개인용품의 부정처분과 관련한 미측 대표의 제의에 관하여 긴급 조치하여 주시고, 당부에도 결과를 통보하여 주시기 바랍니다.

첨부 : 동 서한 사본 1 부.

수신처 : 내무부장관 (치안국장)
법무부장관 (검찰국장)
국방부장관

89

JOINT COMMITTEE
UNDER
THE REPUBLIC OF KOREA AND THE UNITED STATES
STATUS OF FORCES AGREEMENT

16 JAN 1973

Dear Mr. Kim:

I should like to bring to your attention a matter of serious and growing urgency. This concerns the continuing high rate of larceny of US Government property from US storage, supply points, and retail outlets in the Republic of Korea, for disposal through black marketing channels, as well as the continuing practice of the black marketing of duty-free personal property by some individuals. These criminal practices, as you are aware, both adversely impact on the Korean economy and on the image and military effectiveness of the US Forces in the Republic of Korea.

Paragraphs 8 and 9 of Article IX of the US-ROK SOFA contain a number of mutual obligations of general nature which not only permit, but require, cooperative action on the part of the authorities of both of our countries to prevent abuse of privileges, customs offenses, larceny of US Government property, and black marketing in general. As you are aware, pursuant to the provisions of Inclosure 12 to the minutes of the nineteenth Joint Committee meeting and Inclosure 14 to the minutes of the twenty-eighth Joint Committee Meeting, US-ROK joint investigative teams currently are functioning to effect close cooperation between our two governments in matters pertaining to illegal transactions in duty-free goods, and to insure enforcement of all laws and regulations prohibiting abuse of duty-free import privileges and illegal transactions in such items.

In accord with our mutual general obligations as expressed in the US-ROK SOFA, and the rights and powers of the joint investigative teams, I propose that these teams be directed, by Joint Committee action, to investigate the great number of local retail and wholesale outlets which are suspected of dealing in goods which have been obtained either by larceny or by other illegal transactions in violation of the SOFA. If this proposal meets with your concurrence, I would further propose that our two Joint Committee Secretaries review the two referenced inclosures of Joint Committee minutes to determine whether any revisions or amplifications to these inclosures may be required to facilitate the operations of these teams in fulfilling this mission, and to recommend to the Joint Committee any revisions or additions to the cited inclosures deemed necessary or appropriate.

In addition to the steps outlined above, I respectfully request that Republic of Korea authorities revoke licenses of black market retail operators, which would have the beneficial result of forcing closure of their illegal operations, and in addition, take punitive measures against black market operators as appropriate under Korean law and regulations. My rationale in proposing this approach to the problem is that the most effective way to eliminate larceny and black marketing is to eliminate the market in which stolen or black-marketed goods are sold. While other measures may be helpful, the most effective solution to the problem is to be found, I believe, in eliminating the profit in black market transactions.

It would be most appreciated if you would give these proposals your careful consideration.

Sincerely,

ROBERT N. SMITH
Lieutenant General
United States Air Force
United States Representative

KIM Dong-Whie
Republic of Korea
Representative

Agreement Relative to the Conduct of Joint ROK-US Investigations in Cases Involving Suspected Illegal Transactions in Goods Constituting the Property of the Korea Regional Exchange

1. Reference the ROK-US Joint Committee approval of operating instructions for the conduct of ROK-US joint investigations at the nineteenth Joint Committee meeting on 21 December 1967, and Joint Committee approval of the amplification of these operating instructions at its twenty-eighth meeting on 3 July 1968.

2. To supplement actions referenced in paragraph 1 above in the joint investigative field, with the specific objective of preventing the diversion to the Korean market of merchandise of the Korea Regional Exchange (KRE), the Republic of Korea Office of Customs Administration (OCA), the US Army Criminal Investigation Command, Korea Field Office (CIDCD-K) and the US Air Force Office of Special Investigation (AFOSI) agree to take the following actions, upon the approval of this agreement by the ROK-US Joint Committee.

a. Two ROK Customs officials from the Inchon Sub-office, Investigative Division, OCA, will be assigned to the Inchon Supply Depot to monitor the transporting activities of Exchange merchandise.

b. US Exchange officials will provide to the Korean Customs officials a copy of the manifests pertaining to merchandise transported from the Inchon Supply Depot to the various destinations throughout the ROK. These manifests will be furnished to OCA officials through the appropriate CIDCD-K or AFOSI agent, prior to the departure of the merchandise.

c. The Inchon Customs officials, upon receipt of a manifest, will apprise Korean Customs officials working with CIDCD-K or AFOSI agents located at the destination point of the merchandise of the data listed in Inclosure 1 to enable a verification to be made of the merchandise upon arrival at its destination. Verification of the merchandise will be made jointly by Korean Customs officials and CIDCD-K or AFOSI agents as appropriate. Where assigned, Exchange Security officers may participate in such verification process.

d. When the verification of arriving merchandise detects diversion or theft, an investigation will be initiated jointly by ROK OCA and CIDCD-K/AFOSI.

92

e. Exchange authorities will acquaint all Exchange Managers with this program to assure that Korean Customs officials receive full cooperation.

f. CIDCD-K and AFOSI will provide a copy of this agreement to all of their operating units to assure maximum cooperation.

g. Any of the parties to this agreement may at any time request the revision of all or portions of this agreement, upon which negotiation among these parties will be undertaken. This agreement will terminate upon the request of any party for such termination.

h. This agreement will become effective upon the date that it is approved by the ROK-US Joint Committee.

WILLIAM H. LEWIS Colonel, USAF Commander, AFOSI District 45	ROBERT N. HULLEY Colonel, MPC Commander, Korea Field Office, 4th Region USACIDC	SHIN, YONG SU Chief, Investigation Division, Surveillance Bureau, OCA

____
Date

93

INCLOSURE 1:

1. Vehicle Number

2. Driver's Name

3. Departing Time

4. Estimated Arriving Time

5. Destination

6. Seal Number

7. Items & Quantity (Counting be made in terms of cases or boxes according to the classification of VRR code from "0" to "9" items)

8. Transfer Voucher Number

9. Remarks

94

JOINT COMMITTEE
UNDER
THE REPUBLIC OF KOREA AND THE UNITED STATES
STATUS OF FORCES AGREEMENT

1-19-73

16 JAN 1973

Dear Mr. Kim:

I should like to bring to your attention a matter of serious and growing urgency. This concerns the continuing high rate of larceny of US Government property from US storage, supply points, and retail outlets in the Republic of Korea, for disposal through black marketing channels, as well as the continuing practice of the black marketing of duty-free personal property by some individuals. These criminal practices, as you are aware, both adversely impact on the Korean economy and on the image and military effectiveness of the US Forces in the Republic of Korea.

Paragraphs 8 and 9 of Article IX of the US-ROK SOFA contain a number of mutual obligations of general nature which not only permit, but require, cooperative action on the part of the authorities of both of our countries to prevent abuse of privileges, customs offenses, larceny of US Government property, and black marketing in general. As you are aware, pursuant to the provisions of Inclosure 12 to the minutes of the nineteenth Joint Committee meeting and Inclosure 14 to the minutes of the twenty-eighth Joint Committee Meeting, US-ROK joint investigative teams currently are functioning to effect close cooperation between our two governments in matters pertaining to illegal transactions in duty-free goods, and to insure enforcement of all laws and regulations prohibiting abuse of duty-free import privileges and illegal transactions in such items.

In accord with our mutual general obligations as expressed in the US-ROK SOFA, and the rights and powers of the joint investigative teams, I propose that these teams be directed, by Joint Committee action, to investigate the great number of local retail and wholesale outlets which are suspected of dealing in goods which have been obtained either by larceny or by other illegal transactions in violation of the SOFA. If this proposal meets with your concurrence, I would further propose that our two Joint Committee Secretaries review the two referenced

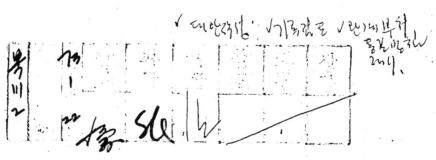

94-1

inclosures of Joint Committee minutes to determine whether any revisions or amplifications to these inclosures may be required to facilitate the operations of these teams in fulfilling this mission, and to recommend to the Joint Committee any revisions or additions to the cited inclosures deemed necessary or appropriate.

In addition to the steps outlined above, I respectfully request that Republic of Korea authorities revoke licenses of black market retail operators, which would have the beneficial result of forcing closure of their illegal operations, and in addition, take punitive measures against black market operators as appropriate under Korean law and regulations. My rationale in proposing this approach to the problem is that the most effective way to eliminate larceny and black marketing is to eliminate the market in which stolen or black-marketed goods are sold. While other measures may be helpful, the most effective solution to the problem is to be found, I believe, in eliminating the profit in black market transactions.

It would be most appreciated if you would give these proposals your careful consideration.

Sincerely,

ROBERT N. SMITH
Lieutenant General
United States Air Force
United States Representative

KIM Dong-Whie
Republic of Korea
Representative

3

94-2

도난사건에 관한 관계 조항

1. SOFA 조항

가. SOFA 제9조 8항

합중국 군대는 대한민국 당국과 협력하여 본조의 규정에 따라 합중국 군대, 동 군대의 구성원, 군속 및 그들의 가족에게 부여된 특권의 남용을 방지하기 위하여 필요한 조치를 취하여야 한다.

(The United States armed forces, in cooperation with the authorities of the Republic of Korea, shall take such steps as are necessary to prevent abuse of privileges granted to the United States armed forces, members of such forces, the civilian component, and their dependents in accordance with this Article.)

나. SOFA 제9조 9항

(가) 대한민국 당국과 합중국 군대는 대한민국 정부의 세관당국이 집행하는 법령에 위반하는 행위를 방지하기 위하여, 조사의 실시 및 증거의 수집에 있어서 상호 협조하여야 한다.

(나) 합중국 군대는 대한민국 정부의 세관당국에 의하여 또는 이에 대신하여 행하여지는 압수된 물품을 인도하도록 확보하기 위하여 그의 권한내의 모든 원조를 제공하여야 한다.

(다) 합중국 군대 당국은 세관검사의 목적으로 군사상 통제하는 부두와 비행장에 파견된 세관 직원에게 가능한 모든 원조를 제공하여야 한다.

95

(a) In order to prevent offenses against laws and regulations administered by the customs authorities of the Government of the Republic of Korea, the authorities of the Republic of Korea and the United States armed forces shall assist each other in the conduct of inquiries and the collection of evidence.

(b) The United States armed forces shall render all assistance within their power to ensure that articles liable to seizure by, or on behalf of, the customs authorities of the Government of the Republic of Korea are handed over to those authorities.

(d) The authorities of the United States armed forces shall provide all practicable assistance to the customs officials dispatched to military controlled piers and airports for the purpose of customs inspection.

2. 제 19차 합동위 합의사항 (inclosure 12)

3. 제 28차 합동위 합의사항 (inclosure 14)

96

기안

결

국 방 부

인사203.1-266 73. 2. 2.

수신 외무부장관

제목 미 정부 재산 도난에 관한 조치

1. 귀부 비이 723-2686(73.1.27)로 조치 의뢰한 건과 관련입니다.

2. 주한미군 재산 도난 방지에 대하여는 72.2.25 주한 미군 사령관의 협조 공한에 의해 첨부와 같이 처리중에 있으며,

3. 군수품 도난및 암시장 근절을 위하여는 기지촌 정화대책(청와대 주관사업)의 일환으로 5부(내무, 재무, 법무, 국방, 상공)합동으로 강력히 단속을 하고 있으며, 72년도 실적은 64,300여점에 달하고 있음을 첨언 합니다.

첨부 : 1. 주한미군 재산 도난 방지를위한 조치 공문 사본 1부.
2. 군수품 도난및 암시장 근절 계획 1부. 끝.

국 방 부 장 관

발송 1973.2.5 국방부

97

외 무 부		결재	
접수 일시	197 . . . 시 분		
접수 번호	제 3680 호		
주무과			
담당자			
관련 근거		197 . . . 까지 처리할것	

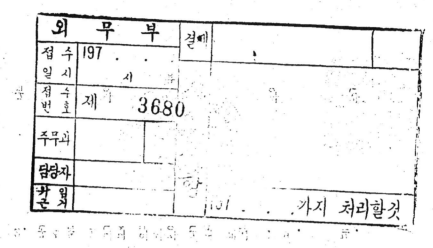

사본

대 한 민 국 국 방 부

주한 미군 사령관 귀하 1972. 3. 28.

귀하의 72.2.25일자 서한에 대한 회신입니다.

본인은 과거 수년간 주한미군의 군수품의 상당량이 도난되었다는 귀하의 서신을 접하고 이에 대하여 심히 유감으로 생각합니다.

그간 수차에 걸친 관계부처와의 협의에 따라 정부는 미 군수품의 도난을 방지하고 미군기지 주변의 정화를 위한 기지촌 정화대책을 수립하여 추진중에 있읍니다.

연이나 귀하의 서신에서 지적한바와 같이 대부분의 군수품 도난사고는 한국인과 미국인의 결탁에 의하여 발생되고 있으므로 범죄수사와 장물 회수를 위하여는 한.미양국 수사진의 긴밀한 협조가 이루어지야 하겠읍니다. 이를 위한 방안으로 본인은 범죄가 발생하였을시는 신속히 범죄내용과 수집된 증거자료를 국방부에 통보하여 줄것을 귀하에게 요청하는 바이며, 이와같은 정보 교환은 당부가 관계 부처에게 적극적인 수사활동을 촉구할수 있는 자료가 되리라 믿습니다.

대한민국 국방부의 통보부서는 국방부 조사대장(육군대령 김정규)을 지정하는 바입니다.

99

본인은 귀하와 공동 노력으로 상호 이익에 배반되는 여사한 사고도 근절 시킬수 있기를 바랍니다.

최대의 경의를 표하면서

경 구

국 방 부 장 관

유 재 흥

99

5부 합동 군수품 단속 계획

1. 목 적

각종 군수품의 시중 암거래를 근절시켜 국가경제 발전의 저해요인을 제거시키고 안보태세를 공고히 하며 국토방위의 전력을 증강시키고저 함에 있음.

2. 방 침

가. 5부 합동 군수품 단속 14개 지구와 겸행한다.

나. 외국군 주둔 11개지역을 우선적으로 중점 단속한다.

다. 국민계몽 사업을 강화한다.

3. 일반계획

가. 연간 단속 계획 : 별첨 (생략)

나. 기구 및 인원편성 : 별첨(생략)

다. 소요 예산 : 2,220,000원

지역별 단속인원 및 실적에 따라 배정

4. 세부 계획

가. 물자별 중점단속과 단속 기일은 지구실정에 알맞게 지구 자체에서 결정한다.

나. 단속물자중 미군물자 (한국군과 공용되는 물자제외)는 그 출처를 규명한후 미군부대에 인계한다.

다. 만일 미군부대에서 압수물자의 인수를 거부할시는 현품을 사진촬영 보고후 처리지시를 받는다.

라. 각지구 상임위원은 경화대책을 위한 군수품 단속 업무에 편성된 단속요원을 확보하고 소요장비를 지원받아 단속업무에 만전을 기한다.

100

마. 11개지구를 관할하는 상임위원은 현지에 설치된 지구 경화 대책본부와 긴밀한 협조를 유지한다.

5. 행정사항

가. 일일 단속결과는 월말로 종합하여 익월5일까지 중앙위원회에 필히 도착토록 한다.

나. 단속 물자중 미군 물자는 기히 시달된 양식에 의거 별도 기입하여 월말 보고서에 유첨한다.

101

관

법 무 부

검찰 820- 2140 (70-2807) 1973. 2.3.

수신 외무부장관

제목 미정부재산 도난에 관한 조치

1. 외무부 미이 723-2686(73. 1. 27)에 대한 것입니다.

2. 귀부를 통하여 당부에 전달된 미정부 재산 도난에 관한 조치의뢰에 대하여는 별첨과 같이 검찰총장에게 지시하였읍니다.

첨부: 미군수물자 관련사범 엄단 1부.끝

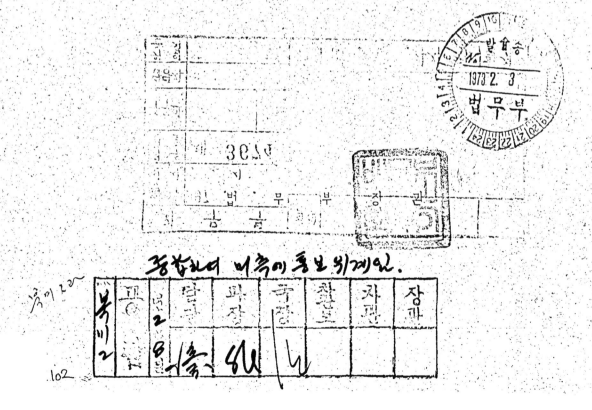

발송 1973. 2. 3 법무부

법 무 부 장 관

종합하여 미측에 통보하게 요.

북미2	과	북2	담당	과장	국장	차관보	차관	장관

외 무 부		결재	
접 수 일 시	197 . . . 시 분		
접 수 번 호	제 3674 호		
주무과			
담당자			
위 임 근 거			197 . . . 까지 처리할것

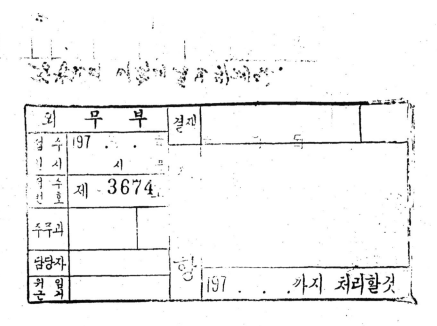

법 무 부

검참 820- (70-2807) 1973. 2. 3.

수신 검찰총장

제목 미군수물자 관련사범 엄단

한미군 대지위에 관한 협정에 의한 한미합동위원회 미측대표로부터 별첨과 같은 공한이 있어 송부하니 업무에 참고하시고,

미군수물자 관련사범을 엄단하여 도난방지 및 피해품 회수에 적극 협조하여 주시기 바랍니다.

첨부: 미정부 재산 도난에 관한 조치의뢰 1부. 끝

법 무 부 장 관

103

내 무 부

수사 821 - P53 1973. 2. 7.

수신 외무부 장관

제목 미 정부 재산 도난에 관한 조치 의뢰

1. 미이 723 - 2768 (73. 1. 27) 관련 입니다.

2. 미군 재산 도난 사건에 관하여 현재 한국 경찰에서 각 사건별로 강력한 수사를 진행 하고 있으며,

3. 면세 도입된 미국인 개인 용품의 불법 유출 암거래 등 관세법 위반 행위에 대하여는 관세청에서 주관하여 단속 하고 있으며 경찰에서 단속 적발시에는 관세청에 이첩 처리 하고 있읍니다.

4. 개인 용품의 불법 유출은 미군측에 서로 협조 하여 그 근원을 봉쇄하여 불법 유출 및 암거래 행위에 대한 사전 예방 조치를 하여 주실 것을 바랍니다. 끝.

발송 No. 2 7 내무부

내 무 부 장

104

외 무 FEB 73 14 : 43			
접수 일시	197 . . . 시 분	결재	
접수 번호	제 4045	지	
주무과			
담당자			
위임 근거			

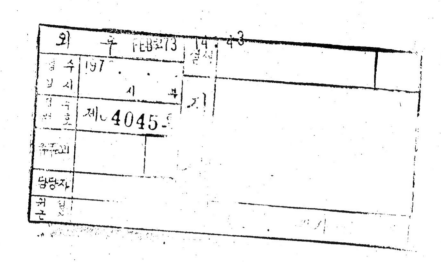

미 정부재산 도난방지에 관한 조치사항

1973. 3. 12.

1. 경 위

   1. 16. 합동위 미측대표 "스미스" 중장의 서한 접수

   1. 27. 당부는 빈번한 미정부재산 도난건에 대하여 강력한 조치를 취해줄 것을 관계부처(내무부, 법무부 및 국방부)에 요청하였음.

2. 관계부처가 취한 조치내용

   가. 내무부 (73. 2. 7.) :

      1) 미군 정부재산 도난건에 관하여 내무부는 전국 경찰에서 각 사건별로 강력한 수사를 진행중에 있음을 재확인하고,

      2) 개인용품의 불법유출에 관하여는 미군측이 자체의 유출근원을 봉쇄하여, 불법유출 및 암거래 행위의 사전 예방조치를 취해줄 것을 건의하였음.

   나. 법무부 (73. 2. 3.) :

      법무부장관은 73. 2. 3.자로 미 군수물자 관련 사범을 엄단하여 도난방지 및 피해품 회수에 적극 협조하여 줄 것을 검찰총장에게 지시함.

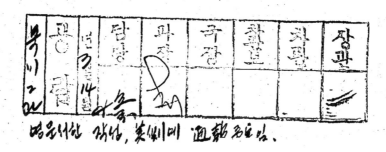

북미2과	공람	년 3월 14일	담당	과장	국장	심의관	차관	장관
			(서명)	(서명)				(서명)

105

영문서한 작성, 美側에 通報 요망임.

다. 국방부 (73. 2. 2.) :

1) 국방부는 군수품의 도난사건에 관련하여 1972. 3. 28. 자로 주한미군 사령관에게 일차 서신을 발송하고, 범죄행위가 발생하였을시는 신속히 그 내용과 수집된 증거자료를 국방부에 통고하여 줄것을 요청하였으며, 또한 국방부는 조사대장 (김정국 대령)을 지정하여 적극적인 수사활동을 전개하고 있음.

2) 또한 국방부는 군수품 도난 및 암시장 근절이 기지촌 정화대책의 일환임을 상기시키고 내무부, 재무부, 법무부, 국방부 및 상공부등 5개부처가 합동으로 강력히 단속하고 있으며 1972년도 실적은 64,300 여점에 달하고 있음을 통보하여 왔음.

106

회의 참석 보고

1. 회의명 : 제 5차 한미 합동 도난 및 암거래 조사반 회의
(ROK-US Larceny & Black Marketing Panel)

2. 일시 및 장소 : 1973. 3. 15. (목) 14:30 -
미측 SOFA 회의실

3. 참석자 : 북미 2과 권 찬 (동 조사반의 한미 양측 위원은 별첨 참조)

4. 안 건 : 미정부 재산 도난방지에 관한 건

** 정부 방침 (별첨 참조)

1. 미 정부 재산 도난 예방법
2. 도난품의 회수책
3. 한미 양측의 보고절차 개선책

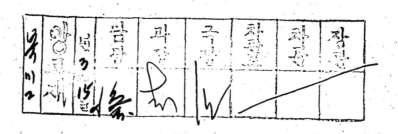

북미2	양 재	3월 15일	담당	과장	국장	차관보	차관	장관

107

공 란

공 란

공 란

공　　란

공 란

1972	US Gov't Property Lost/Stolen	US Gov't Vehicles Lost/Stolen	1 Total US Gov't Prop Lost/Stolen	US Gov't Prop Recovered	US Gov't Veh's Recovered	2 Total US Gov't Prop Recovered	3 Total Net Loss US Gov't Prop	Nonapp Fund Lost/ Stolen	Nonapp Fund Recovered	Total Net Loss Nonapp Fund
JAN	$132,837	$12,808	$145,695	$52,178	$3,000	$55,178	$90,517	$6,727	$101	$6,626
FEB	95,390	-	95,390	801	-	801	94,589	5,800	-	5,800
MAR	58,500	2,800	61,300	13,525	2,800	16,325	44,975	-	-	-
APR	62,471	-	62,471	24,168	-	24,168	38,303	2,219	-	2,219
MAY	121,632	10,879	132,511	21,248	-	21,248	111,263	580	-	580
JUN	246,263	-	246,263	11,764	-	11,764	234,499	9,008	-	9,008
JUL	94,850	-	94,850	23,121	-	23,121	71,729	843	-	843
AUG	120,088	-	120,088	5,728	-	5,728	114,360	8,258	57	8,201
SEP	67,369	2,880	70,249	30,728	-	30,728	39,521	-	42	(-)42
OCT	74,199	-	74,199	10,819	-	10,819	63,380	299	-	299
NOV	118,123	-	118,123	5,940	-	5,940	112,183	206	234	(-)28
DEC	192,570	3,195	195,765	2,353	-	2,353	193,412	308	-	308
[illegible]	1,384,342	32,563	1,416,904	202,373	5,800	208,173	1,208,73[illegible]	34,24[illegible]	[illegible]	35,814

The dollar value of lost/stolen, recovered and net loss of US Government Property, US Government Vehicles, and Nonappropriated Funds Property listed above, reflect the figures reported to the Eighth Army PM by Major Subordinate Commands for the period 1 Jan 72 to 30 November 1972.

113

美軍物資盜難狀況

區分 / 市道別	發生	檢擧	%	被害額	回收額	措置 計	拘束	不拘束	移牒
計	282	206	73.1	161,271,814	(未140,765,256) (15.3%) 25,501,558	420	208	142	70
서울	8	23	287.5	3,732,160	2,877,800	35	30	3	2
釜山	4	5	125.0	10,942,100	1,842,100	13	11		2
京畿	181	119	65.7	121,345,459	11,240,860	259	97	104	(送致43) 58
江原	6	6	100	156,200	63,900	6	6	.	.
忠北	2	2	100	13,500	13,500	4	3	1	.
忠南	15	10	66.7	1,606,980	1,299,400	19	9	7	3
慶北	28	27	96.4	13,865,938	2,453,718	54	32	20	2
慶南	9	5	55.6	2,779,902	1,325,650	14	8	4	2
全北	28	8	28.6	11,689,575	4,250,830	14	12	1	1
全南	1	1	100	140,000	140,000	2	.	2	.
濟州	.	.		.	.	.	.	.	.

註:

※ 檢擧被疑者所屬別內訳 ~ 別添

※ 美軍側集計 差額

72年度 美軍側算出은 {被害額 1,416,904$ (566,761,600원), 回收額 208,173$ (83,269,200원), 未回收 1,208,731$ (483,492,400원)}

差額 ~ {被害額(+) 400,489,786원, 回收額(+) 57,762,642원, 未回收(+) 342,727,144원}

114

檢擧被疑者所屬別內訳表

72. 1 ~ 12

區分 / 市道別	檢擧件數				檢擧人員			
	計	美軍人	韓國人	從業員	計	美軍人	韓國人	從業員
計	206	33	58	115	420	49	123	248
서울	23	·	8	15	35		25	10
釜山	5	·	2	3	13	·	11	2
京畿	119	29	16	74	259	43	33	183
江原	6	·	6		6	·	6	·
忠北	2	·	1	1	4	·	2	2
忠南	10	2	8		19	4	15	·
慶北	27	1	7	19	54	1	7	46
慶南	5		4	1	14	·	12	2
全北	8	1	6	1	14	1	12	1
全南	1	·	·	1	2	·	·	2
濟州	·	·	·	·				
註	※ 從業員 248名中 카추샤 31名 包含							

115

[illegible]

PX Ration System
proved failure
by Don C Terrell
the Korea Times, March 11.

1. It has been the practice of some persons to compromise or to bribe a ration control MP in order that he does not record the purchases. this privilege that buyer an unlimited supply of black market goods. ~~these people become the source of~~

2. The ration plate is used ~~when GIZ~~ for the purchase of liquor & cigarette & household goods.

The PX & Commissary systems are controlled & operated by Americans

And the American MP make no genuine effort to discourage ~~[illegible]~~ the illegal flow of goods into the black-market.

116

On the occasion of my last attendance at this meeting, I want to express to you the personal privilege & pleasure it has been for me to have had the opportunity to work together with you all great personality on this panel.

I was originally scheduled to bring the new member with me today, but he was recruited for the exercise of CPX.

117

SUBJECT: Improved procedures on the subject of larceny and ~~&~~ blackmarketing involving US Government & property

c. That US & ROK law enforcement authorities meet at least four times a year, on a quarterly basis, to discuss methods to improve notification procedures for all acts of larceny (of US Government property), to discuss measures to prevent the larceny of US Government property and blackmarketing

1190 and the recovery of lost or

stolen U.S Government property

119

공 란

공 란

공 란

공 란

強賣·不良상품등 集中단속

商工部 商去來淨化 3·단계로

'73. 5. 22.

不正외래품 闇去來도

店員복장統一 同一商品 점포制限

상공부는 상도의앙양을 위해 오는7월10일부터 강매행위、부당가격징수및 불량상품취급、부정외래품의 암거래등을 집중단속키로했다。21일하오열린 관계기관의 관·민연석회에서는 현재 말썽이되고있는 商去來상의 문젯점이 ①呼客및 强賣행위、고객에 대한 시비행위、買入상품의 교환거부 ②부당가격및 불량상품취급 ③부정외래품의 암거래등이라고 지적、이를 해소키위해 제1단계로는 6월말까지 상가의 자율적인 정화를 실시토록하되 제2단계로 7월10일부터는 집중지도단속을 실시하며 3단계로 제도적인 항구적방안을 수립키로 했다。

① 6월까지 商街自律로
② 7월10일부터 指導도
③ 제도적恒久방안 수립

이날 업계에서는 이러한 불미스러운 상행위가 근본적으로는 백화점、상가등 판매기관의 직영체제미확립과 동일업종취급점포의 난립에 의한 파당 경쟁때문이라는 의견을 제시했는데 이에따라 상공부는 商街개설자에 대해 점포를입대함에 있어 동일취급상품점포의 개설수를제한시키도록할방침이다。

이날회의에는 내무、농수산、문화공보부、국세청、서울市와 大韓商議등 비롯한 각 백화점대표등 21명이 참석했다。상거래 정화를위한 3단계실천방안의 내용은 다음과같다。

◇자율적정화실시(1단계)

상공부 商易次官補를 위원장으로하는 실무위원회를 설치、지도계몽「캠페인」전개(5월21일부터 6월30일까지)

▲6월을 商道義앙양의달로선정、商店員의 윤리강령을 채택하고 상점및商街경진대회를개최

▲각백화점、市場、商街에 忠告「센터」를 설치

▲百貨店、商街、외국인관광객専用賣店、市場상점원의 복장통일및 명찰부착

◇집중指導團束(2단계)

▲7월10일부터 31일까지 경찰및 관계기관합동단속반을편성、집중단속

▲1차적으로 輕犯法으로 처벌하고 다음에는 店舗임대계약취소、市場開設허가취소등관계법규에의한처벌병행

◇항구적방안수립(3단계)

▲商去來관계법령의 개정보완

▲直營백화점등 대량판매기관의 지원육성

경 새마을노동교실개관 축
전국연합노조청계피복지부 '73.5.21

◇청계피복상가에서열린 새마을노동교실개관식。2백여명의 근로자들이 참석했다。

뉴스 스포트

市民누구나 겪어본 不快感
자발적「캠페인」先行돼야

강매、불량식품등 악덕상행위에 대한 관계당국의 강력한시정책 마련은 오히려 때늦은 감이없지 않다。지난 17、18 이틀동안 서울시경이 전격적으로 벌인 악덕상인단속에서 적발된 내용만보아도 그동안 우리나라의 상도의가 어떠했나를 그대로 들여다볼수가있다。

이날 경찰은 서울의 東大門、南大門동 번화시장가와 반도·조선「아케이드」등 주로 외국인 관광객이 많이 드나드는곳등 모두 11개소에서 총1천7백9명의 악덕상인을적발、그중 경미한사범 4백40명만을 훈방한후 나머지 1천2백79명을 무더기로 즉결에 회부、새 경범법이나 도로교통법을 적용해 벌금 또는 구류처분을 받도록했는데 특히 서울시민이 주로 한용하는 南大門、東大門등 두시장에서만 전체의 3분의1이 넘는 6백49건이 적발됐고 외국인이 많이 드나드는 반도·조선「아케이드」에서는 65건이 적발됐었다。

이단속에서 적발된 악덕상인들의 유형을 보면 ①국산품을 외제로 속여파는행위 ②물건값만물어보고 사지않는다고 욕설을 퍼붓는행위 ③물건을 만져보고 마음에 들지않아 사지않는경우 부덥대는 불친절 ④가게앞을 지나는 손님의 옷자락을잡아끌며 물건을사라고 강요하는행위 ⑤외국인 관광객에게 억지로 매달리며 물건을사도록 강청하는행위 ⑥지방상경객에게바가지요금을 씌우는 행위 ⑦도로상에 노점을 차리고 강매하는행위 ⑧수학여행온 학생들을 붙들고 불량상품을 비싼값으로속여파는행위등 갖가지。적발된 상인중 어느 포목점주인은 첫손님이 값만 물어보고 그냥 지나간후 재수가 없다며 가게문앞에 소금을 뿌리기도 했고 규격이 맞지않아 옷을 바꾸러온 손님에게 웃돈을 더 요구하다 적발되기도 했다。

이번단속에 걸려든 상인들중 즉결에넘겨진 상인들은 모두 개정경범법 또는 도로교통법의 적용을받아 10일내외의 구류처분 또는2~5천원의과료에 처해졌는데 경찰은 앞으로 이같은단속을 전국에확대、지방도시에 대해서도 단속을펴 지금까지 누적된 상가의 병폐를 일소할 방침을 세우고있다。아뭏든 명랑한 상거래를위한 정부의 이같은 3단계 淨化방안은 특히 대도시의 시민이면 누구나 한번쯤겪는불쾌감을 시 맛보지않기위해서라도 강력히 실천에 옮겨져야 할일들。

이번 서울시경이 집중단속을편 다음날 어느시민은『후련한 일이었다』며 철저하게 단속을 펼것을 당부하기도했는데 단속에 나섰던 대부분의경찰은『일시적인 단속에앞서 이미 각경찰서、구청、보건소등에 설치돼 있는「새생활신고센터」의 적극적인 활용과 시장 또는 상인조합의 자발적인 상도의앙양「캠페인」이면저 이뤄져야 할것』이라고 입을모았다。

124

[redacted]

공 란

공 란

공　　　란

공 란

Project Padlock Effective In Curbing Stolen Property

SEOUL (Special) — A trend of "rapid and dramatic reductions" in stolen U.S. property in Korea was cited during an in-progress review of Project Padlock, the 8th U.S. Army's asset control and security program, at U.S. Forces Korea headquarters here.

The asset control task group told USFK asset control representatives and coordinators that these reductions coincide with Padlock's improvements in personnel, security and logistics thus indicating the program's effectiveness.

Lt. Col. Eugene R. Belcher, chief of the task group, said it appeared from "all indicators" that now is the time to switch Padlock from a remedial action to a long-range preventive effort.

The task group's study of thefts showed that monthly net average of stolen U.S. property fell from $132,000 in 1972 to $61,000 during the first five months of 1973.

Net losses are calculated by subtracting total recoveries from total losses. Project Padlock began full scale operations in January of this year. Statistics from the same five month period in 1972 are not available, but total net losses for the year were said to be at least $1.5 million.

Of the four property categories (government, Korea Regional Exchange, nonappropriated and private) government thefts showed the greatest decline, falling 71 per cent. On the other hand, private per property thefts fell only 8 per cent, although the report's statistics showed a $2,000 decline in the net monthly average. Task Group Director Brig. Gen. Max Etkin, assistant chief of staff, G4, told the audience private property theft was "an area of this program that needs special attention."

Improved logistic management and security formed the spearhead of the drive to reduce thefts. Project Padlock's goals for increased security "have been or are being met." According to the task provost marshal representative.

More stringent security measures are in effect at the gates of most U.S. installations, and direct coordination has been established between U.S. and Republic of Korea law enforcement agencies. In addition, increased cooperation between the provost marshal and the criminal investigation division helped bring a reduction in Korea Regional Exchange losses.

Belcher said the program's logistical improvements have shown what "logistical and professionalism really are." Some of the logistical achievements have been improved inventory of supplies, better control over goods while they are enroute to their destination, increased turn-in of excess supplies and the consolidation of logistical facilities wherever operational requirements permitted.

Padlock's personnel program generally aims to stock Korea with the best possible personnel, obtain the most qualified people for key security and supply positions and to increase continuity of operations within the Korean theater.

Lt. Col. R. C. Horn, chief, military personnel division, G1, said 8th Army has requested the Department of Defense not to assign personnel with sustandard records to Korea. The records of those people who are assigned here receive a careful screening.

The command is now working closely with U.S. Army Pacific and DA to find qualified school trained personnel for critical security and supply positions. A concrete effort is also underway to encourage people to remain in Korea.

DA has been asked to rescind Korea's restricted area status and housing for command sponsored personnel has been more than doubled in the past year.

Belcher said the initial Padlock efforts brought about the remedial results for which they were designed but added that the time has come to implement a long-range preventive program intended to perpetuate these gains. The long-range effort would be a system of checks "that will measure the compliance and verify the adequacy of managerial procedures and operational staffing."

An asset control task force would meet on call or at least quarterly to analyze and review the program's effectiveness. It will then recommend corrective and preventive actions to the 8th U.S. Army command group.

In summary, Etkin said the overall purpose of the asset control program is to control "so we can have what we need, when we need it and where we need it."

내 무 부

수사 821 - P61 1973. 6. 12.

수신 외무부 장관

참조 외무부 북미 2과
서기관 양 세 훈

제목 한, 미간 도범 및 암거래 실무반 회의 사항 협의

73. 6. 1 외무부 회의실에서 개최된 SOFA 도범 및 암거래 실무반 회의에서 미 정부 재산과 미국인 개인용 재산의 도난 및 암거래에 관하여 미측 으로 부터 3개 사항을 제의 해 왔으므로 그 에 대한 한국측 대안을 별첨과 같이 작성 회람 하오니 검토 하신후 그 의견을 73. 6. 16. 까지 제출 하여 주시기 바랍니다.

첨부 : 미국측 제안에 대한 한국측 대안 1부. 끝.

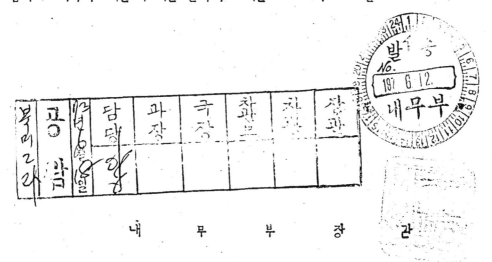

북미2과	공람	6/13	담당	과장	국장	차관보	차관	장관

내 무 부 장 관

130

외 무 부

접수 일시

22896

미국 측 제안에 대한 한국측 대안

미 측 제 안	한 국 측 대 안
1. 한미 법 집행 당국은 미정부 재산의 도난 및 암거래 문제를 토의키 위하여 회합을 갖이며 토의는 탁송 되는 미정부 재산 및 미 군인 미국 민간인 구성원 과 그들 부양 가족의 개인용 재산이 포함 된다	가. 한,미 양당국은 미 정부 재산의 도난 및 암거래 문제를 토의키 위한 회합은 갖이되 나. 그외 민간인 및 부양 가족의 도난 문제는 별도로 일반인 도난 사건에 준해서 취급되여야 함으로 본 토의에 포함시킬 필요가 없음.
2. 도난 및 암거래 된 미 정부 재산이라는 것을 한국 당 정부 당국에 증명키 위하여 이에 조력하는 한미 합동반을 설치 한다	가. 미 정부 재산 및 미군인 개인 용품의 암거래 행위에 대하여 한국 관세청 당국과 미군 당국간에 현재 운영중인 합동 수사반을 기능으로 암거래 물품 유출원 및 암시장 을 더욱 효과적으로 봉쇄 할수 있으므로 별도의 합동반 설치는 불 필요함. 나. 한국 경찰은 암거래의 단속 강화를 위하여 계속 노력 하고 있음.
3. 한국 법 집행 당국은 미 당국이 증명한 도난,암거래된것 뿐만 아니라 불법으로 운반되는 미정부 재산 및 미국인 개인 재산에 대하여도 압수 반환에 대한 즉각적인 조치를 취한다	가. 도난 사건에 접한 한국 당국은 신속히 수사에 착수하고 피해품이 압수된경우에는 한국법에 규정된 절차에 따라 조속 반환 조치 한다 나. 미군 영내에서 도난 사건이 발생 하여 한국 수사당국이 수사할 필요한 조치를 요청할시는 미당국은 최대한 편의를 도모 한다.

121

분과위원명단

한국측		미군측	
위원장	내무부 치안국 수사지도계장	위원장	미8군 헌병대장
	총경 유명두		육군소령 오웬에이스. 세이키
위원	외무부 북미 2과	위원	육군대령 투미스.이. 헤디크
	서기관 양세훈		
"	법무부 검찰과	"	육군중령 칼빈,씨 퀜스델
	검사 연홍주		
"	법무부 송무과	"	" 씨,제이, 벨드저
	검사 박희태	"	육군대령 존 엠. 벤.
"	재무부 관세청 심리과장		
	서기관 양성법	"	군속 프랜시스,케이.쿠-크

132

기 안 용 지

분류기호 문서번호	미이 723 -	(전화번호)	전결규정 9 조 2 항 국장 전결사항
처리기간			
시행일자	1973. 6. 22.		
보존년한		국 장	
보조기관	과 장		협조
기안책임자	양세훈	북미 2 과	
경 유		발송	통제
수 신	내무부장관		
참 조	치안국 수사지도과		
제 목	한미간 도범 및 암거래 실무반 회의시 협의		

대 : 수사 821 - 961

SOFA 도범 및 암거래 실무반 회의에서 제시된 미측의 3개안에 대한 귀부 대안에 관하여 당부가 검토한 내용을 아래와 같이 회보합니다.

1. (1) 귀부 대안에서 군인에 관하여 명시되어있지 않으며,
   (2) 민간인 및 부양가족의 도난문제는 일반인 도난사건에 준해서 취급되어야함으로 본 토의에 포함시킬 필요가 없다고 하였는 바, 이는 SOFA 제 25조 및 동합의 양해사항 규정과 상치되는 처사가 아닌지 여부가 검토되어야 할 것으로 사료됨.
2. 한미 합동반 설치가 불필요하다는 귀견과 같은 의견임.
3. 도난사건에 한하여 즉각 조치한다는 귀안에 동의하나 미군당국에 의하여 식별 확인하는 문제는 신중을 기하여야 할 것임. 끝.

정서 / 관인 / 발송

공통서식 1—2 (갑)
1967. 4. 4 승 인

190mm×268mm (1급인쇄용지70g/m²)
조 달 청 (500,000매 인 쇄)

133

Korea Times Photo

A Korean woman shops for PX goods at a black market in downtown Seoul. Numerous rationing systems have been used by the U.S. Forces in Korea since their first arrival in 1945. But Korean "Yankee markets" still enjoy business due to many problems and shortcomings in the systems.

Black Markets

PX Ration System Proved Failure

...ween the practice to issue each man a myriad of little folded paper cards and stamp books which were to be punched, marked, or ripped as ration allowance was consumed. Today, the single plastic plate is used for every type of purchase, and the card is coded to indicate ration allowances.

When a purchase is made in the PX or commissary, an ink impression of the ration plate is made on a blank IBM card together with a figure showing the amount of the purchase, and these cards are wrapped and sent to Seoul every four days and entered into a computer. Each soldier is limited to $75 a month in the PX and each dependent is allowed to spend $50. If he or his wife spend more than that, he risks being court-martialed.

If a single item valued at $25 or more is bought from the PX, the purchase is recorded on still another form, and these are sent to Seoul for the computer every 20 days. Some of these items are rationed so that a person is allowed to purchase only one during his entire tour in Korea. These items include radios (over $25), electric fans, cameras (over $40), and sixteen other items.

'Letter of Authorization'

Some items are rationed so severely that none may be purchased without special permission of the area commander, and he must issue a "Letter of Authorization" after the applicant submits written justification for wanting to own the item. This list includes television sets, diamond rings, air conditioners, and nine other items. As before, all these items are entered in a permanent computer record in Seoul.

Many other items are rationed by the commissary. For example: A family of seven is limited to 40 ounces of instant coffee a month and five jars of Tang. In addition, a single soldier (receiving separate ration pay) is limited to $70 a month in the commissary.

The ration plate is used -

5) The PX and commissary systems are controlled by Americans in name only, while day-to-day operations are controlled by Koreans (sort of like giving a fox his own chicken farm). The pay of these Korean employes is low, and the profits from black marketing are high. Being caught black-marketing carries little social stigma among Korean people, and Korean police can be bribed by their fellow citizens. Often vast quantities of goods disappear from the warehouse — sometimes paid for, sometimes outright stolen, but always blackmarketed. On one occasion a giant PX warehouse was burned down just before inventory apparently as a cover-up for merchandise diversion. The rationing system makes no attempt to control warehouse inventory, only sales.

6) The Korean National Police make no genuine effort to discourage the open sale of black market goods. "Yankee Markets" are busy, well stocked, and open seven days a week. Approximately two days a year the police "crack down" for the benefit of newspaper reporters and cameramen. The remainder of the year there is no real enforcement.

There is no practical rationing system which can reverse this hopeless problem. It is clear that no rationing system will be effective short of hiring enough policemen to follow each and every member of USFK and their dependents twenty-four hours a day. The answer to the problem would be for the Korean police to aggressively close "Yankee Markets," arrest the operators, and confiscate the goods, on a daily basis.

In summary, numerous rationing systems have been used by U.S. Forces in Korea, but black marketing continues as usual. And, dispite a continuous, unbroken history of failure, it is not likely that the USFK will give up its rationing mentality.

* * *

The writer is a resident in Taegu.

deficiency

Off-post activities

$100,000 a week

in Two hours

① New I.D.

② Letter of Auth.

③ Ration Card — Korean approach

18 Electric App..

134

Joint Team To Battle Black Mart

S&S Korea Bureau

SEOUL — A special joint U.S.-Korean investigative team has been formed to monitor post exchange and commissary goods in an attempt to curtail their flow onto the black market, a U.S. Army spokesman announced Tuesday.

The team was formed on May 30 and, according to the spokesman, has already been responsible for the confiscation of 30 ration control plates and $1,500 in post exchange and commissary items.

He added that over $6,000 in fines had been levied against offenders apprehended by the team.

U.S. officials here claim that an average of over $120,000 in government property (mostly post exchange items) was lost to illegal markets each month last year. The joint team is the newest of several methods that are being employed to combat the problem.

The spokesman said that measures were being taken to establish similar teams in all areas of Korea where U.S. installations are located.

'73. 7. 13. <S&S>

135

회의
~~면담~~ 기 록

(북미 2과)

1. 제 목 : 도난 및 암거래방지 실무소위원회 회의
2. 일 시 : 1973. 8. 28. 14:00 - 16:00 미측 SOFA 회의실
3. ~~면담~~자 : 한미 양측 위원

4. 내 용 :

가. 한국측은 3개 미측 제안에 대하여 동 제안에 따라 취하여질 조치가 한국경찰 당국의 독자적 조치로서 충분하다는 이유로 전면 수락거부함.

나. 한국측은 만약 미측이 본건의 토의가 더 필요하다고 생각한다면 미측안에 대한 대안으로서 현 한미 합동 수사반의 기능을 최대로 활용한다는 것을 골자로 한 별첨 (1)안을 제시함.

다. 차기회의 개최시기 : 미정

136

한, 미, 도범 및 암거래 소 위원회

1. 제목 : 미국측 제안에 대한 한국측 대안

2. 내용 : 한, 미 양 당국은 미정부 재산의 도난 및 암거래 문제를 토의키 위하여 계속 회합을 가지며,

이를 뒷받침 하기 위하여 현지 운영중인 한국 관세청 당국과 미군 당국간의 합동 수사반 기능을 충분히 발휘케 하여 부정 물품의 유출원을 효과 있게 봉쇄하는 동시에 회수된 미 정부 재산에 대하여는 73. 3. 19. 에 이미 합의된 동 문서 제3항에 의거 한국 당국은 신속 통보 조치 하고 미군 영내 도난 사건에 있어서는 한국 수사 당국이 수사상 필요한 조치를 요청할시 미 당국은 즉각적으로 최대한 편의를 도모한다.

1317

"참 고"

(군복 및 군용 장구의 단속)

1. 정부는 73. 1. 30. 제정 공포된 군복 및 군용 장구 단속에 관한 법률에 따라 73. 8.21. 동법 시행령을 마련 하여
내무, 재무, 법무, 국방, 상공의 5부 합동으로 아래와 같이 강력히 단속 함.

2. 단속 내용

가. 73. 8. 21 - 73. 10. 31 까지 국민 계몽 기간 설정

나. 73. 11. 1 부터 계속으로 단속 개시

3. 단속 대상 및 처벌

가. 허가 없이 군복 또는 군용 장구를 제조 판매 하거나 판매 목적으로 소지 한자. 또는 허가 받은자가 정당히 착용 사용 또는 휴대 할수 없는자를 위하여 제조, 판매 하거나 판매 목적으로 소지한자와 유사 군복 또는 군용 장구 제조, 판매 또는 판매 할 목적으로 소지한자

※ 1년 이상의 징역 또는 30만원 이하의 벌금

나. 군인 아닌자로서 정당한 이유 없이 군복 또는 군용 장구를 착용 사용 휴대한 자와 유사 군복 군용 장구를 착용 사용 휴대하는 행위

※ 10만원 이하의 벌금이나 구류, 과료

139

공 란

공 란

공 란

공 란

공 란

공　　란

공 란

공 란

Fighting Sophisticated Thieves

'73.10.5. <S&S>

'Padlock' Aims at Black Market

SEOUL (Special) — A new method of cracking down on black marketeers is in operation at larger exchanges in Korea, a member of the 8th U.S. Army Asset Control Padlock Investigating Team has said.

Capt. Dennis L. Edwards said that investigating team members and CID agents are now monitoring controlled items as they are taken through the PX ration control checkout lines.

He said that customers purchasing unusual amounts of controlled items would be informed in the store that they "appear to have the kind of items that sometimes end up on the black market." The agent or team member then notes the person's name and the goods he purchased.

The buyer's controlled items purchasing record is checked on-the-spot to see if it exceeds the purchasing limit, and the buyer may have to buy the controlled merchandise at a later date.

Edwards talked about the new program during an interview on the AFKN radio show "Daybreak." He said that so far, about 60 per cent of the controlled items checked in this way have been returned to the PX by the following day. The spot-checks "tend to put a little fear into them (those checked) if they have been doing anything illegal," he added.

Edwards emphasized that the average shopper need not fear the new system since he is given ample opportunity to prove the item's whereabouts, either by showing it or providing written proof that it was sold, or sent home.

"A lot of people have the mistaken impression that you just don't get caught if you make a ration control violation," Edwards pointed out, adding that in August alone 465 ration plates were processed for exceeding the control limits.

Commenting on the American role in the theft of private and U.S. government property, Edwards said, "We find that practically every major case of theft, diversion or black marketing always has an American involved in it somewhere.".

He went on to point out that aside from the actual theft, Americans sometimes just turn their heads to what is happening.

During the 60-minute program, Edwards also said:

— That the individual soldier is Padlock's first line of defense;

— That the Padlock effort has paid off in the steady decline of U.S. government losses and that August's losses were the lowest "in two or three years;"

— That some thieves have become sophisticated enough to use the Army supply system to their own advantage;

— That about 75 of the 80 calls received on the Padlock hotline have helped lead the Padlock investigating team to an area of property loss.

Edwards said there have been no "real large thefts or diversions since the (asset control) program has started." He added that the ample supply of merchandise on exchange shelves compared to past years is another indication of the Padlock success.

He pointed out that much of the success of 8th Army's program to stop property losses in Korea can be attributed to the cooperation between the various USFK agencies. He explained that 8th Army G4 has provided its expertise on the supply system and that the 8th Army Provost Marshal has aided in the security field.

Edwards also praised the efforts of Koreans. He said, "A lot of the success is due to their fine efforts."

In commenting on the sophistication of today's thieves, he recalled one case of larceny in the 2nd Inf. Div. that was accomplished by altering computer ordering cards. He said a supply sergeant detected the computer discrepancy and was responsible for breaking the case.

He cited the sergeant's alertness as an example of the kind of individual effort Padlock needs to be successful.

Edwards said the Padlock hotline is the best way individuals can give tips without becoming involved in the investigation.

He assured callers that his team is not concerned with who the tip comes from, but what information they have when they call the hotline number — "Lock," or (293-5625).

145

'73. 11. 5.
<SLS>

Pinpoints PX Violators

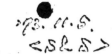

Project Padlock Hits ROK Blackmarket

SEOUL (Special)—"We suspect PX shoppers are now the major suppliers of Korea's blackmarkets," the Project Padlock investigating team chief said Thursday.

Maj. Owen Saiki said that a year ago the blackmarket merchandise supply source was fairly evenly divided between PX items obtained after they were legally purchased and those diverted from Korea Regional Exchange supply lines.

"But recent spotchecks at the Yongsan PX, the blackmarket areas and the supply lines themselves, indicate that the blackmarketeers have been forced to the retail level," he said.

Saiki is head of the five-man investigative arm of Project Padlock, 8th U.S. Army's organized drive to stop U.S. property losses in Korea.

He made the comments while talking about a front-page article in Oct. 26 edition of the U.S. Free Forces Korea Newspaper (KORUS.)

The article claims that one of every five shoppers stopped by Saiki's team during a recent spotcheck at the Yongsan PX in Seoul had violated ration control laws by purchasing large amounts of "highly blackmarketable" goods.

The article said the Padlock team stopped only those shoppers who passed through the stores ration control checkout line with items possessing high potential blackmarket value.

These persons were assured they were not being accused of blackmarketing but that their records would be checked on the spot, the KORUS article said.

In the Thursday interview Saiki said the spotchecks were undertaken on the suspicion that blackmarketeers "had been driven to the front doors" of the PX to get their merchandise.

According to the team chief, increased security measures have virtually cut off the KRE warehouses and transportation system as a source of blackmarket goods.

"Now," he said pointing out that the blackmarkets continue to flourish "the blackmarketeers are forced to buy good after the merchandise has been legally purchased. It's a little less profitable for them but a lot safer."

Padlock team members also said that more goods on blackmarket stalls now bear original PX price stickers. "Merchandise diverted before it hits the store shelves usually doesn't have a price tag," one of them said.

Commenting on the ration control system as a whole, Saiki said that many people are under the mistaken impression that ration control plates can no longer be confiscated for over-purchases.

And, as a result of their PX spotchecks, his team was studying the ration control system's ability to pinpoint offenders.

Saiki said 8th Army made an administrative change in plate confiscating procedures in July to inject more fairness into the ration control system. The move shifted the emphasis for confiscating a violator's ration plates from the store MP's to the unit commanders.

Eighth Army felt this would allow for fairer consideration of all the factors involved in an individual case.

The Padlock team reserved its criticism of a system which allowed one of the violators they caught to purchase more than 25 controlled items in less than a year without being detected.

"There are so many factors to be considered," said team computer specialist Capt. Cleveland Edwards. "It could be that the ration control system is working as well as possible under its inherent limitations. The 77 violators we stopped at the Yongsan PX might have been routinely picked up by the computer system."

Edwards pointed out that the number of ration control violators caught by the computer has steadily increased in recent months. He cited this as another indication that the blackmarket is being supplied by PX shoppers.

Saiki said that the Padlock team would continue to evaluate the ration control system to weed out any possible shortcomings, but that it would be some time before they had definite answers.

In the meantime, he said, the team will continue spotchecking post exchanges and contacting unit commanders to find out what action has been taken against offenders.

148

분류번호	729.419 군1972-73	등록번호	514	보존기간	영구
기능명칭	SOFA 한미합동위원회 군민관계 임시분과위원회 - 한미친선협회, 1972-73.				
생산과	안보담당관실		생산년도	1973	

주;

1. 한미친선위원회 구성

1-1 한미친선위원회 설치규정(안)

1-2 미8군 예규 550-5호에 대한 검토

1-3 미8군 예규 550-5(英)

1-4 한미 친선위원회 계층별 구성도

2 한미 친선위원회 설치규정 제정

2-1 한미 친선위원회 설치규정 결과보고

2-2 OO도(시·군) 한미친선 협의회 조례 준칙(안)

2-3 한미친선 협의회 설치규정 제정 결과보고 (책자 제본)

0186

	M/F No.	180

내 무 부

관리 723 - 5283 1972. 5. 8.

수신 외무부장관

참조 북미 2 과장

제목 한미친선위원회 구성

1. 미이 723-5162(72.2.18)의 관련 임.

2. 제 70 차 SOFA 한미합동위원회가 협의 채택한 "한미친선위원회의 설치"에 대하여 당부의 시안을 별첨 (1)과 같이, 미군측 친선위원회규정(미 8 군 예규 550-5)에 대한 당부의 조정의견을 별첨 (2)와 같이 각각 송부하오니 한미친선위원회가 보다 효율적으로 운용될 수 있도록 이를 Panel on Local Community & Governmental Relations 의 의제로 상정 하시되 귀부 에서 규정서식에 의한 영문 안건화등 적절한 조치를 취하여 주시기 바랍니다.

발송 No. 1972. 5. 8. 내무부

첨부 : 1. 한미친선위원회 규정(안) 1부

2. 미8군 예규에 대한 의견 1부 끝.

내 무 부 장

내무부장관인

정부공문서 규정 제27조 제2항의 규정에 의하여	(관리 과장) (새마을 …) 전결

2

외 무 부		결재	
접수 일시	197 . . . 시 분	지시사항	'72 16:09
접수 번호	제15659호		
주무과			
담당자			
위임 근거			197 . . .까지 처리할것

Panel on Local Community
&
Governmental Relations

討議資料

案件
1. 韓美親善委員會 設置規程(案)
2. 美八軍 例規 第550-5號 檢討

提案者: 內務部 管理課長 白世鉉
(ROK Chairman,
Panel on Local Community
and Governmental Relations)

3.

(별첨 1)

韓美親善委員會 設置規程(案)

内 務 部

4

4

韓美親善委員會 設置規程 "小題目"

1. 目的
2. 設置部署
3. 名稱
4. 機能
5. 構成
6. 委員의 辭退
7. 委員長등의 職務
8. 節次
가. 會議
나. 會議主管
다. 會議開催通報
라. 小委員會
마. 未解決事案의 處理
9. 委員會解散
10. 參示人의 委員會 出席
11. 報告
12. 其他事項
13. 既存委員會 廢止

5

韓美親善委員會設置規程(案)

1. 目的: 韓國人과 美軍人間의 理解를 促進하고 關係의 改善으로 相互間의 友誼를 增進하여 親善을 圖謀하는데 있다.

2. 設置部署: 委員會는 美合衆國의 陸海空軍이 駐屯하고 있는 市, 区, 邑 面과 이 地域을 管轄하는 特別市, 道, 郡에 設置한다.

3. 名稱: 委員會의 名稱은 ○○道(特別市, 市, 郡, 邑, 面) 韓美親善委員會라 한다.

4. 機能: 委員會는 韓美間의 共同關心事와 韓美間에 發生 또는 發生의 憂慮가 있는 아래 事項에 關하여 相互 不詳事의 事前防止 對策을 講究하고 下級委員會에서 建議된

問題를 相互 理解와 協調로서 調整하고 解決한다.

가. 接客業所의 人種差別 및 서-비스 改善策

나. 保菌者 및 接待婦의 善導對策

다. 麻藥의 所持, 販賣 및 團束對策

라. 衛生 檢察 對策

마. 勞使紛糾 對策

바. 軍票所持와 密輸防止 및 暗市場對策

사. 其他 相互間의 權益의 侵害 및 親善阻害要素에 關한 對策

5. 構成: 委員會는 委員長 1人과 委員 5~7人 및 幹事 1人으로 構成한다.

委員長은 地方行政機關의 長 (道知事, 市長

공통서식 1-1 (을) 190mm×268mm

郡守, 区廳長 및 邑面長)이 되고 委員과 幹事는

委員長이 다음 機関의 代表또는 構成員中

에서 任命 또는 委嘱한다.

가. 司法機関(検察, 警察 및 税関)

나. 労動行政機関

다. 保健衛生機関

라. ○○諮問委員會 또는 開發委員會

마. 情報機関

바. 觀光業体, 遊興 및 料食業協會

사. 業態婦代表

아. 其他 有関機関 또는 住民代表

6. 委員의 辭退 : 委員長은 委員中 다음 事由가 發生

하였을 때는 그 職을 辭任케 하고 即時

8

관문서식 1—1 (을)   190mm×268mm(인쇄용지 2급 40g/m²)

後任者를 交替選任한다.

가. 本人이 辭任코자 願할때

나. 他機關으로 轉出되었을 때

다. 會議參席이 徹底的이고 委員會運營에 消極的일때

라. 韓美親善을 害치는 行爲를 하였거나 그러한 行爲가 있다고 認定될때

마. 其他 委員長이 必要하다고 認定될때

7. 委員長 등의 職務 : 委員長은 委員會를 代表하고 會議의 議長이 된다. 다만 委員長이 事故가 있을 때에는 委員中에서 委員長이 指定한 者가 그 職務를 代行한다.

委員은 委員長의 命을 받아 委員會에

9

공통서식 1-1 (을) 190mm×268mm(…)

出席하여 發言하며 附議된 案件은 相互 協議하고 討論한다.

幹事는 委員長의 命을 받아 委員會에 出席하되 發言할 수 없으며 委員會의 庶務를 處理한다.

8. 節次 : 가. 會議 : 委員會는 每月 1回 定期的으로 開催하되 日字는 韓美 兩側의 協議로 定한다. 다만 어느 一方의 要求가 있을 때는 隨時 開催할 수 있다.

나. 會議主管 : 定期會는 相互交代로 他方 委員을 招請하여 開催하되 招請한 機關이 主管한다. 다만 어느 一方의 要求에 의하여 隨時 開催하는 會議에서는 要求機關

10

공문서식 1-1 (을) 190mm×268mm(인쇄용지 45g/m²)

에서 主管함을 原則으로 한다.

○ 다. 會議開催通報 : 主管機關은 늦어도 會議 開催 5日前에 他方代表에게 아래 事項이 記載된 內容을 書面으로 通知하여야 한다

(1) 會議開催 日時

(2) 會議開催 場所

(3) 附議案件 또는 開催코자 하는 事由

(4) 招請者와 被招請者의 機關및 代表名

다만 下級委員會의 未解決事案을 上級委員會에서 協議코자 할때에는 兩側의 事前 協議로 會議日時와 場所는 따로히 定할수 있다.

○ 라. 小委員會 : 委員會의 效率的 運營과 附議된 事項을 円滑히 處理하기 爲하여

0111

공문서식 1-1 (을)
1967. 4. 4. 승인

190mm×268mm(...)
조달청 (1,000,000 매 ...)

委員會의 協議를 거쳐 小委員會를 構成할 수 있다.

小委員會의 委員은 委員長이 指名하고 委員의 數는 2人 내지 3人으로 한다.

小委員會는 委任받은 事案이 完結되었을 때 自動的으로 解体된다.

○ 마. 未解決事案의 處理 : 下級委員會에서 合議되지 못한 事案은 韓美 双方의 指揮系統에 따라 漸次 次上級委員會에 建議한다. 이 境遇 上級委員會의 美軍側部隊가 韓國側 行政官署의 管轄地域外에 所在하고 있을 때에는 小委員會로 하여금 相對方의 委員會와 協議토록하여 解決한다.

12

공통서식 1-1 (을)
1967. 4. 4. 승인

190mm×268mm(...)
조달청 (1,000,000매 인쇄)

上級委員會에서도 解決되지 못한 事案은

韓美合同委員會에 建議한다.

9. 委員會解散: 被對象機關이 移動하거나 兵營이 廢鎖되는 때는 自動的으로 解体된다. 새로운 部隊가 같은 兵營에 駐屯하게 되거나 前任部隊의 業務를 引受받았을 때는 委員會를 다시 構成한다.

10. 參考人의 委員會出席: 委員會는 必要하다고 認定할 때는 附議된 案件에 關聯되는 關係人, 參考人의 出席發言이나 參考資料의 提示를 要請할 수 있다.

11. 報告: 道知事는 每月 道와 傘下 市郡邑面의 委員會開催狀況을 別紙 書式에 의거 翌月 10日

13

공통서식 1-1 (을)
1967. 4. 4. 승인

190mm×268mm(··· 40g/m2)
(1,0··,000 매 ···)

까지 內務部長官에게 報告한다.

韓美間의 不詳事나 兩側의 親善을 沮害할 要因이 發生 또는 發生의 憂慮가 있는것은 即刻 內務部長官에게 指揮 報告한다.

12. 其他事項: 委員會運營에 必要한 其他事項은 委員會의 協議를 거쳐 따로히 定한다.

13. 既存委員會廢止: 既存의 各種 韓美親善組織은 이 委員會에 廢置 統合한다.

14

(書式 2.)

○○道 韓美親善委員會
第 次 會議錄

1. 開催日時

2. 開催場所

3. 議 題

가.

나.

다.

4. 討議및 協議事項

(○ 提案側의 提案說明및 要望또는 措置事項을 略述
○ 相對方의 意見및 同意與否)

5. 對策및 措置狀況

(○ 合意與否의 結果에 따른 對策또는 措置事項을 略述)

6. 特記事項

(其他 參考事項)

15

(별첨 2)

美8軍 例規 550-5號에 對한 檢討

區 分	例 規	意 見	備 考
1. 목 적	......위원회의 목적은 미군인과 한국인간의 이해를 촉진하고 개선하며 대한민국의 사회적 경제적 발전에 기여하는데 있다.	......위원회의 목적은 미군인과 한국인간의 이해를 촉진하고 관계의 개선으로 상호간의 우의를 증진하고 친선을 도모하는데 있다.	委員会의 方向転換 ○韓国에 対한 認識態의 刷新 ○國威宣揚
4. 정의	다. 지역사회와 관련된 계획 : 사령부의 기능은 .....및 지역사회의 존경과 신의를 받도록 계획을 작성한다.	다. 지역사회와 관련된 계획 : 사령부의 기능은 .... 및 지역사회의 협조와 친선을 도모하도록 계획을 작성한다.	同等한 立場에서의 協調와 親善
6. 지침	타. 대민관계 활동(8군 예규 550-7) 및 민간활동 계획의 건실한 이행과 착수를 의론하는 위원회로 최대한 활용되어야 한다.	타. 민간활동 계획의 건실한 이행과 착수를 의론하는 위원회로 최대한 활용되어야 한다.	"対民関係活動" 削除
7. 신위원회 설립	나. 신위원회는 특정한 지역 군부대장과 기획된 위원회를 대표하는 지역사회의 지방공무원간의 협정으로 설립된다. 지역군부대장은 지방공무원에 대하여 위원회가 합의와, 그리고 자문적성질 및 위원회의 능력과 한계; 이 위원회의 설립과 운영으로 얻어지는 상호간의 이익에 대하여 분명히 밝혀야 한다.	나. 신위원회는 .... 된다. 지역군부대장은 지방공무원에 대하여 위원회가 한미합동위원회의 협의로 설립되었음과 위원회의 협의사항은 한미상호간에 신의와 성실로서 준수하고 이행할 의무를 지며 이 위원회의 설립과 운영으로 얻어지는 상호간의 이익에 대하여 분명히 밝혀야 한다.	協議事項의 遵守義務를 明示

0098

16

區分	例規	意見	備考
8. 위원회의 예산	가. 부대의 폐쇄에 관하여(군보안이 허용하는 내) 승인을 받는대로 지역사회대표에게 통지한다.	가. 부대의 폐쇄에 관하여(군보안이 허용하는 내) 승인을 받는대로 한국측 위원회 의장에게 통지한다.	
9. 구성	나. 한국측 구성원 : 한국측 대표는 지역사회지도자에 의하여 결정된다. 일반적으로 한국측위원은 도, 특별시, 군, 면, 시, 읍, 구 혹은 동의 최고위자로서 한국측구성원의 의장이 되며 미군구성원에 대한 민간인상대역이 된다. 고위공무원과 동급이고 그들과 독립된 한국경찰의 대표는 한국측구성원의 필수요원이 된다. 대표자는 존경받는 부락의 고령자, 방위군, 건강, 위생, 교육관계공무원과 지역사업가, 신문사대표 및 노동관계공무원이 포함된다.	나. 한국측 구성원 : 한국측 대표는 지방관서의 장에 의하여 위촉된다. 일반적으로 한국측위원은 도, 특별시, 군, 면, 읍, 구의 최고위자로서 한국측 구성원의 의장이 되며 미군 구성원에 대한 민간인 상대역이 된다. 한국측 구성원에는 아래기관의 대표 또는 요원이 포함된다. 0 사법기관(검찰, 경찰, 세관) 0 노동행정기관 0 보건 위생기관 0 정보기관 0 지문위원회 또는 개발위원회 0 관광업체, 유흥업및 요식업협회 0 업태부 대표 0 기타 유관기관 또는 주민대표	委員 住民代表者를 明示하고 播民으로 限定. ○第70次(72.1.28) SOFA 韓美合同委에서 "適切한 水準의 代表"로 構成토록한 바 있음.

17

區分	例規	意見	備考
11. 절차	가. 회합 : 회합은 매월 개최되어야 한다. 회합을 최소 60일간 개최하지 못한때는 회합을 갖일수 없는 상황을 서면으로 제출하여야 한다. 장군이 주재하는 위원회에서는 위의 조항이 적용되지 아니하며 적당하다고 생각되는 때를 예정할 수 있다.	가. 회합 : 회합은 매월 1회 정기적으로 개최하고 일방의 요청이 있을 때는 수시 개최한다. 회합을 최소 60일간 개최하지 못한때는 회합을 갖일수 없는 상황을 서면으로 제출하여야 한다. 도지사와 장군이 주재하는 위원회에서는 위의 조항이 적용되지 아니하며 적당하다고 생각되는 때를 예정할 수 있다.	隨時 開催할 수 있는 融通性 부여
	사. 소위원회의 이용 : .... 규모가 큰 위원회에는 안전, 방화, 문화행사, 기타 관심을 끌 필요가 있을 때는 다른 사항의 상설 소위원회를 두어야 한다. 대부분의 위원회는 군인의 날, 식목일, 재해구호등 다른 특별활동을 위한 특별 소위원회의 지정을 희망하고 있다.	사. 소위원회의 이용 : - 소위원회의 위원은 (각각) 2명 내지 3명의 위원으로 구성하고 위원회의 의장이 지명한다.	小委員會의 委員數를 制限.

18

區分	例規	意見	備考
	아. 미해결된 사안 : 하급위원회 수준에서 미해결된 사안은 상급 사령부에 이관한다. 위원회에서 해결되지못한 안전문제는 육군성 직업안전국에게 제출하여야 한다.	아. 미해결된 사안 : --. 이 경우 대방의 상급 기관이 지리적으로 원격한 곳에 위치하고 있을 때에는 소위원회로 하여금 상대방의 위원회와 접촉하고 협의토록 하여 해결한다. 상급 사령부에서도 해결되지못한 사안은 한미합동위원회에 건의하여 처리토록 한다. 카. 참고인의 위원회 출석 위원회는 필요한 경우에 부의된 안건에 관련되는 관계인 참고인의 출석발언이나 참고자료의 제시를 요청할 수 있다.	o 小委員会에서 解決토록 하여 委員会開催를 爲해 全委員이 他地域으로 出張가는 번잡을 避하고자 함 (特히 任務圈域이 다른 경우) o 協議事項의 円滿, 迅速한 解決을 爲하여 追加挿入.

공 란

공 란

공 란

공 란

공 란

공 란

공 란

공 란

공 란

공 란

공 란

공 란

공 란

공 란

공 란

공　　　란

공 란

공 란

공 란

공　　　란

공 란

공 란

공 란

(첨부 3)

韓美親善委員會 階層別 構成圖

43

서울特別市

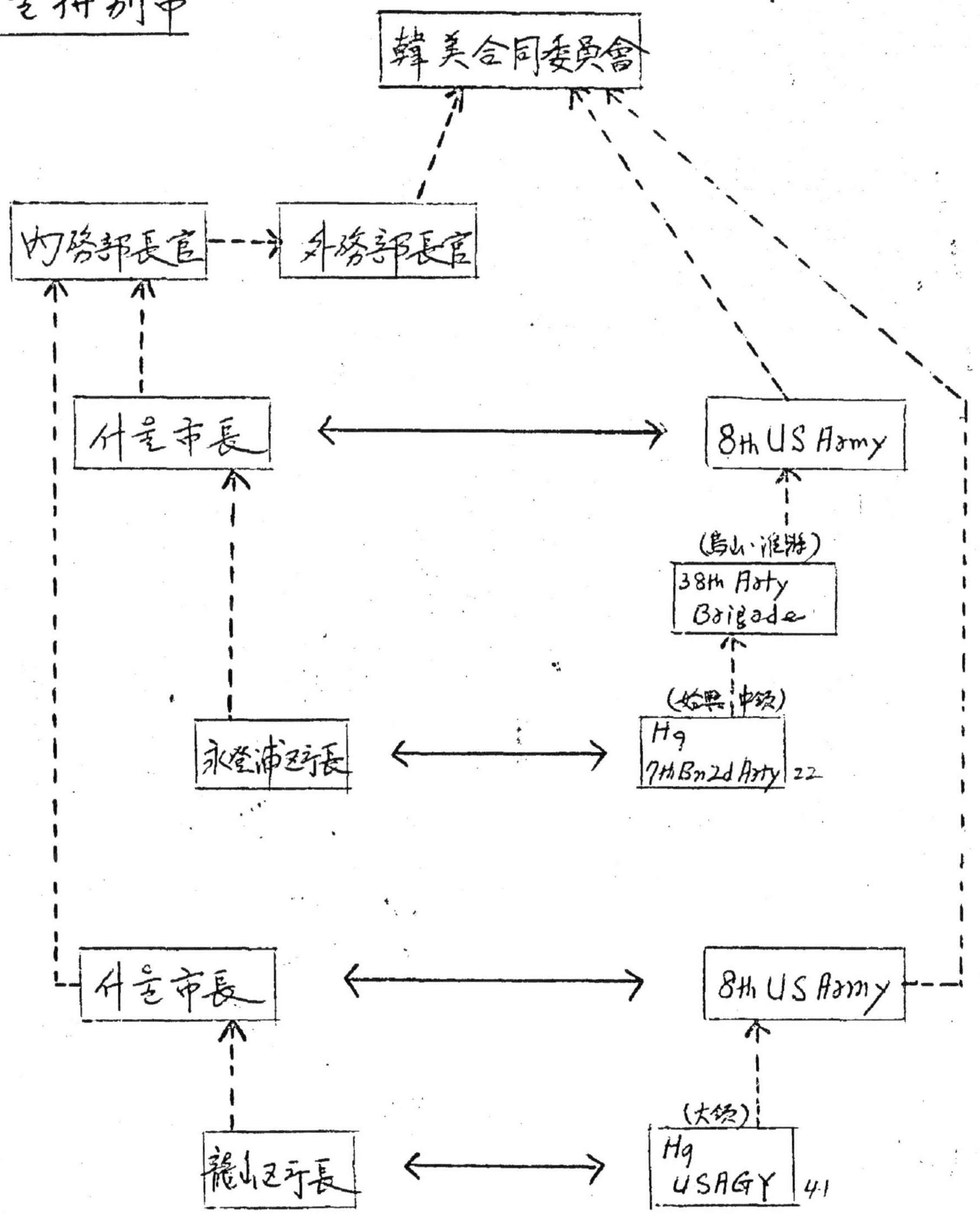
韓美合同委員會
內務部長官
外務部長官
서울市長
8th US Army
38th Arty Brigade
Hq
7th Bn 2d Arty
22
永登浦區廳長
서울市長
8th US Army
(大領)
Hq
USAGY
41
龍山區廳長

釜山市

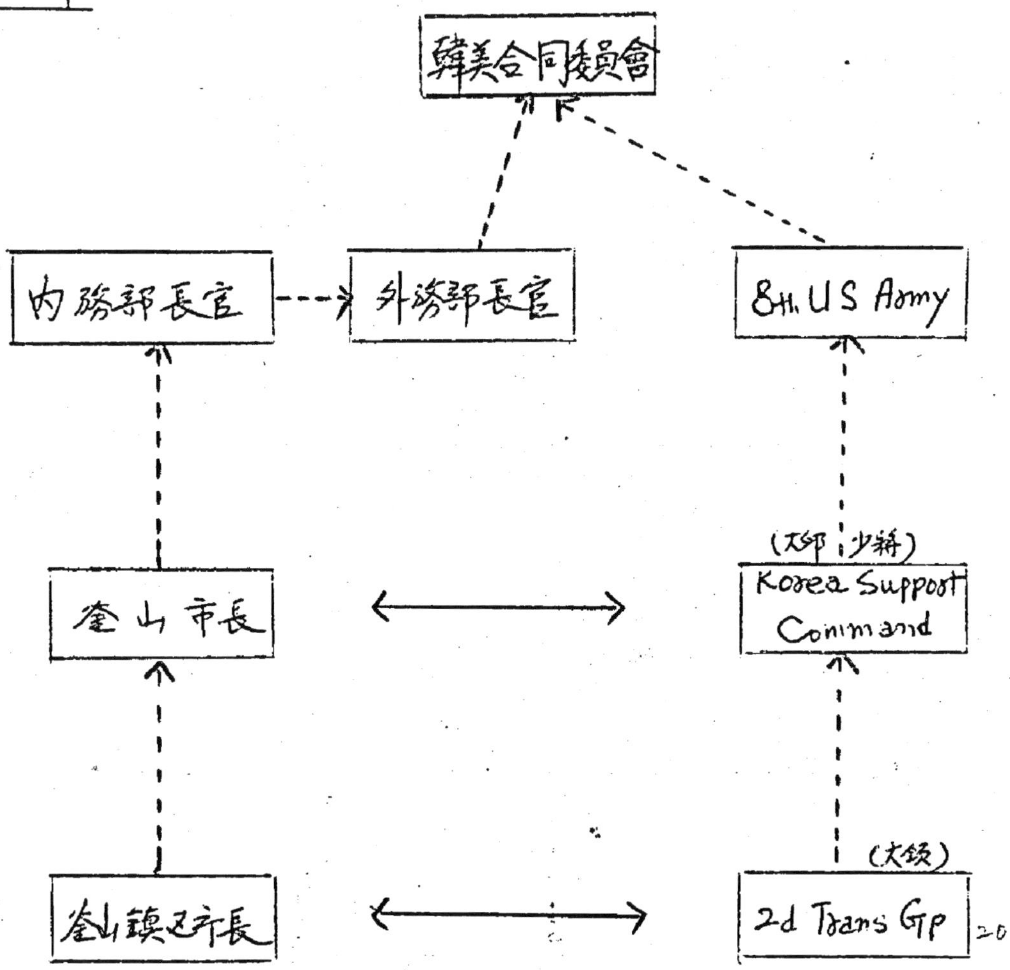

韓美合同委員會
內務部長官
外務部長官
8th U S Army
(大邱 少將)
Korea Support Command
釜山市長
(大領)
釜山鎭區廳長
2d Trans Gp

45

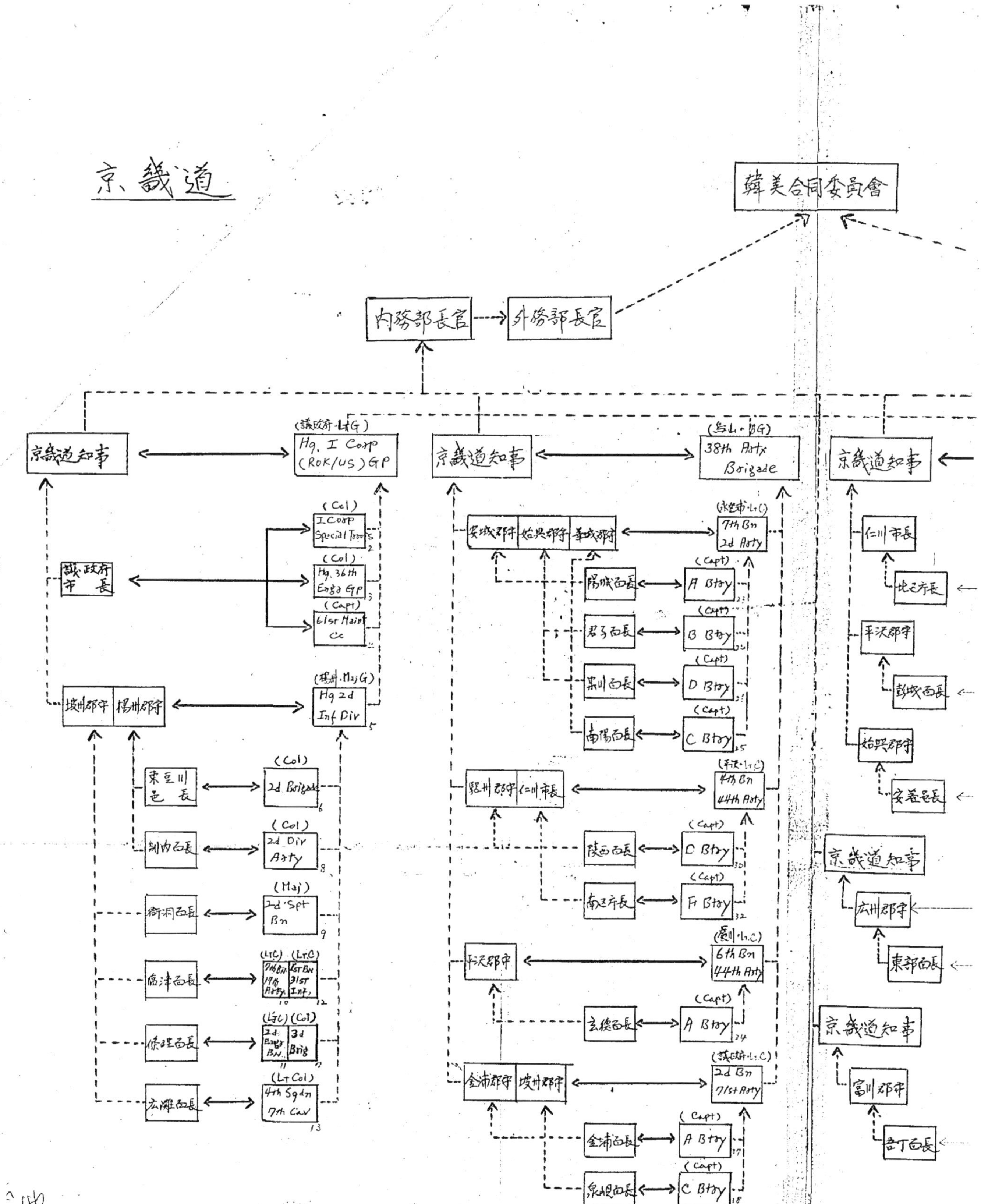
京畿道
韓美合同委員會
內務部長官
外務部長官
京畿道知事
Hq. I Corp (ROK/US) GP
38th Arty Brigade
I Corp Special Troops
Hq. 36th Engr GP
61st Maint Co
Hq 2d Inf Div
2d Brigade
2d Div Arty
2d Spt Bn
4th Sqdn 7th Cav
7th Bn 2d Arty
A Btry
B Btry
D Btry
C Btry
4th Bn 44th Arty
6th Bn 44th Arty
2d Bn 71st Arty
仁川市長
平沢郡守
始興郡守
広州郡守
富川郡守

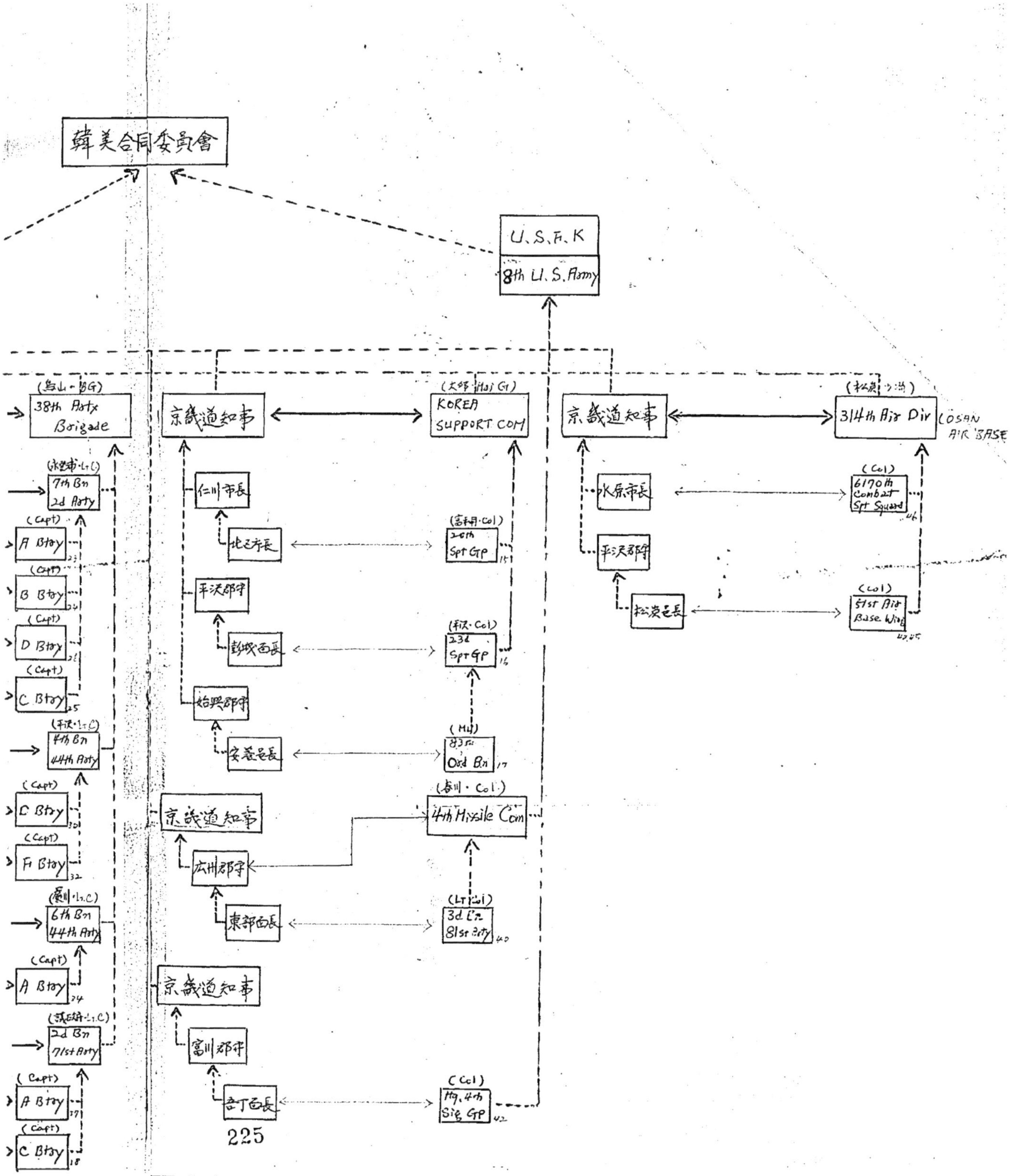

韓美合同委員會
U.S.F.K
8th U.S. Army
38th Arty Brigade
京畿道知事
KOREA SUPPORT COM
京畿道知事
314th Air Div
OSAN AIR BASE
7th Bn 2d Arty
A Btry
B Btry
D Btry
C Btry
4th Bn 44th Arty
C Btry
F Btry
6th Bn 44th Arty
A Btry
2d Bn 71st Arty
A Btry
C Btry
仁川市長
平沢郡守
始興郡守
安養邑長
京畿道知事
広州郡守
東部面長
京畿道知事
富川郡守
4th Missile Com
3d Bn 81st Arty
Hq. 4th Sig GP
水原市長
6170th Combat Spt Squard
平沢郡守
松炭邑長
51st Air Base Wing

225

江原道

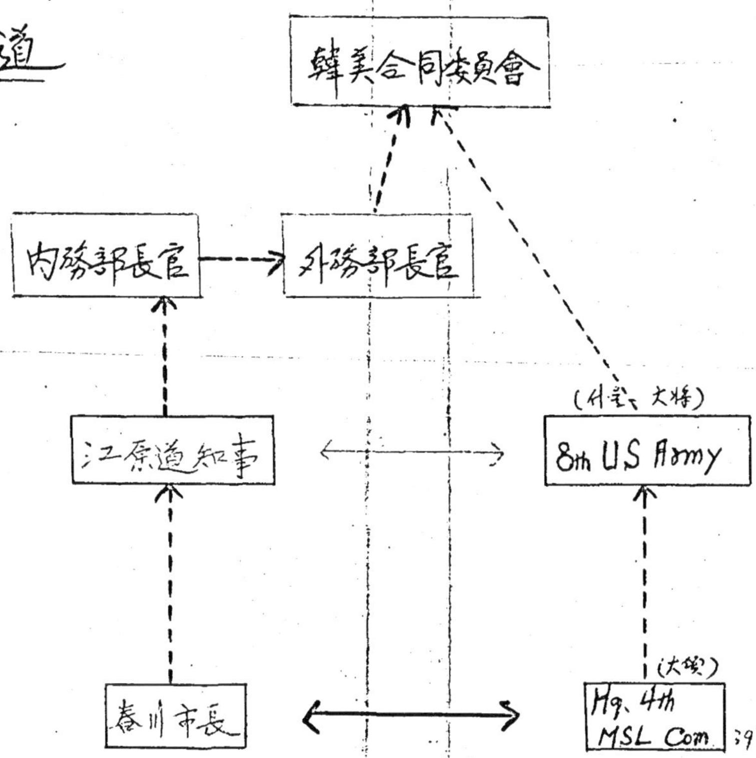
韓美合同委員會
內務部長官
外務部長官
(서울、大將)
江原道知事
8th US Army
(大領)
春川市長
Hq. 4th
MSL Com

6

47

忠清北道

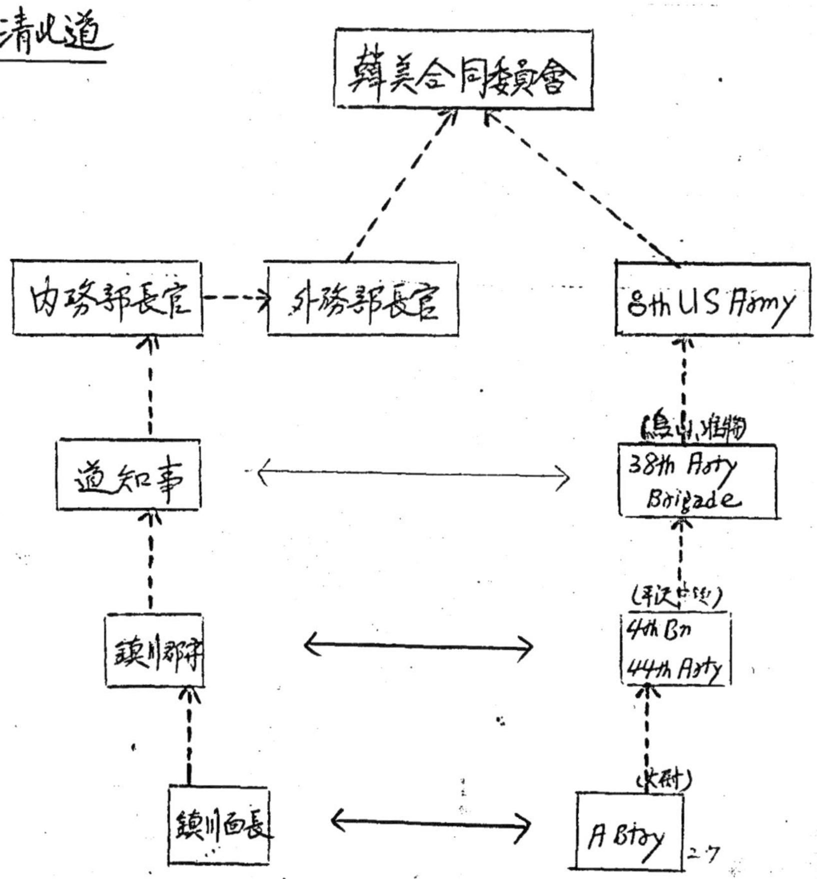
韓美合同委員會
内務部長官
外務部長官
8th US Army
道知事
38th Arty Brigade
鎮川郡守
4th Bn 44th Arty
鎮川面長
(大尉)
A Btry

48

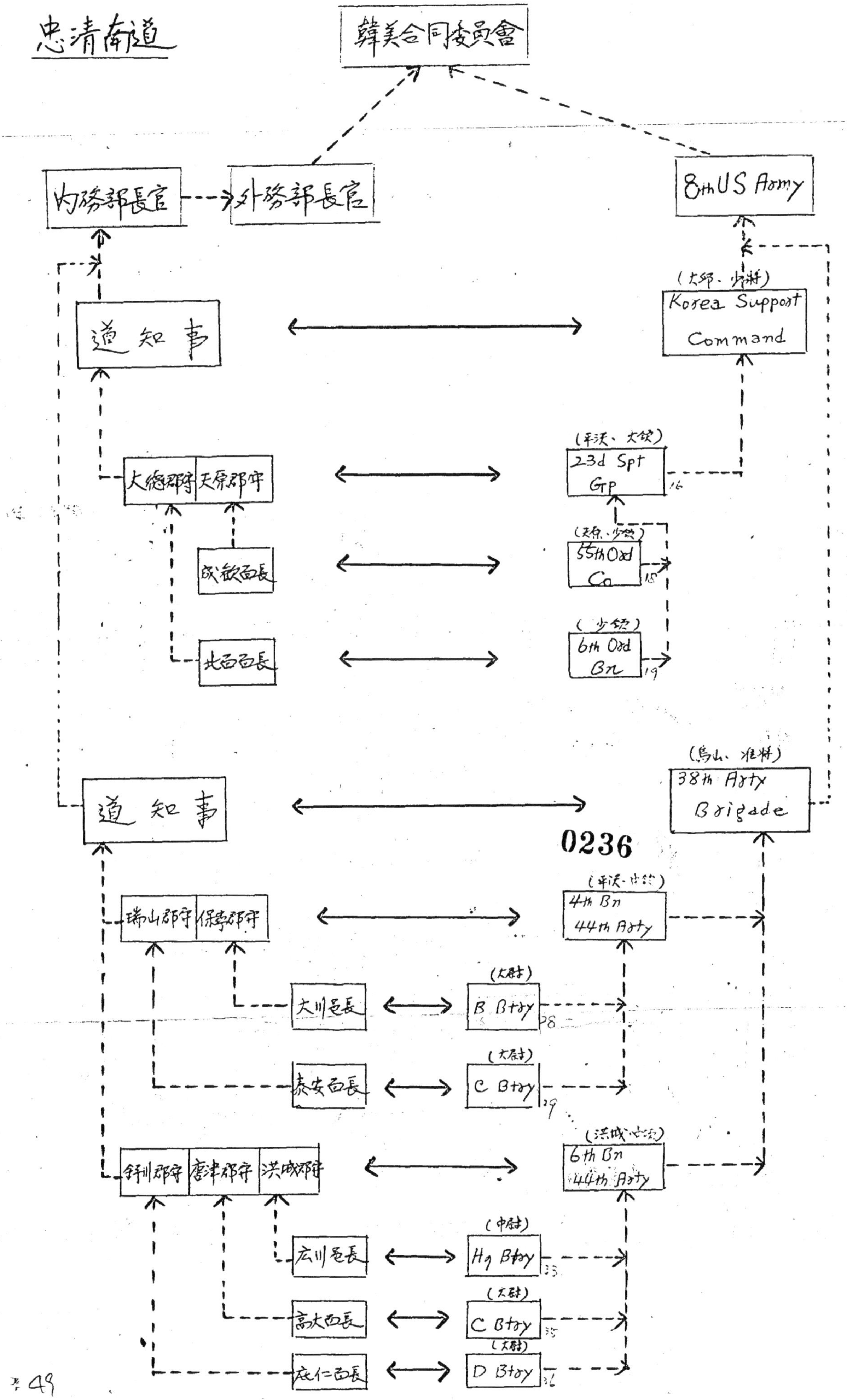
忠清南道
韓美合同委員會
內務部長官
外務部長官
8th US Army
(大邱、少將)
Korea Support Command
道知事
(平澤、大領)
23d Spt Gp
16
大德郡守
天原郡守
(天原、少領)
55th Ord Co
18
成歡面長
(少領)
6th Ord Bn
19
北面面長
(烏山、准將)
38th Arty Brigade
道知事
0236
(平澤、中領)
4th Bn 44th Arty
瑞山郡守
保寧郡守
(大尉)
B Btry
28
大川邑長
(大尉)
C Btry
29
泰安面長
(洪城、中領)
6th Bn 44th Arty
舒川郡守
唐津郡守
洪城郡守
(中尉)
Hq Btry
33
廣川邑長
(大尉)
C Btry
35
高大面長
(大尉)
D Btry
36
庇仁面長
49

全羅北道

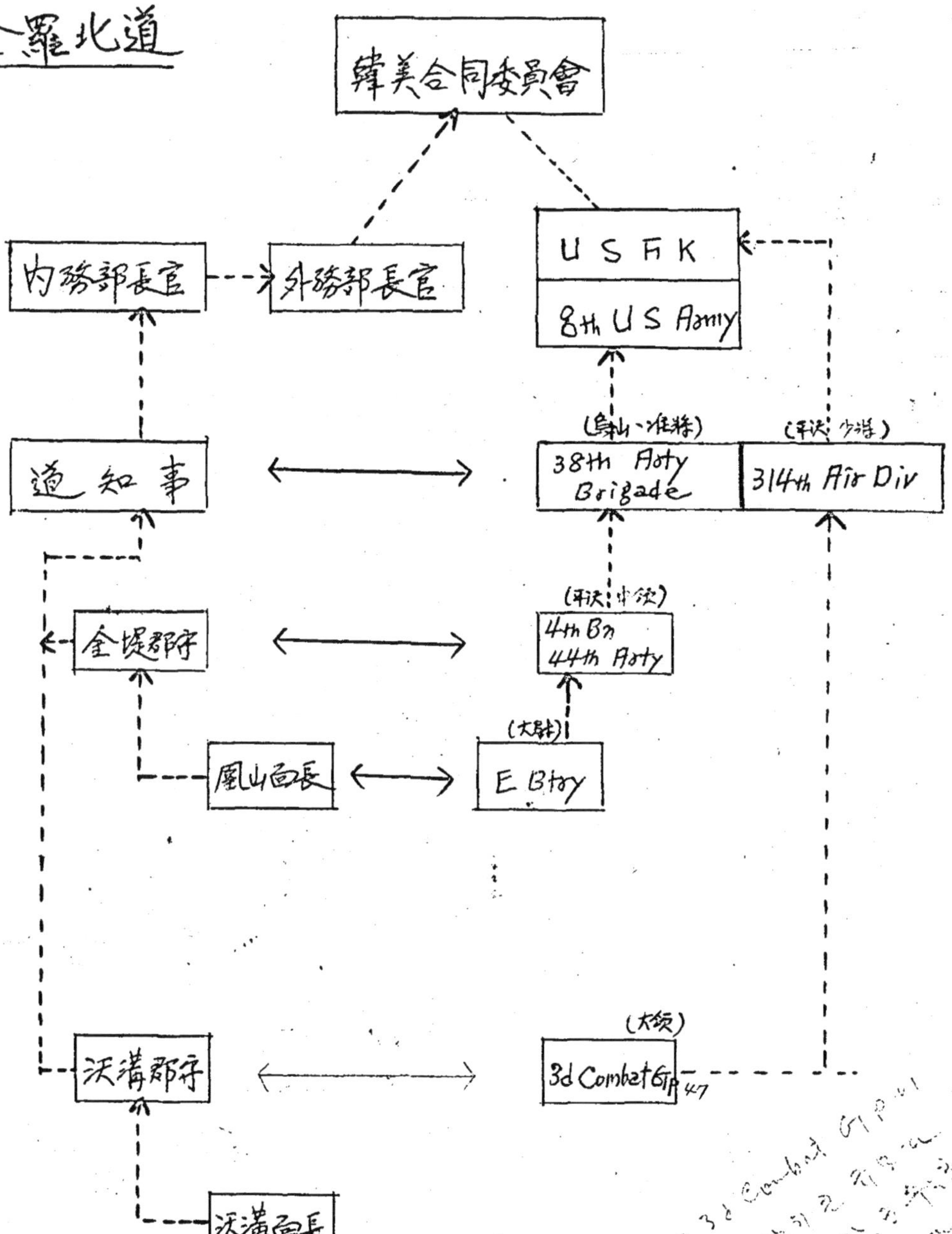
韓美合同委員會
内務部長官
外務部長官
USFK
8th US Army
道知事
38th Arty Brigade
314th Air Div
金堤郡守
4th Bn 44th Arty
鳳山面長
E Btry
沃溝郡守
3d Combat Grp
沃溝面長

50

慶尙北道

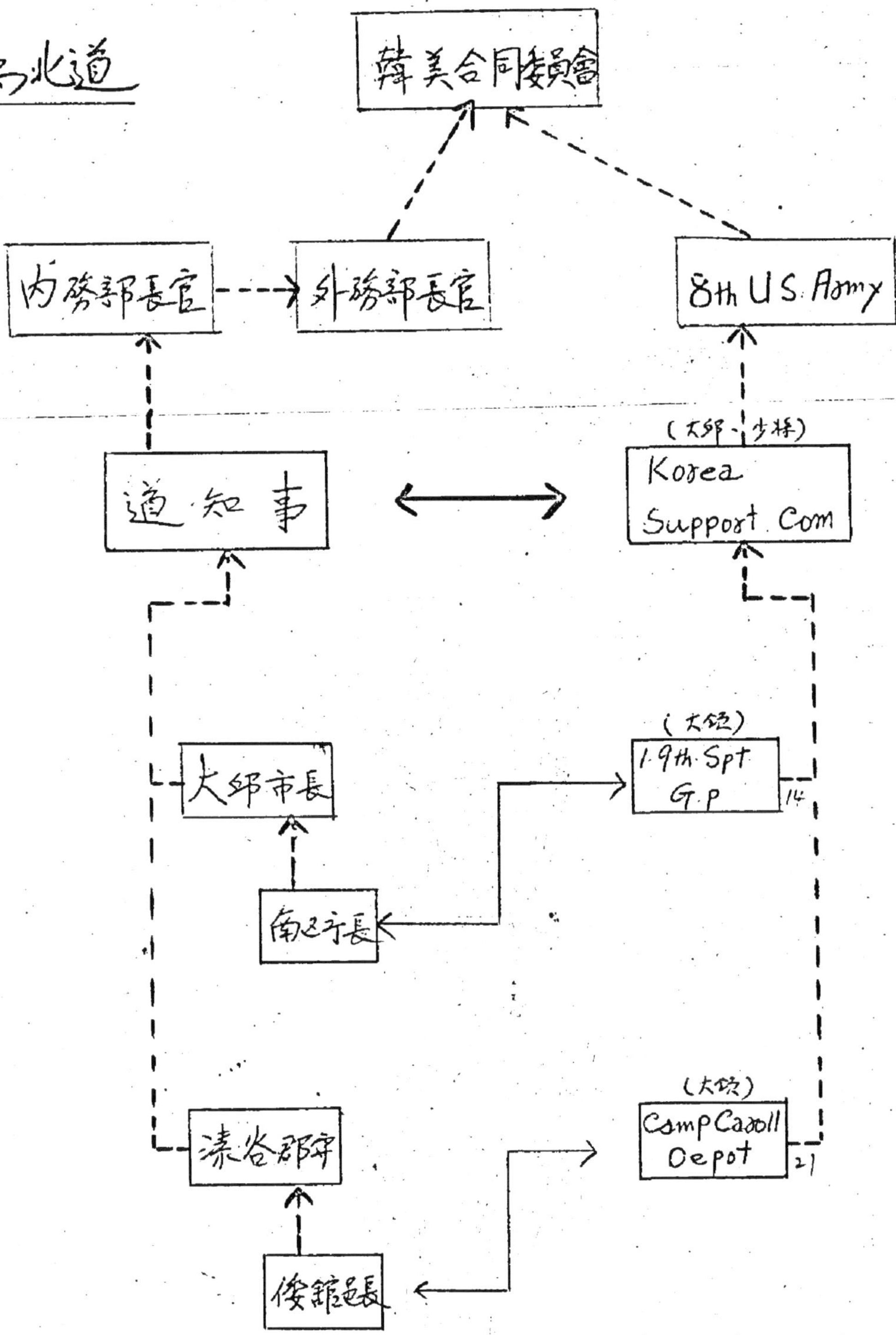
韓美合同委員會
內務部長官
外務部長官
8th U.S. Army
(大邱-少將)
Korea Support Com
道知事
(大領)
19th Spt G.P
14
大邱市長
南區廳長
(大領)
Camp Carroll Depot
21
漆谷郡守
倭館邑長

251

慶尙南道

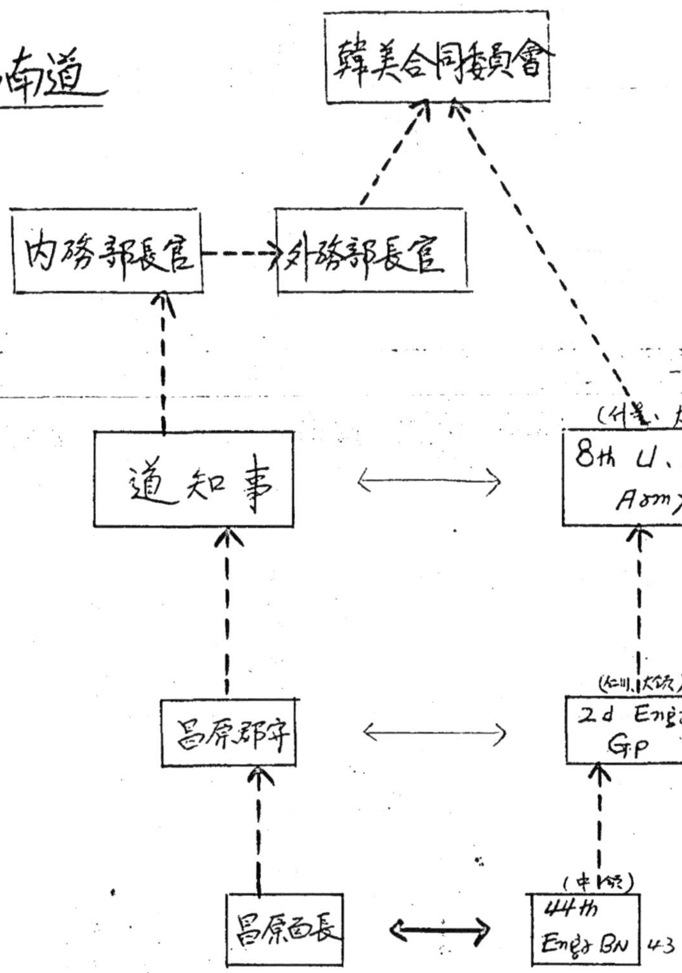

韓美合同委員會
內務部長官
外務部長官
(서울、大將)
8th U.S. Army
道知事
(仁川、大佐)
2d Engr Gp
昌原郡守
(中佐)
44th Engr BN
43
昌原面長

52

○○道(市·郡)韓美親善協議會條例準則(案)

53

韓美親善協議会設置条例(準則)(案)目次

-1-

54

○○道 韓美親善協議会設置条例準則(案)

※○○市(郡)
○○市○○区
○○郡○○面 (1973.6. ○○道条例第 号)

第1条(目的) 이 条例는 ○○道 韓美親善協議会
※1.
(이하 "協議会"라 한다)의 設置와 運営에 関한 事項을 規定함을 目的으로 한다.

※1 市(郡): ○○市(郡) 韓美親善協議会
区 : ○○市○○区 〃
邑(面): ○○郡○○邑(面) 〃

第2条(設置) 駐韓美軍과 地域社会間의 올바른 理解促進 및 友誼增進으로 相互協調 및 紐帯強化를 為하여 協議会를 둔다.

第3条(機能) ①協議会는 駐韓美軍과 地域社会間의 共同関心事와 両側에 発生 또는 発生의 憂慮가 있는 諸般事項 및 市郡協議会
※4.
에서 建議된 事項에 対하여 相互間의 理解協調로서 適切한 対策을 講究하고 調整하며 提起된 問題를 両側의 合議로서 解決한다.

※4 市: 区 協議会에서 建議된
郡: 邑(面) 〃
邑(面): 傍線部分削除

②前項의 共同関心事는 아래와 같다.

1. 駐韓美軍을 顧客으로 하는 接客業所의

o 써-비스 改善

-2-

55

o 内外施設 改善

o 衛生監督

2. 性病 保菌者 및 業態婦의 啓導

3. 麻薬의 所持 및 販売団束

4. 美軍票去来 密輸 및 美軍需物資의 暗去来団束

5. 駐韓美軍機関에 従事하는 韓国雇傭人과의 労使紛糾

6. 其他 相互間의 権益의 侵害 및 親善의 沮害

第4条(構成 및 委員의 委解嘱) ①協議会의 韓国側 構成員은 委員長1人과 委員5내지 7人 및 幹事 1人으로 構成한다.

②委員長은 道知事가 되고 委員은 委員長이 다음 機関의 代表
※5.
또는 構成員中에서 委嘱하고 幹事는 所属 公務員中에서 任命한다.

※5 市(郡):市長(郡守)이 되고
区 :区庁長이 되고
邑(面):邑長(面長)이 되고

1. 司法機関(検察,警察 및 税関)

2. 労動行政機関

3. 保健衛生機関

4. 道路間委員会 또는 開発委員会

5. 情報機関

6. 観光業体遊興 및 料食業協会

-3-

56

7. 業態婦組合(協会)

8. 其他 有関機関 또는 道民代表

③委員長은 委員中 다음 事由가 発生하였을 때는 그 職을 辞任케 하고 即時 後任者를 選任하여야 한다.

1. 本人이 辞任코자 願할 때.

2. 他機関으로 転出되었을 때.

3. 会議参席이 微温的이고 協議会 運営이 消極的일 때.

4. 韓美親善을 害치는 行為를 하였거나 그러한 行為가 있다고 認定될 때.

5. 其他 委員長이 必要하다고 認定될 때.

第5条(委員長등의 職務) ①委員長은 協議를 代表하고 会議의 議長이 된다. 다만 委員長이 事故가 있을 때에는 委員中에서 委員長이 指定한 者가 그 職務를 代行한다.

②委員은 委員長의 命을 받아 協議会에 出席하여 発言하며 附議된 案件을 相互 協議하고 討議한다.

③幹事는 委員長의 命을 받아 協議会에 出席하되 発言할 수 없으며 協議会의 庶務를 処理한다.

第6条(分任協議会) ①協議会의 効率的 運営과 附議된 事項을 円滑히 処理하기 위하여 協議会의 協議를 거쳐 分任協議会를 構成

-4-

57

할 수 있다.

②分任協議会의 委員은 委員長이 指名하고 委員의 数는 2내지

3人으로 한다.

③市郡協議会에서 解決되지 못하여 建議된 事項은 分任協議会에서
※6.
協議할 수 있다.

※6 市：区 協議会에서
郡：邑(面)協議会에서
区邑面：③項 削除

④分任協議会는 受任받은 事案이 完結되었을 때 自動的으로 解体

된다.

第7条(会議) 協議会는 毎月1回 定期的으로 開催하되 開催日은

兩側의 協議로 定하며 会議는 円滑한 意思交換을 図謀하기 위하

여 非公式的이어야 한다.

다만 어느 一方의 要求가 있을 때는 随時 開催할 수 있다.

第8条(会議主管) ①定期会는 相互交代로 他方委員을 招請하여 開

催하되 招請한 機関이 主管한다.

다만 前条 但書의 경우에는 要求機関에서 主管함을 原則으로

한다.

②主管機関은 늦어도 会議開催 5日前에 他方 代表에게 아래 事

項이 記載된 内容을 書面으로 通知하여야 한다.

-5-

58

1. 会議開催日時

2. 会議開催場所

3. 附議案件 또는 開催코자 하는 事由

4. 招請者와 被招請者의 機関 및 代表名

③第6条第3項의 規定에 의한 分任協議会는 両側의 事前 協議를 거처 会議日時와 場所를 따로히 定하여 開催할 수 있다.

第9条(協議会解散) 駐韓美軍이 移動하거나 兵営이 廃鎖되는 때는 自動的으로 解体된다.

第10条(参考人의 協議会出席) 協議会는 必要하다고 認定할 때에는 附議된 案件에 関聯되는 関係人 또는 参考人의 出席発言이나 参考資料의 提示를 要請할 수 있다.

第11条(未決事案의 処理) 協議会에서 合議되지 못한 事案은 韓美合同委員会에 建議한다.

※7 市(郡):道委員会에 建議한다.
区(邑,面):市(郡) 〃

第12条(報告) ①委員長은 아래 各号에 対하여 内務部長官에게 報告한다.
※8.

1. 所属協議会와 管内 全 協議会의 協議会開催状況
※9.

2. 第9条에 의한 協議会 解散事項

59

3. 駐韓美軍과 地域社会間의 不祥事나 両側의 親善을 沮害하는 問題의 発生 또는 発生의 憂慮가 있는 事項

4. 其他 中央部処의 支援 또는 調整이 必要하거나 参考될 事項
※10.

②第1項第1号의 報告는 前月分을 翌月 10日까지 第2号와 第4号의 報告는 即時 各各 書面 報告하고 第3号의 報告는 指揮 報告로 한다.
※11.

※8 市(郡): 道知事에게 報告한다.
区 : 市長에게 〃
邑(面): 郡守에게 〃

※9 区(邑, 面): 傍線部分 削制

※10 市(郡): 道의
区(邑, 面): 上級機関의

※11 市(郡): 翌月 7日까지
区(邑. 面): 翌月 5日까지

第13条(其他事項) 協議会運営에 必要한 다른 事項은 協議会의 協議를 거쳐 따로히 定한다.

附 則

①(公布日) 이 条例는 公布한 날로 부터 施行한다.

②(既存委員会廃止) 이 条例 公布 当時에 設置되어 있는 既存의 各種 韓美 親善 組織은 本条例에 의하여 構成되는 委員会에 廃置 統合한다.

60

REPORT ON THE PROGRESS OF ESTABLISHING REGULATIONS FOR ROK-US FRIENDSHIP COUNCIL

Baek Se Hyun
ROK Chairman
Panel on Local Community & Governmental Relations

6

Report on the Progress of Establishing Regulations for ROK-US Friendship Councils

Progress

1. There were created a number of various community advisory committees, both military and civilian, in the areas where the US Army units were stationed in order to promote friendship between US servicemen and Korean nationals. On the contrary to the original intention, they had stand in the way to friendly relations between the two people and what was worse had created troubles and discord.

2. In compliance with a suggestion made by the Panel on Local Community and Governmental Relations, the Ad Hoc Sub-Committee suggested on November 19, 1971 to the SOFA joint committee that the above mentioned various community advisory committees be unified into a ROK-US friendship councils

3. At the 70th SOFA meeting held on Jan. 28, 1972 over the said suggestion, it was agrred that there would be established regulations concerning the ROK-US Friendship Councils in order that local problems would be solved by local level through mutual consultations, and the following were adopted.

A. THE ROK government and US Forces in Korea authorities would change the name of the community advisory committees to a ROK-US Friendship Councils.

B. There would be organized a ROK-US friendship councils on equal levels

4. The ROK representative for the Sub-Committee for Community and Government (Chairman: the Chief of the Management Div., MHA) worked out

-62

on March 30, 1972 a working rule of the Local Autonomy Regulations concerning the ROK-US friendship councils and it was agrred that the ROK representative would present to the US representative an opinion of the ROK representative regarding an organization and operation principles of the ROK-US Friendship Councils in compliance with the working rule for the establishment of the Conncils and the Eighth US Army Regulations 550-5 concerning community development.

An opinion on the Eighth US Army Regulations 550-5, attachment 1

5. The Chairman on the ROK side presented on September 1, 1972 to the US side an opinion of the ROK side in accordance with the previous paragraph.

Notification, attachment 2

A. Working rule for the establishment of the ROK-US Friendship Councils

B. An organization chart

C. Working principles

D. An opinion on the study of the Eighth US Army Regulations 550-5

6. The chairman on the US side presented in March 1973 to the chairman on the Korean side 5 suggestions to the previous ROK opinion. The ROK side in turn sent back on April 11, 1973 to the chairman on the US side an opinion of the ROK side as attached.

63

ROK Reply to US Suggestions

US Suggestions	Reviewed by ROK Side
"In the Working Rule for Regulations concerning the Establishment of ROK-US Friendship Councils"	
1. Change the word "the Committee" in paragraph "Organization" to "members on ROK side of the Committee"	1. No objection
2. Paragraph A "Procedures" Insert a sentence"meetings should be held with closed doors in order to maintain a smooth exchange of opinions	2. No objection
3. Change the word "entrusted committee" in Paragraph D "Procedures" to the word "panel"	3. Objection Reasons: US side proposal was in the contrary to the original intention to unify the existing various friendship (advisory) committees into such a single unit like ROK-US friendship councils because such committees had stand in the way to promotion of friendship between the two people and their heavy reliance on US authorities had given US servicemen bad impression about Korea
4. Change the word "abolishment of existing committees" in Paragraph 2, Addenx to the "disposition of existing committees"; the sentence in the said paragraph "existing various advisory committees" should be abolished and amalgamated into a ROK-US friendship councils" to the sentence "existing various advisory committees may be joined to a ROK-US friendship councils upon concurrence with the chairmen on the both sides	
ROK-US Friendship Council Organization Chart	

64

1. Insert USFK | 1. No objection

7. The chairman on the both sides met on April23 and 26, 1973 and discussed the above matters and came to a final conclusion at the meeting held on April 30, 1973. They were:

US Side Chairman

He expressed his' concern about a gap that might be occured with the abolishment of the existing committees and the establishment of a proposed new councils, and requested there must be some steps to be taken so that a ROK-US friendship councils takes over the functions of the existing committees without delay.

ROK Side Chairman

He reassured that every means would be taken to have a newly established councils absorb not all but some necessary functions of the defunct organizations which would be disorganized in accordance with the agreement made at the ROK-US SOFA joint meeting on Jan. 28, 1972.

Matters Agreed Upon

It was agreed that the matters agreed upon would be presented in writing by the US side chairman to the ROK side .

8. The US skde chairman presented on May 14, 1973 to the ROK side chairman a letter of agreement in accordance with the previous paragraph.

A Letter of Agreement, attachment 3

Agreed the ROK proposal

No existing committee disorganized before new regulations come into effect

Matters To Be Suggested

1. Matters to be taken by both sides

ROK Side: Working rules that would be enforced by the local autonomous bodies would be presented by end of June 1973 for necessary actions

65

① US Side: US Army Regulations 550-5 should be revised in line with such as attached

② The AD-HOC Committee would report above matters to ROK-US SOFA joint committee.

③ The AD-HOC Committee would discuss the establishment of a ROK-US friendship councils on central government level.

66

Working Rule for Regulations concerning the Establishment of Provincial ROK-US Friendship Councils (Draft)

* City (County)

City District

County Myon

Provincial Regulation No

Dated

Article 1 (Purpose)

These regulations shall be to provide provisions concerning the establishment and operation of Provincial ROK-US friendship councils (hereinafter referred to as the Council).

* 1 City (County):	City (County) ROK-US Friendship Council		
District :	District,	City ROK-US Friendship Council	
Up (Myon) :	Up (Myon),	County ROK-US Friendship Council	

Article 2 (Establishment)

There shall be established the Council in order to strengthen mutual cooperation and ties between the US Army stationed in Korea and the Korean community through promoting understanding and friendship,

Article 3 (Functions)

1) The Council shall, through mutual agreement , study, coordinate and/or settle matters of common interest, matters that have occured or are likely to occure, or matters that have been brought about by city or county councils.

*)4 City: brought about by district council

Couty: brought about by Up (Myon) council

Up (Myon): delete underlined partion

2) matters of common interest

2) Above mentioned matters of common interest shall be as follows:

i. Improvement in service, of facilities, interior and exterior, and supervision over entertainment facilities for US servicemen.

ii. Guidance for VD carriers or entertainment girls

iii. Control over those in possesion of drugs or drug peddlers

iv. Control over transaction of US military payment certificate, smuggling activities, illegal transaction of US military goods

v. Labor dispute between US Army units and their Korean national employes

vi. Intrusion of common interest or any act that hampers friendship

Article 4 (Appointment and Dismissal of Council Members)

1) Council members on the ROK side shall be one chairman, five to seven members and one secretary.

2) The chairman shall be the provincial governor.

The council members shall be appointed from among the representatives of the following offices.

The secretary shall be appointed from among officials of the offices concerned.

* 5 City (County): City mayors or county chiefs

District: District chiefs

Up or Myon: Up or Myon chiefs

i. Judiciary agencies (public prosecutors offices, police stations, customs offices)

ii. Labor administration agencies

iii. Health and sanitation agencies

iv. Provincial advisory committees or provincial development committees

-68

v. Intelligent agencies

vi. Tourist service associations, entertainment associations, restaurant associations

vii. Entertainment service girls associations

viii. Other related organizations or representatives of the provincial society

3) The chairman shall dismiss any council member from the office for any of the reasons given below:

i. When he wants to resign

ii. When he transfers himself to other agency

/ iii. When he has less interest in the operation of the Council

iv. When he behaved that hampers friendship or when found any behavior that is likely to hamper

v. When the chairman deems it necessary

Article 5 (Responsibilities of Chairman)

1) The Chairman shall represent the Council and shall take the chair at the meeting. When the chairman is unable to take office, a member of the Council appointed by the chairman shall carry out functions of the chairman.

2) Members of the Council shall, by order of the chairman, attend the Council, propose and/or discuss matters proposed.

3) The secretary shall, by order of the chairman, attend the Council but shall not propose. He shall carry out general affairs of the Council.

Article 6 (Sub-Committees)

1) There may be established sub-committees in order to operate the Council efficiently and to dispose of matters presented for consideration.

2) Members of sub-committees shall be appointed by the chairman and

69

and number of each sub-committee shall be two to three persons.

3) Any proposal that has not been settled at the city or county council may be handled at a sub-committee of the Council.

* City : at District council

County: at Up or Myon council

District, Up or Myon: Paragraph 3) deleted

4) Sub-committees shall be automatically disorganized when entrusted matters are carried out.

Article 7 (Meetings)

There shall be held meeting once every month periodically and the day fixed for a meeting shall be decided through agreement of the both sides. There shall be closed door meetings for a frank exchange of views. Meetings may be held at any time upon request by one party.

Article 8 (Presiding Office)

1) 1) A regular meeting shall be held by turns and a sponsor agency shall be presiding the meeting. Provided that any agency who has requested such a meeting as has been mentioned in a Proviso of the previous article shall in principle be presiding the meeting.

2) A sponsor agency shall notify in writing the other side representative that there will be held a meeting 5 days prior to such a meeting, with the following information contained:

i. Date and time of meeting

ii. Place of meeting

iii. Matters to be presented or reasons for meeting

iv. Agencies and representatives involved

3) Sub-council meetings under Paragraph 3), Article 8 may be held

70

through consultation in advance, with fixture of date and place.

Article 9 (Disorganization of the Council)

There shall automatically be disorganized the council when the US Army unit is moved to other place or is disbanded.

Article 10 (Attendance of Persons concerned at Meetings)

The Council may, whenever it deems necessary, request persons who are concerned with matters presented for their testimony or for presentation of data for reference.

Article 11 (Disposition of Unsettled Matters)

Any matters that have not been settled at the Council shall be presented to the SOFA. *7

* 7 City (County) : present to the provincial council

District (Up or Myon): present to the city (County) council

Article 12 (Reporting)

The chairman shall report to the Minister of Home Affairs *8 the following:

1) Progress of meetings of his council and all councils

2) Disorganization of any council under Article 9

3) Any dispute between the US Army unit and community; occurance of problems that hamper good relations or such problems which are likely to occur.

4) Matters that require the central government support or coordination *10

Report under Paragraph 1) should be made in writing no later than 10th of the following month; report under Paragraphs 2) and 3), in writing immediately; and report under Paragraph 3), by telephone.

71

*8 City, Gun: report to the provincial governor

District: report to the city mayor

Up, Myun: report to the Gun chief

*9 District (Up, Myun): delete partion underlined

*10 City, Gun: provincial

District (Up, Myun): higher level agencies

*11 City (Gun): no later than 7th the following month

District (Up, Myun): no later than 5th the following month

Article 13 (Other Matters)

Other necessary matters for the operation of the Council shall be decided through consultation.

ADDENX

These regulations will be effective upon promulgation.
The existing various Korean American friensship organizations at the time these regulations are promulgated will be either abolished or unified into the Conncil.

12

Operation Principles for Korean American Friendship Council

1. Purpose

These councils will be established with a view to strengthen mutual cooperation and friendship between the two people on an equal footing, with erasing such thinking from Koreans' mind that the existing friendship organizations are merely for obtaining US Army support and with making US servicement understand what Korea and Koreans really are.

2. Establishment

All areas where US armed forces are stationed should have been included in this program but only areas where such friendbhip organizations have already been established are included in this program. Other areas which are not included in this program would take action by separate orders.

2) There should be established different levels of councils according to the size of military units ~~[illegible]~~ with which local government offices keep contact, as follows:

A corps or higher - provincial level

Battalion or higher - City, Gun, District level

Company - Up or Myun level

3) No council should be established for the size of platoon or for Ri or Dong level.

4) There should be established only one council where there are more than one unit in an area or where there are more than one unit in a camp. In this case, ~~[illegible]~~ any of units a commander of which has the highest rank of the other unit

73

commanders should be selected and the other units should cooperate.

3. Title The name of administrative district should be put before Korean American Friendship Council.

Example: Kyonggido Korean American Friendship Council

Pyongtaek Korean American Friendship Council

Hwasung Gun Osan Up Korean American Friendship Council

4. Functions 1) To promote mutual understanding and friendship, thereby enhansing the national prestige

2) To render positive cooperation for prevention of conflicts that may occur between US servicemen and local nationals.

3) Every effort should be made to create environment in which matters brough about would be settled through understanding and dialogue. Matters that are connected with welfare of villages and national interest should be carried through with understanding the other side position.

4) The following are what US Army authorities is concerned about, which should be fully taken into consideration when ~~supervising~~ controlling facilities or issuing permits:

a. Entertainment facilities: They must be located on the broad road side where vehicles can access. They must have outside lights installed.

There must be installed such inside lights that can help recognize others.

There must be installed a satisfactory fire syatem.

There must be installed a lavatory system for each sex.

There must not be served any food or drink.

74

There must not be displayed or shown any signboard or indication for or against any particular race.

b. Control over possesion of arms

c. Control over possesion or sale of drugs

d. Control over illegal exchange of MPCs; over money lending on the security of PX cards or ID cards; over sale of goods on credit

e. Strengthen police patrol around entertainment facilities

5) Matters that have not been settled should be referred to the next higher level council for settlement.

6) The provincial level council should supervise the city and Gun level councils.

5. Organization

1) Number of members of the both side councils should in principle be the same.

2) Higher councils (provincial level) should have more members than lower ones and the provincial level council should consist of representatives of various agencies. Number of members of the counterpart should be taken into consideration when fixing number of members.

3) The chairman should be the chief of local administrative agency.

4) US side should organize their own councils with unit commanders chairmen and staff-officers members. (Councils are not ROK-US combined).

5) The chairman should present letters of appointment or dismissal to members concerned in his name.

6. Meetings

1) There ~~will~~ should be held one meeting once a month and date for next meeting ~~will~~ is be decided at the meeting.

75

2) Meetings ~~will~~ should be held by turns. Meetings should be convened when called by the Korean side even if there is any matter to be taken up but for friendly relations. Minimum entertainment (for example: Bulgogi) would be provided.

3) Meeting places ~~would~~ should be arranged by the side who called the meeting.

4) Tables and chairs ~~would~~ should be arranged in such a way that the chairman sits in the middle of other members. Members of the both sides ~~would~~ should face each other.

5) Agenda ~~would~~ should be presented to the US side 5 days before so as to give time for review by members.

6) Formal dress is desirable at the table and proper etiquette would be observed before the speaker and at the table.

7) The chairman of the side who called the meeting should be a speaker.

8) Interpreters may be employed if necessary.

7. Sub-Committee

1) Sub-committee members should be appointed by the chairman from among those who are familiar with matters to be taken up. Number of each sub-committee should be 2 to 3. For example: for smuggling, customs officers; for health and sanitation, health center officials. One person can be a member of several sub-committee.

2) Any matter that has been referred to the higher council by the lower council for settlement should be settled, with formation of sub-committees when a US counterpart concerned is located in a very far distance.

8. Disposition of Unsettled Matters

1) Unsettled matters should be referred to the higher councils to the SOFA in the last resort.

-26

2) When the Minister of Home Affairs receives through the Chief of the Management Division of the Ministry such a report as has been mentioned in the previous paragraph, the Ministry of Home Affairs ~~would~~ should refer the case to the SOFA.

3) When referring the case to the Ministry of Home Affairs there should be presented full information, together with references and date.

9. Witnesses — ~~Witnesses should not be forced to present themselves before testimony~~

Neither witnesses nor evidences should be forced to be presented for testimony but every means should be used to make witnesses or evidences presented voluntarily.

10. Announcement — Announcement of results of council meetings should be made with agreement between the both sides.

11. Reporting — 1) All reports to the Minister of Home Affairs should ~~be~~ go through the Management Division Chief of the Ministry.

2) Progress report should be made on the form 1) and 2) attached.

3) A summary of progress should be reported by telephone and details should be reported in writing immediately afterward.

12. Abolishment of Existing Committees — All existing committees and similar organizations which are excluded ~~from~~ in these regulations should be either unified into this council or abolished.

17

Form 1

Progress Report on Provincial Korean Americal Friendship Council Meeting

COUNCIL	DATE	AGENDA	AGREED OR DISAGREED	ACTIONS TAKEN	REMARKS

78

Form 2

Minutes of the th Meeting of

Provincial Korean American Friendship Council

1. Date

2. Place

3. Agenda

a

b

c

4. Discussion or Consultation

5. Action taken

6. Special References

79

HEADQUARTERS, UNITED STATES FORCES, KOREA
APO SAN FRANCISCO 96301
OFFICE OF THE ASSISTANT CHIEF OF STAFF, J5

EJ 14 May 1973

MEMORANDUM FOR: Mr. BAEK Sae Hyun, ROK Chairman, Panel on Local Community and Governmental Relations

SUBJECT: Korean-American Friendship Council Directive

1. To respond to your Memorandum of 11 April 1973, I requested the views and comments of the US members of the Panel on Local Community and Governmental Relations. Their reactions have been most favorable and note with appreciation the proposal to formally recognize the Korean-American Friendship Councils (KAFCs).

2. In line with our conversation on 30 April, I was most pleased to know that you share my concern that local coordination through the several KAFCs should not be interrupted during the period of implementation of the new directive. I believe that KAFC activities assume additional importance as we progress into the summer months. It has been traditional that this season provides the greatest influx of US Forces personnel into the local communities; and, consequently, there is a more urgent need to maintain effective civil-military coordination and cooperation.

3. I recommend that you brief the members of the Ad Hoc Subcommittee on Civil-Military Relations concerning the Ministry of Home Affairs directive at the next Ad Hoc Subcommittee meeting. This certainly represents a major step in enhancing effective Korean-American civil-military relations.

FRANK W. ATKINSON, JR.
LTC, USA
US Chairman
Panel on Local Community and Governmental Relations

80

韓美親善協議會設置規程制定

經 過 報 告

(73. 6.5. SOFA)

1973 [illegible]

內務部管理課長 白 世 鉉

BAEK, SE HYUN

ROK CHAIRMAN

PANEL ON LOCAL COMMUNITY

&

GOVERNMENTAL RELATIONS

81

韓美親善協議会設置規程制定에 対한経過報告

制 定 経 緯

1. 現在 各基地村 地域에는 軍民間에 雑多한 地域 諮問委員会가 構成되어 있으며, 이들 委員会의 活動은 韓美間의 親善을 図謀하고 友誼를 增進하기 보다는 오히려 軍民間의 親善을 沮害하고 非協調 또는 不和를 이르키는 事例가 許多하였음.

2. 71.11.19 "軍民関係特別分科委員会" (SOFA의 AD-HOC SUB-COMMITTEE)는 "地域社会 및 政府関係小委員会" (PANEL ON LOCAL COMMUNITY & GOVERNMENTAL RELATIONS)의 建議에 따라 前述한 雑多한 地域諮問委員会를 単一한 "韓美親善協議会" (THE KOREAN AMERICAN FRIENDSHIP COUNCILS)로 統合整備할 것을 "SOFA 合同委員会"에 建議하였음.

3. 72.1.28 "SOFA 合同委員会" 第70次会議에서는 前項의 建議事項에 対하여 地域問題는 地域単位에서 相互協議 処理할수 있도록 韓美親善協議会에 関한 規程을 制定 施行할것을 다음과 같이 合議 採択하였음.

가. 韓国政府와 駐韓美軍当局은 "地域問題諮問委員会"를 "韓美親善協議会" (THE KOREAN AMERICAN FRIENDSHIP

COUNCILS) 로 名称을 改正할것.

나. 韓美両側 共히 適正한 "LEVEL"에서 "韓美親善協議会"를 組織할것

4. 前項에 依拠 72.3.30 "地域社会 및 政府関係小委員会" 韓国側(議長 内務部管理課長)은 韓美親善協議에 関한 地方自治団体条例準則(案)을 作成하고 韓国側 議長이 韓美親善協議会設置条例準則에 따른 韓美親善協議会 階層別 構成図와 運営要綱 및 地域社会 発展과 関聯되는 美8軍 例規 550-5号에 対한 韓国側 意見을 美側과 協議키로 하였음.

o 美8軍例規 550-5号 検討에 따른 意見

※ 別添1

5. 前項에 依拠 72.9.1 韓国側議長은 韓国側 意見을 美側議長에게 通報하였음.

o 通報事項 (※別添2)

가. 韓美親善協議会 設置条例準則

나. " 階層別構成図

다. " 運営要綱

라. (美8軍例規 550-5号 検討内容)

6. 前項에 対하여 73.3 美側議長은 5個 項目의 建議事項을 韓国

側 議長에게 提示하였으며 이에 対하여 韓国側意見을 73.4.11. 美側議長에게 回示 하였는바 그 內容은 다음과 같음.

回 示 內 容

美側建議內容	検 討 結 果
韓美親善協議会 設置条例 準則(案)中	
1. "構成項" 中 "委員会"라는 用語를 "委員会의 韓国側 構成員"으로 改正	1. 賛 成
2. "節次-가項" "会議는 円滑한 意思交換을 図謀하기 為하여 非公式的 이어야 한다"를 挿入	2. "
3. "節次-라.마項"에서 "委任委員会"라는 用語를 "Panel"로 使用	3. "
4. 附則第2項 "既存委員会廃止"를 既存委員会処理로 改正	4. 不 賛 <理 由>

84

하고, 才2項의 內容인 "既存의 各種 韓美親善組織을 韓美親善協議会에 廃置 統合한다"를 "既存의 各種 韓美親善組織을 韓美両側議長의 同意下에 韓美親善協議会에 加入될 수 있다"로 改正	乱立된 既存 各種 親善団体가 軍民間의 友誼増進과 親善을 오히려 沮害하고 美側에 依存하는 低姿勢를 取함으로서 一部 美軍들이 韓国에 対해 나쁜 認識을 갖게 되어 乱立된 既存団体를 単一韓美親善協議会로 統合코저 하는 本来의 目的에 違背됨
韓美親善協議階層別 構成図에있어 1. USFK(駐韓UN軍司令部)를 挿入	1. 賛 成

7. 前項에 対하여 韓美両側議長은 73.4.23, 73.4.26 両次에 걸쳐 相互 協議한바 있으며. 73. 4. 30 両側議長間의 最終協議를 거쳐 合議된 事項은 아래와 같음.

o 美側議長

既存委員会를 廃止하고 韓美親善協議会를 設立하는 境遇 廃止 新設에 따라 空白期間의 発生이 憂慮되므로 既存委員会의 機能을 新設 協議会에서 吸収하여 차질이 없도록 措置하여 줄 것을 要請

o 韓国側 議長

72.1.28 «韓美合同委員会» 合議事項 本来의 趣旨에 立脚하여 廃止되는 既存委員会의 必要한 機能을 新設되는 韓美親善協議会에 統合吸収되도록 함이 妥当함을 再確認하였음

o 合議事項

위 事項을 美側議長이 書面으로 韓国側에 提示키로 合議하였음.

8. 前項에 依拠 73.5.14. 美側議長은 韓国側議長에게 合議文書를 伝達

<合議文書内容> (別添 3)

o 韓国側案에 対하여 同意함

o 어떤 特定 KAFC 도 新規程 施行前에 廃止 되어서는 아니됨.

-5-

86

建 議 事 項

1 . 雙方措置事項

韓国側 : 各地方自治団体에서 施行할 規則準則 (案) 을 示達하여

73 . . 까지 KAFC를 発足토록 한다.

美 側 : 美軍例規 550-5号를 # 別添 1 内容과 같이 修正토록

한다.

2 . AD - HOC COMMITTE 에서는 위 措置事項을 韓美合同委員

会에 報告할 것

3 . AD-HOC COMMITTE 에서는 中央政府 LEVEL 에서의 韓

美親善協議会 構成을 検討할것.

0817

(# 別添 1)

美八軍例規才 550-5号 検討

-7-

89

美 8 軍 例規 550-5 号에 대한 検討

区分	例規	意見	備考
1. 目的	....委員会의 目的은 美軍人과 韓国人間의 理解를 促進하고 改善하며 大韓民国의 社会的, 経済的 発展에 寄与하는데 있다.	....委員会의 目的은 美軍人과 韓国人間의 理解를 促進하고 関係의 改善으로 相互間의 友誼를 増進하고 親善을 図謀하는데 있다.	委員会의 方向転換 0 韓国에 対한 認識感의 刷新 0 国威宣揚 同等한 立場에서의 協調와 親善
4. 定義	다. 地域社会와 関聯된 計劃: 司令部의 機能은 .... 및 地域社会의 尊敬과 信義를 받도록 計劃을 作成한다.	다. 地域社会와 関聯된 計劃: 司令部의 機能은 ... 및 地域社会의 協調와 親善을 図謀하도록 計劃을 作成한다.	
6. 指針	아. (新設)	아. 韓美合同委員会에서 相互合意된 事項은 両側이 誠実하게 이를 遵守하고 履行할 義務를 진다.	
7. 新委員会 設立		"新委員会設立" 을 "委員会設立" 으로 修正	
	나. 新委員会는 特定한 地域 軍部隊長과 計劃된 委員会를 代表하는 地域社会의 地方公務員間의 協定으로 設立한다. 地域軍部隊長은 地方公務員에 対하여 委員会가 任意의, 그리고 諮問的性質 및 委員会의 能力과 限界, 이 委員会의 設立과 運用으로 얻어지는 相互間의 利益에 대하여 分明히 밝혀야 한다.	나. 委員会는 ....된다. 地域軍部隊長은 隷下将兵으로 하여금 本委員会가 韓美合同委員会의 決定으로 設立된 点과 委員会의 目的과 機能 等을 周知케 하여야 한다.	地域部隊長의 遵守義務를 明示
8. 委員会의 解散	가. 部隊의 閉鎖에 関하여 (軍保安이 許容하는 内) 承認을 받는 대로 地域社会代表에게 通知한다.	가. 部隊의 閉鎖에 関하여 (軍保安이 許容하는 内) 承認을 받는대로 韓国側委員会 議長에게 通知한다.	

-8-

89

89

区 分	例 規	意 見	備 考
9. 構 成	가. 韓国側 構成員: 韓国側 代表는 地域社会指導者에 依하여 決定된다. 一般的으로 韓国側 委員은 道・特別市・郡・面・里・邑・区 或은 洞의 最高位者로서 韓国側構成員의 議長이 되며 美軍構成員에 対한 民間人 相対役이 된다. 高位公務員과 同級이고 그들과 独立된 韓国警察의 代表는 韓国側 構成員에 必須要員이 된다. 代表者는 尊敬받는 部落의 高齢者, 予備軍, 健康, 衛生 教育関係公務員과 地域事業家, 新聞社代表 및 労勵関係公務員이 包含된다.	나. 韓国側 構成員: 韓国側 議長은 地方行政機関의 長(道知事・市長・郡守・区庁長 및 邑・面長)이 되고 委員은 아래機関의 代表 또는 構成員中에서 議長이 指名 또는 委嘱한다. o 司法機関(検察, 警察, 税関) o 労勵行政機関 o 保健衛生機関 o 情報機関 o 諮問委員会 또는 開発委員会 o 観光業体, 遊興業 및 料食業協会 o 業態婦 代表 o 其他 有関機関 또는 住民代表	o 委員長은 当然職으로 하고 構成員도 限定 o 第70次(72.1.28) SOFA 韓美合同委에서 "適切한 水準의 代表"로 構成토록한바 있음.

-9-

90

90

区　分	例　規	意　見	備　考
11. 節　次	가. 会合 : 会合은 每月 計劃되어야 한다. 会合을 最小 6 0 日間 開催하지 못한 때는 会合을 가질 수 없는 状況을 書面으로 提出하여야 한다. 将軍이 主宰하는 委員会에서는 위의 条項이 適用되지 아니하며 適当하다고 생각되는 때를 予定할 수 있다.	가. 会合 : 会合은 每月 1 回 定期的으로 開催하고 一方의 要請이 있을 때는 随時 開催한다. 会合을 最小 60 日間 開催하지 못한 때는 会合을 가질수 없는 状況을 書面으로 提出하여야 한다. 道知事와 将軍이 主宰하는 委員会에서는 위의 条項이 適用되지 아니하며 適当하다고 생각되는 때를 予定할 수 있다.	随時 開催할 수 있는 融通性 賦与
	사. 小委員会의 利用	사. 小委員会의 利用 : 削除 : 不要	
	아. 未解決된 事案 : 下級委員会 水準에서 未解決된 事案은 上級司令部에 移管한다. 委員会에서 解決되지 못한 安全問題는 陸軍省 安全官에게 提出하여야 한다.	아. 未解決된 事案 : .... 이 경우 他方의 上級機関이 地理的으로 遠隔한 곳에 位置하고 있을 때에는 委任委員会로 하여금 相対方의 委員会와 接触하고 協議토록 하여 解決한다. 上部司令部에서도 解決되지 못한 事案은 韓美合同委員会 (軍民関係分科委員会) 에 建議하여 処理토록 한다.	o 委任委員会가 解決토록 하므로써 全委員이 他地域으로 出張가는 煩雑을 避하고자 함 (特히 行政区域이 다를 경우)

91

区分	例規	意見	備考
		카・參考人의 委員会 出席 委員会는 必要한 경우에 附議된 案件에 関聯되는 関係人 參考人의 出席発言이나 參考資料의 提示를 要請할 수 있다.	o 協議事項의 圓滑, 迅速한 解決을 為하여 追加挿入

-11-

92

92

(# 別添 2)

1. 韓美親善協議会 設置規程 (案)

2. 韓美親善協議会 階層別 構成図 (案)

3. 韓美親善協議会 運営要綱 (案)

93

1. 韓美親善協議会設置規程要旨

韓美親善協議会設置規程 "小題目"

1. 目　　的
2. 設置　部署
3. 名　　称
4. 機　　能
5. 構　　成
6. 委員의辞退
7. 委員長등의　職務
8. 節　　次
　가. 会　　議
　나. 会議　主管
　다. 会議開催通報
　라. 分任委員会 (Panel)
　마. 未解決事案의　処理
9. 協議会解散
10. 参考人의　協議会出席
11. 報　告
12. 其他　事項
13. 既存委員会　廃止

-13-

94

韓美親善協議会設置規程 (案)

1. 目　　的：韓国人과 美軍人間의 理解를 促進하고 関係의 改善으로 相互間의 友誼를 増進하여 親善을 図謀하는데 있다.

2. 設置部署：委員会는 美合衆国軍隊가 駐屯하고 있는 市・区・邑・面과 이 地域을 管轄하는 特別市・道・郡에 設置한다.

3. 名　　称：協議会의 名称은 〇〇道 (特別市・市・郡・邑・面) 韓美親善協議会라 한다.

4. 機　　能：協議会는 韓美間의 共同関心事와 韓美間에 発生되었거나 또는 発生 憂慮가 있는 事項에 関하여 事前事後 対策을 마련하고 下級協議会에서 建議된 問題를 相互理解와 協助로서 調整하고 解決한다.

가. 相互対話의 通路마련

나. 懸案問題点의 確認

다. 相互関心事인 問題解決의 方案模索

라. 相互間의 利益을 増進하는 事業의 企劃 및 執行

마. 駐屯軍部隊와 地域住民과의 有益한 協調

5. 構　　成：協議会의 韓国側 構成員은 委員長 1人과 委員 5~7人 및 幹事 1人으로 構成한다.

委員長은 地方行政機関의 長 (道知事・市長・郡守・区庁長 및 邑・面長)이 되고 委員과 幹事는 委員長이

95

다음 機関의 代表 또는 構成員中에서 任命 또는 委囑한다.

가. 司法機関(検察·警察 및 税関)

나. 労動行政機関

다. 保健衛生機関

라. 諮問委員会 또는 開発委員会

마. 情報機関

바. 観光業体·遊興 및 料食業協会

사. 業態婦代表

아. 其他 有関機関 또는 住民代表

6. 委員의 辞退: 委員長은 委員中 다음 事由가 発生하였을 때는 그 職을 辞任케 하고 即時 後任者를 交替選任 한다.

가. 他機関으로 転出되었을 때

나. 会議参席이 徴温的이고 委員会運営에 消極的일 때

다. 韓美親善을 害치는 行為를 하였거나 그러한 行為가 있다고 認定될 때

라. 其他 委員長이 必要하다고 認定될 때

7. 委員長등의 職務: 委員長은 協議会를 代表하고 会議의 議長이 된다. 다만 委員長이 事故가 있을 때에는 委員中에서 委員長이 指定한 者가 그 職務를 代行한다. 委員은 委員長의 命을 받아 委員会에 出席하여 発

-15-

96

言하며 附議된 案件을 相互協議하고 討論한다.

幹事는 委員長의 命을 받아 委員会에 出席하되 発言할 수 없으며 委員会의 庶務를 処理한다.

協議会의 運営費(韓国側負担分)는 地方自治団体에서 予算이 許容하는 範囲内에서 最大限 確保한다.

8. 節 次:

가. 会 議 ······ 協議会는 每年 1回 定期的으로 開催하되 日字는 韓美 両側의 協議로 定하며 会議는 円滑한 意思交換을 図謀하기 위하여 非公式的이어야 한다. 다만 어느 一方의 要求가 있을 때는 随時 開催할 수 있다.

나. 会議主管 ······ 定期会는 相互交代로 他方委員을 招請하여 開催하되 招請한 機関이 主管한다. 다만 어느 一方의 要求에 의하여 随時 開催하는 会議에서는 要求機関에서 主管함을 原則으로 한다.

다. 会議開催通報 ·······主管機関은 늦어도 会議開催 5日前에 他方代表에게 아래 事項이 記載된 内容을 書面으로 通知하여야 한다.

(1) 会議開催 日時

(2) 会議開催 場所

(3) 附議案件 또는 開催코자 하는 事由

(4) 招請者와 被招請者의 機関 및 代表者

다만 下級協議会의 未解決 事案을 上級委員会에서 協議코자 할 때에는 両側이 事前協議로 会議日時와 場所를 따로히 定

할 수 있다.

라. Panel……協議会의 効率的 運営과 附議된 事項을 円滑히 処理하기 為하여 協議会의 協議를 거쳐 Panel을 構成할 수 있다.

Panel의 委員은 委員長이 指名하고 委員의 数는 2人 내지 3人으로 한다.

Panel은 受任받은 事案이 完結되었을 때 自動的으로 解体된다.

마. 未解決事案의 処理……下級協議会에서 合議되지 못한 事案은 韓美 双方의 指揮系統에 따라 漸次 次上級協議会에 建議한다. 이 境遇 上級協議会의 美軍部隊가 韓国側 行政官署의 管轄地域 外에 所在하고 있을 때에는 Panel로 하여금 相対方의 協議会와 協議토록 하여 解決한다.

上級協議会에서도 解決되지 못한 事案은 韓美合同委員会(軍民関係分科委員会)에 建議한다.

9. 協議会解散 : 被対象機関이 移動하거나 兵営이 廃鎖되는 때는 自動的으로 解体된다. 새로운 部隊가 같은 兵営에 駐屯하게 되거나 前任部隊의 業務를 引受받았을 때는 協議会를 다시 構成한다.

10. 参考人의 協議会 出席 : 協議会는 必要하다고 認定할 때는 附議된 案件에 関聯되는 関係人, 参考人의 出席発言이나 参考資料의 提示를 要請할 수 있다.

11. 報 告 : 道知事는 每月 道와 傘下 市郡邑面의 協議会開催状況

-17-

98

을 別紙書式에 依拠 翌月 10日까지 內務部長官에게 報告 한다.

韓美間의 不詳事나 両側의 親善을 沮害할 要因의 発生 또는 発生의 憂慮가 있는 것은 即刻 內務部長官에게 指揮 報告한다.

12. 其他事項 : 協議会運営에 必要한 其他 事項은 協議会의 協議를 거쳐 따로히 定한다.

13. 既存委員会 廃止 : 既存의 各種 韓美親善組織은 이 委員会에 廃置 統合한다.

99

2 . 韓美親善協議会階層別構成図

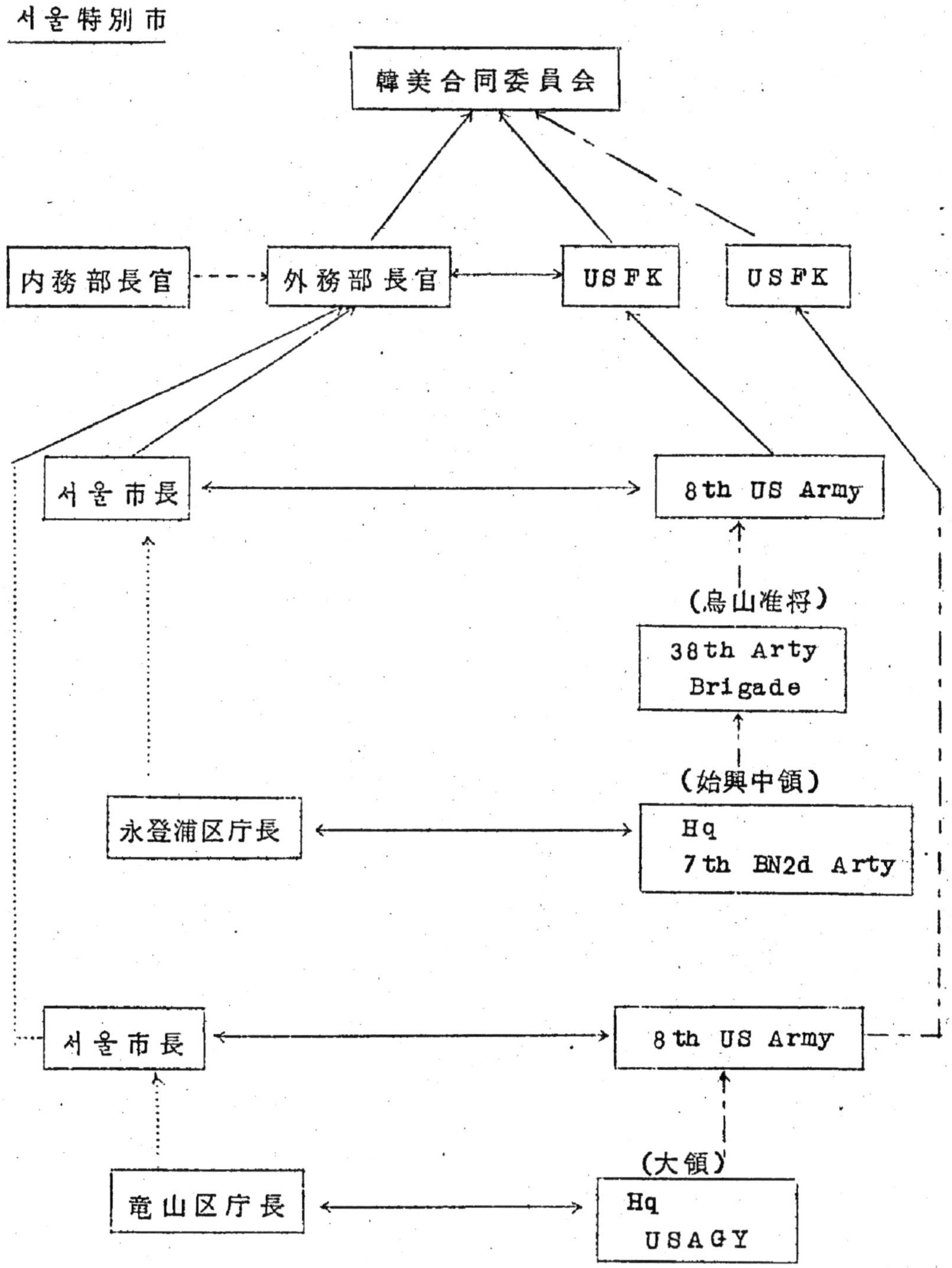

-19-

100

釜 山 市

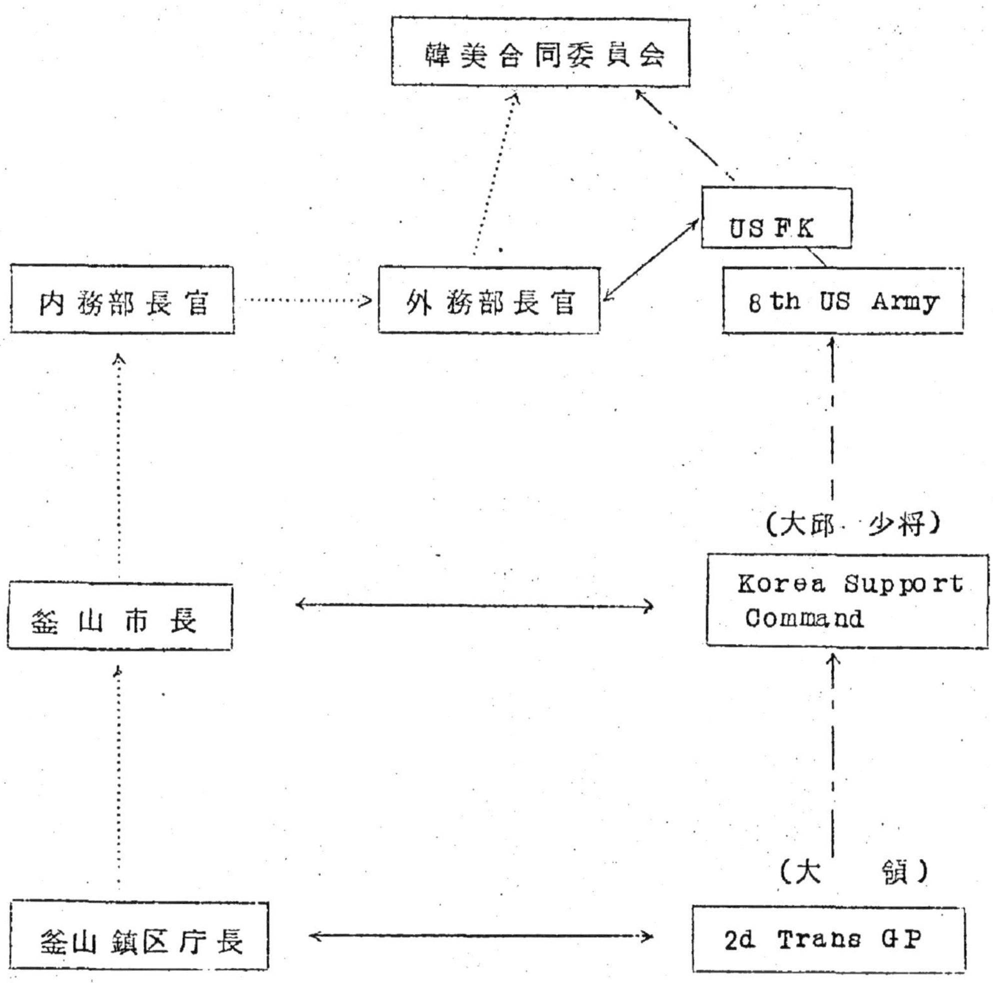

韓美合同委員会
USFK
8th US Army
內務部長官
外務部長官
(大邱 少将)
Korea Support Command
釜山市長
(大 領)
釜山鎮区庁長
2d Trans GP

101

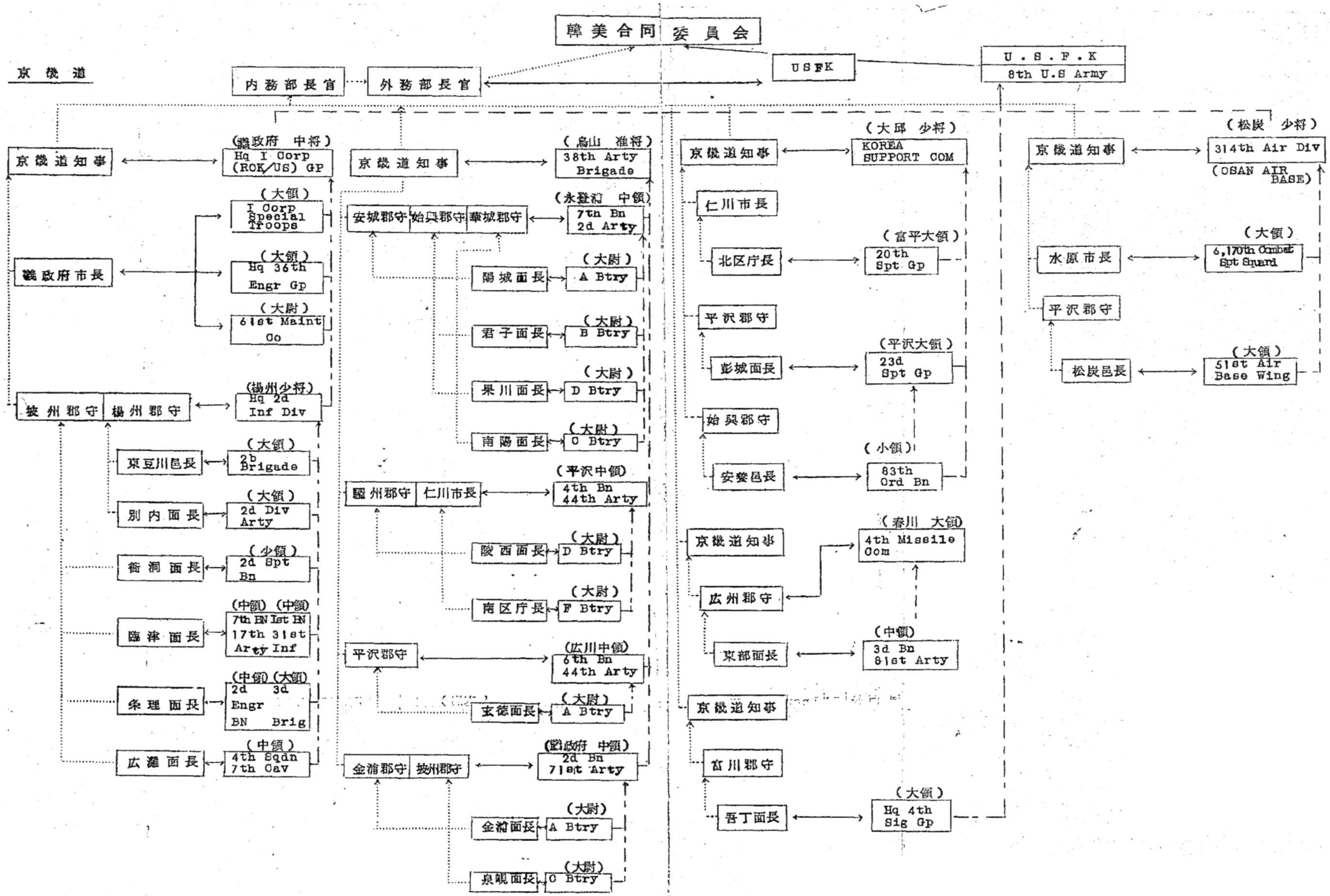
韓美合同委員会
京畿道
内務部長官
外務部長官
USFK
U.S.F.K
8th U.S Army
京畿道知事
(議政府 中将)
Hq I Corp (ROK/US) GP
(大領)
I Corp Special Troops
議政府市長
(大領)
Hq 36th Engr Gp
(大尉)
61st Maint Co
坡州郡守
楊州郡守
(楊州少将)
Hq 2d Inf Div
東豆川邑長
(大領)
2b Brigade
別内面長
(大領)
2d Div Arty
榆洞面長
(少領)
2d Spt Bn
臨津面長
(中領) (中領)
7th BN 1st BN
17th 31st
Arty Inf
条理面長
(中領) (大領)
2d 3d
Engr Brig
BN
広灘面長
(中領)
4th Sqdn
7th Cav
京畿道知事
(烏山 准将)
38th Arty Brigade
安城郡守
始興郡守
華城郡守
(永登浦 中領)
7th Bn
2d Arty
陽城面長
(大尉)
A Btry
君子面長
(大尉)
B Btry
果川面長
(大尉)
D Btry
南陽面長
(大尉)
C Btry
富川郡守
仁川市長
(平沢中領)
4th Bn
44th Arty
陵西面長
(大尉)
D Btry
南区庁長
(大尉)
F Btry
平沢郡守
(広川中領)
6th Bn
44th Arty
玄徳面長
(大尉)
A Btry
金浦郡守
坡州郡守
(議政府 中領)
2d Bn
71st Arty
金浦面長
(大尉)
A Btry
泉峴面長
(大尉)
C Btry
京畿道知事
(大邱 少将)
KOREA SUPPORT COM
仁川市長
北区庁長
(富平大領)
20th Spt Gp
平沢郡守
彭城面長
(平沢大領)
23d Spt Gp
始興郡守
安養邑長
(小領)
83th Ord Bn
京畿道知事
(春川 大領)
4th Missile Com
広州郡守
東部面長
(中領)
3d Bn
81st Arty
京畿道知事
富川郡守
吾丁面長
(大領)
Hq 4th Sig Gp
京畿道知事
(松炭 少将)
314th Air Div
(OSAN AIR BASE)
水原市長
(大領)
6,170th Combat Spt Squard
平沢郡守
松炭邑長
(大領)
51st Air Base Wing

-21-

102

江 原 道

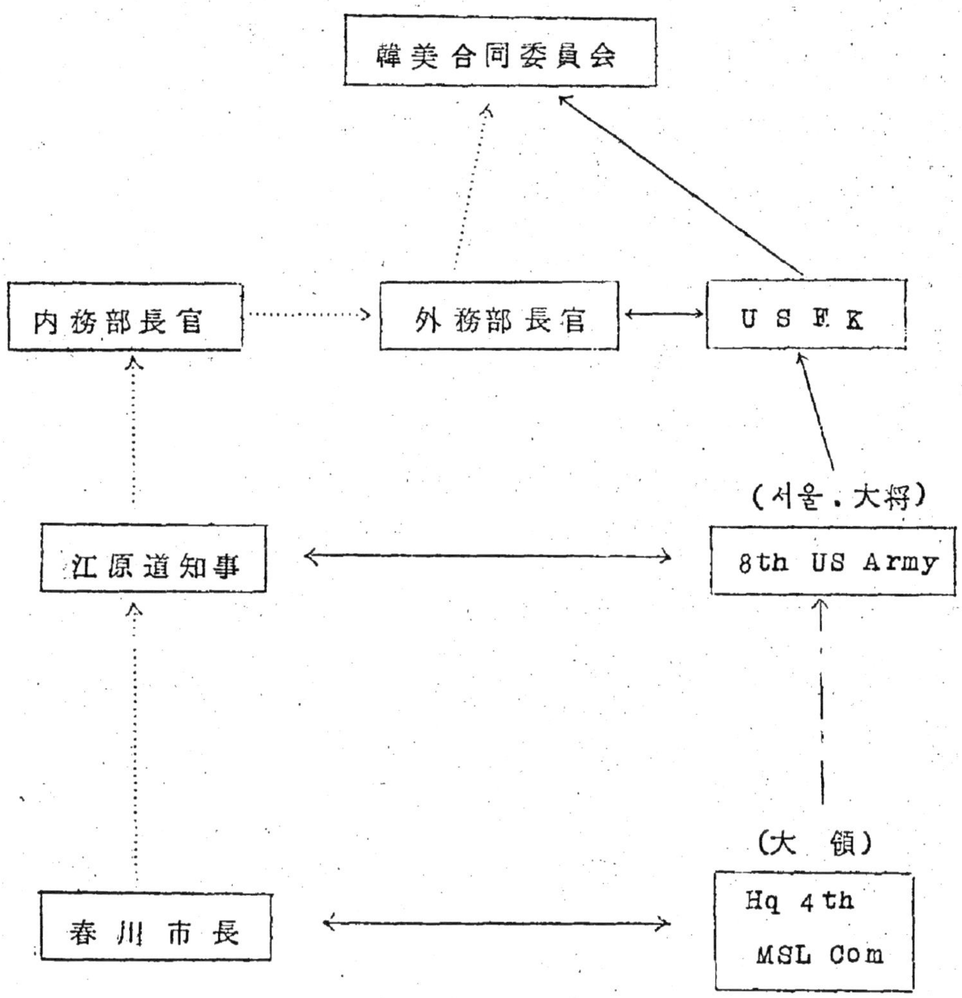
韓美合同委員会
內務部長官
外務部長官
U S F K
(서울 . 大將)
江原道知事
8th US Army
(大 領)
春川市長
Hq 4th
MSL Com

-22-

103

忠 淸 北 道

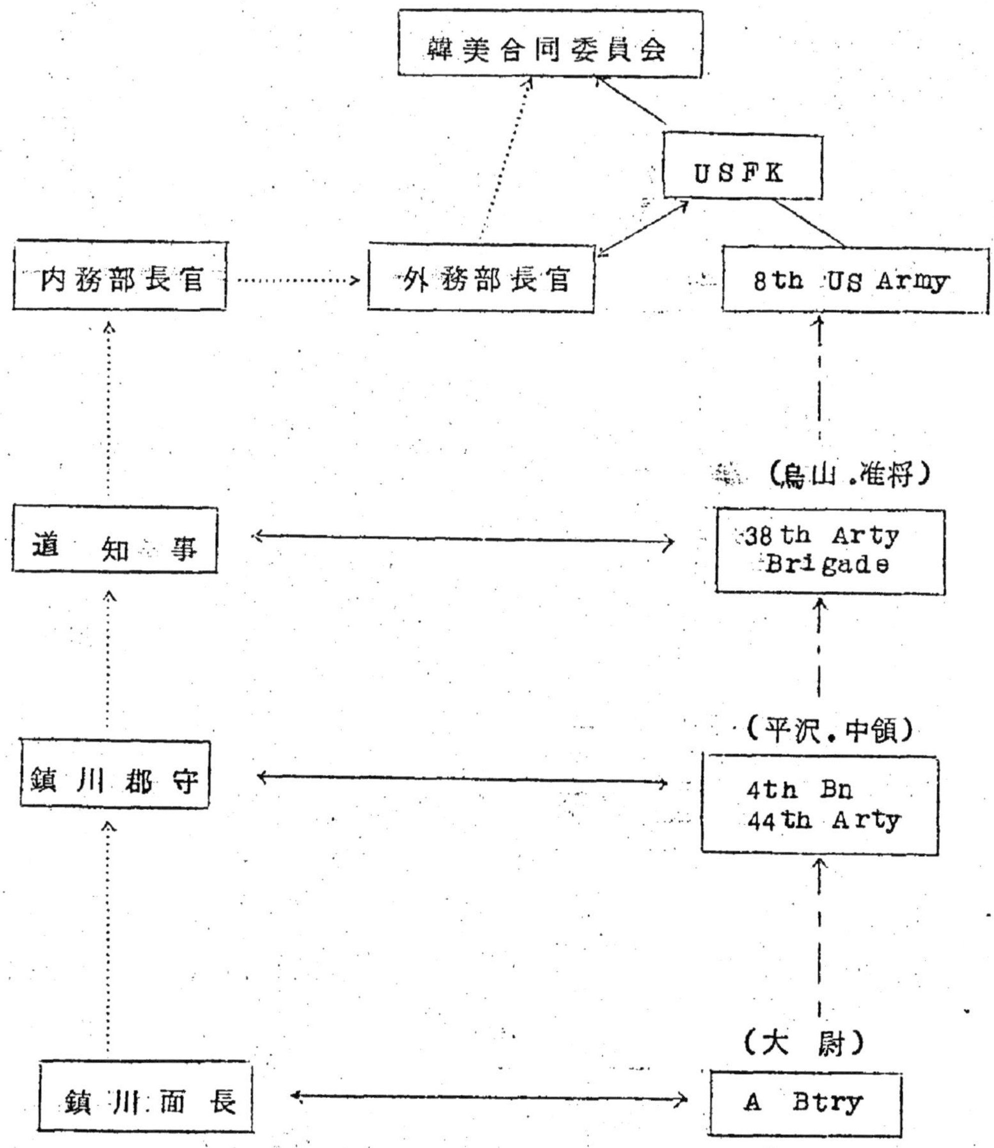
韓美合同委員会
USFK
內務部長官
外務部長官
8th US Army
(烏山.准將)
道 知 事
38th Arty Brigade
(平沢.中領)
鎭 川 郡 守
4th Bn 44th Arty
(大 尉)
鎭 川 面 長
A Btry

-23-

全羅北道

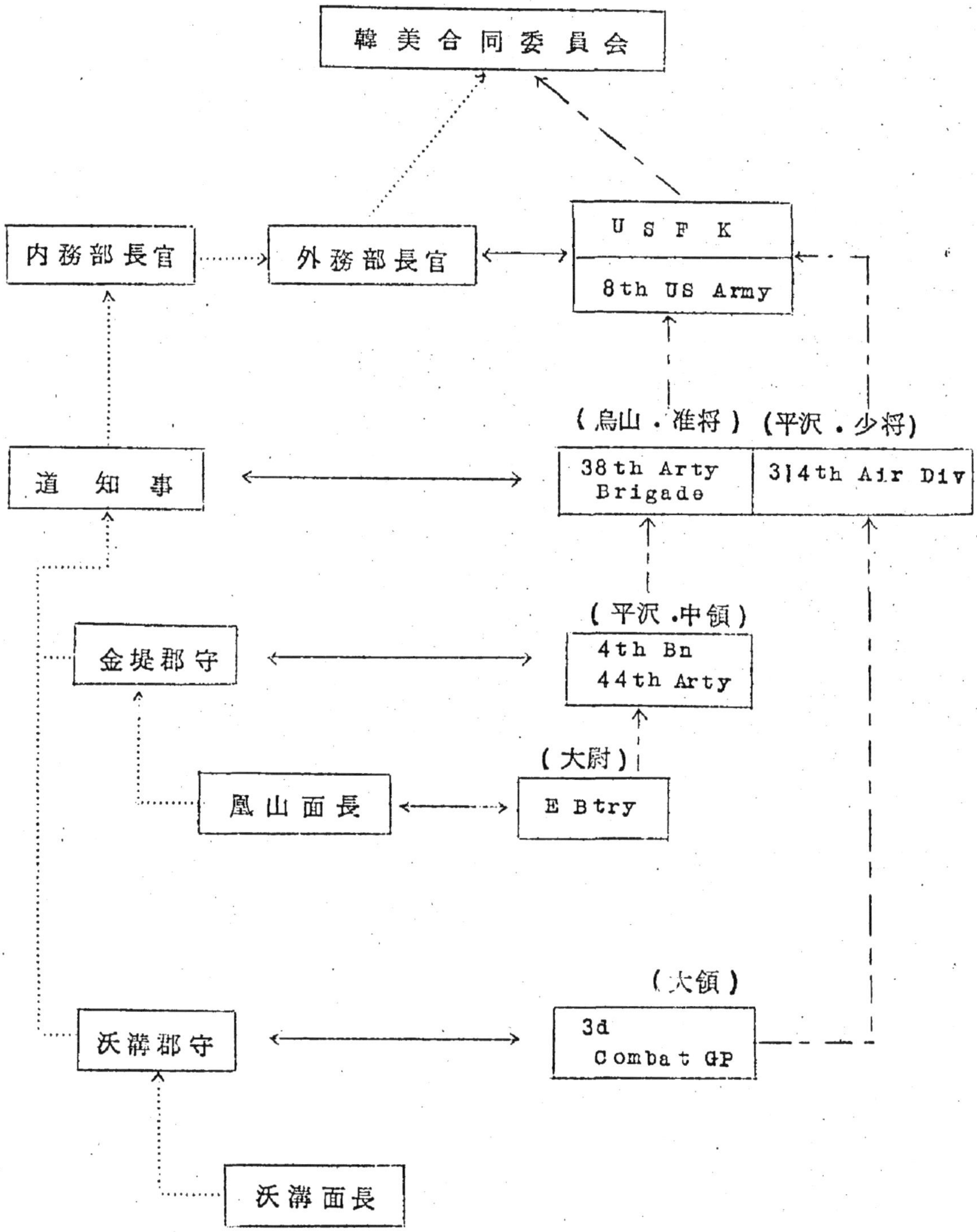

韓美合同委員会
内務部長官
外務部長官
U S F K
8th US Army
(烏山・准将)
(平沢・少将)
道 知 事
38th Arty Brigade
314th Air Div
(平沢・中領)
金堤郡守
4th Bn 44th Arty
(大尉)
凰山面長
E Btry
(大領)
沃溝郡守
3d Combat GP
沃溝面長

105

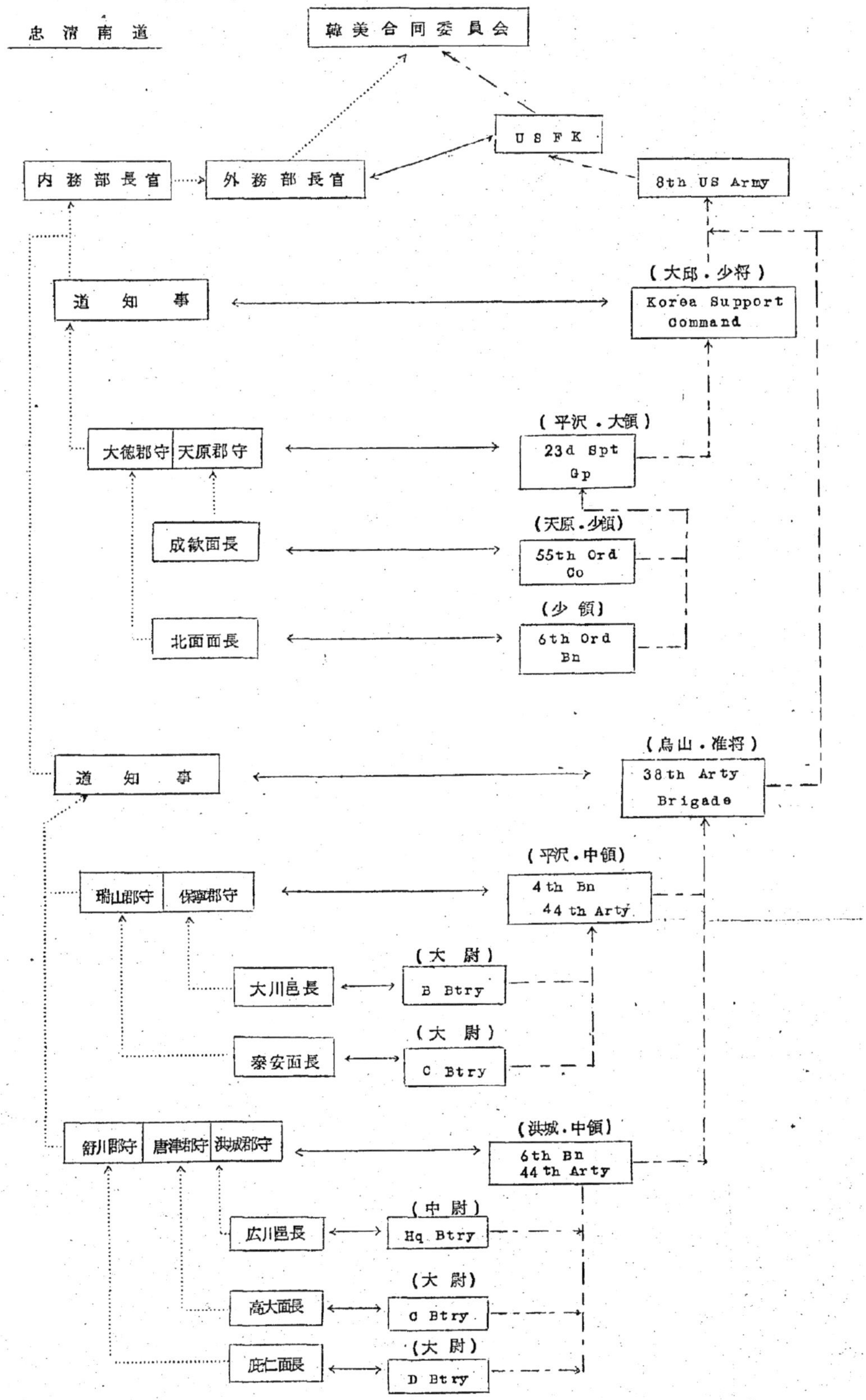

忠清南道
韓美合同委員会
USFK
内務部長官
外務部長官
8th US Army
(大邱・少将)
道知事
Korea Support Command
(平沢・大領)
大徳郡守
天原郡守
23d Spt Gp
(天原・少領)
成歓面長
55th Ord Co
(少領)
北面面長
6th Ord Bn
(烏山・准将)
道知事
38th Arty Brigade
(平沢・中領)
瑞山郡守
保寧郡守
4th Bn 44th Arty
(大尉)
大川邑長
B Btry
(大尉)
泰安面長
C Btry
(洪城・中領)
舒川郡守
唐津郡守
洪城郡守
6th Bn 44th Arty
(中尉)
広川邑長
Hq Btry
(大尉)
高大面長
C Btry
(大尉)
庇仁面長
D Btry

-24-

106

慶尚北道

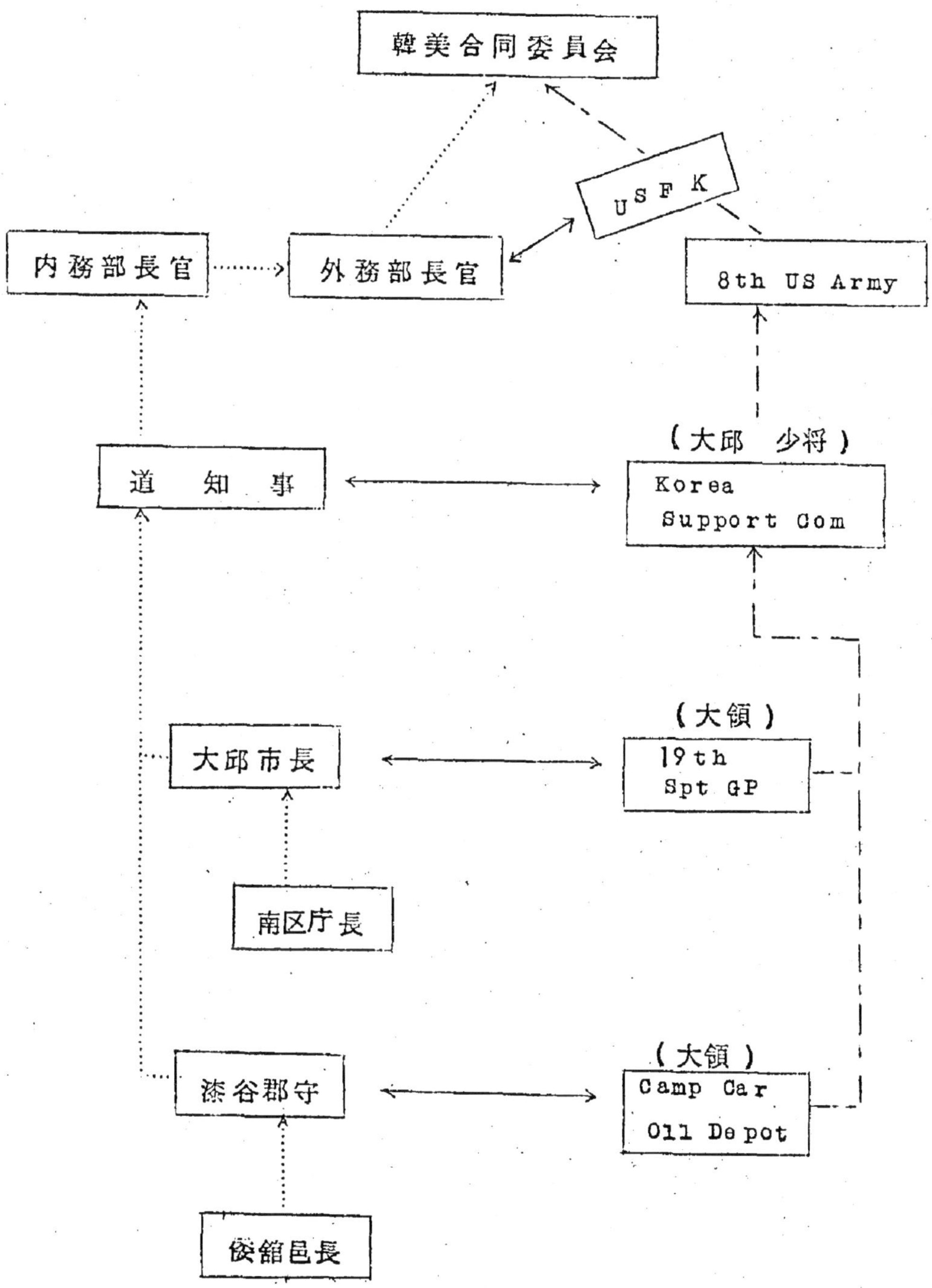
韓美合同委員会
USFK
内務部長官
外務部長官
8th US Army
(大邱 少将)
道 知 事
Korea
Support Com
(大領)
大邱市長
19th
Spt GP
南区庁長
(大領)
漆谷郡守
Camp Car
Oil Depot
倭舘邑長

107

慶尙南道

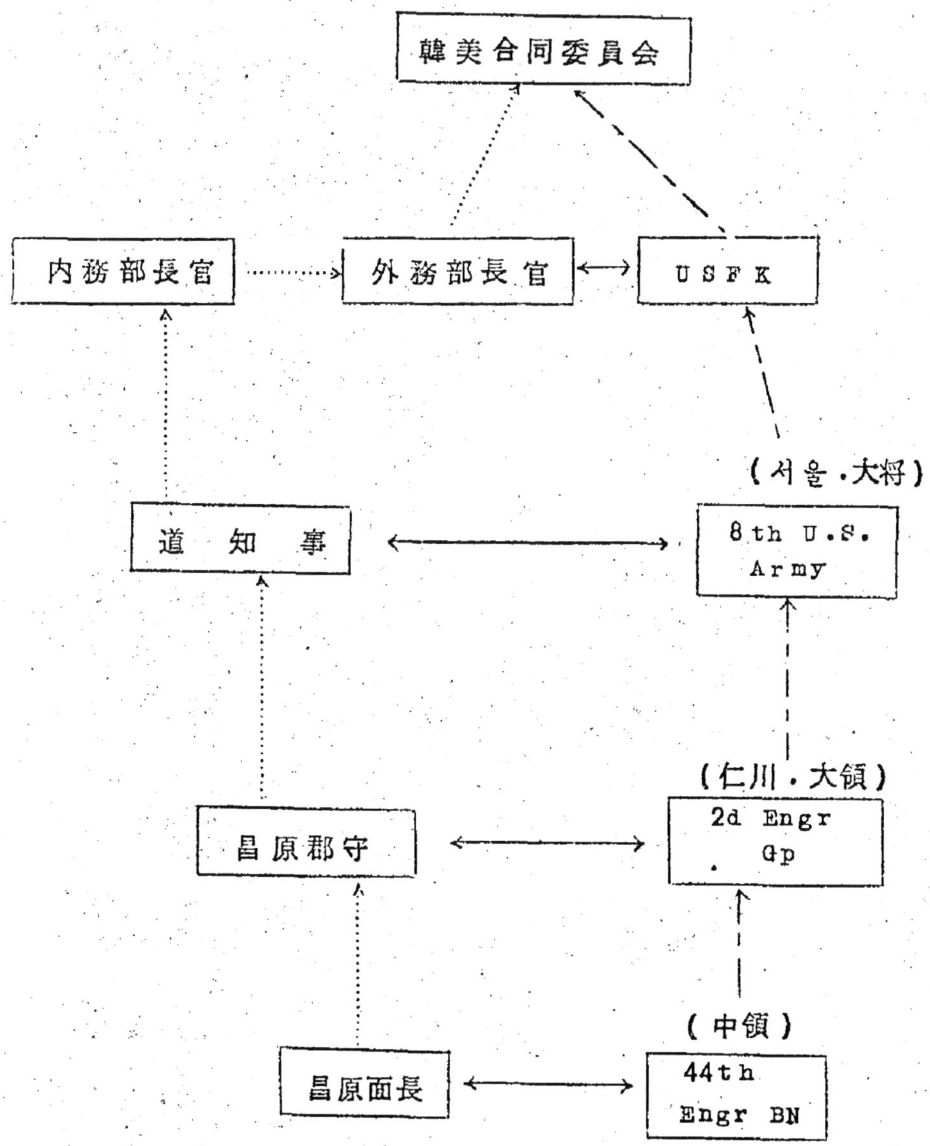

韓美合同委員会
內務部長官
外務部長官
USFK
(서울 .大將)
道 知 事
8th U.S. Army
(仁川 . 大領)
昌原郡守
2d Engr Gp
(中領)
昌原面長
44th Engr BN

-27-

108

題 目	内 容
	対話를 通하여 妥協하고 調整하는 雰囲気를 維持하는데 努力하되 住民의 福利◦国家利益에 関한것은 相対方의 立場을 理解하면서 韓国側의 意見을 説得으로 貫徹토록 할것 4. 美軍側의 関心事는 아래와 같으니 施設의 許可 監督에 十分 反映되도록 할것 가. 接客業所 : o 車輛이 接近할수 있는 大路辺에 位置하고 保安燈이 있을것 o 内部照明은 身分을 確認할수 있는 程度를 維持할것 o 暖房, 通風装置가 充分할것 o 火災安全対策이 講究되어 있을 것 o 男女別区分 便所를 갖출것 o 一切의 飲食物, 얼음類의 提供을 禁할것 o 特定人種만을 為하거나 이를 表示하는 商標, 看板을 使用하지 말것 나. 武器販売団束 다. 麻薬의 所持, 販売団束一各種薬品의 購入이 部隊周辺에선 容易함 라. 性病感染에 対한 対策

題　　目	內　　容
	마. 美軍票의 交換, PX 物品購入証과 身分証을 担保로한 金錢貸与行為 및 外上販売의 禁止 바. 業所周辺의 警察巡察強化 5. 下級 協議会에서 解決하지 못한 事案은 階層別로 次上級協議会에 報告하여 解決토록 할것 6. 市, 郡協議会에 対한 一般的監督權을 行使할것
5. 構　　成	1. 委員数는 両側이 同数로 함을 原則으로 하고 2. 上級協議会(道)는 下級協議会보다 많은 委員을 各機関에서 委嘱하되 相対方의 構成人員도 参酌하여 定할것 3. 委員長은 반드시 地方行政機関의 長이 되어야 함 4. 美軍側도 部隊長을 委員長으로 参謀를 委員으로 하여 別途委員会를 構成하는 것임(韓美混成委員会가 아님)

110

題目	内容
	5. 委員長은 委員의 選任時는 委嘱状을, 解任時는 解任通知書를 委員長名義로 交付할 것
6. 会合	1. 会合은 月1回定期로 開催하되 最初会議에서 時日을 指定할것 2. 会合은 相互交代로 開催하며 附議案件이 없드라도 親睦図謀를 為하여 韓国側이 主催가될 때는 반드시 開催할 것이며 会食은 最少의 経費 ("불고기 파티" 程度)로 할 것 3. 会議場은 主催側의 施設物을 利用하고 主催側이 準備할것 4. 椅子의 配列은 両側 委員長을 中心으로 左右에 両側委員들이 各各配席토록 할것. 그러므로 卓床은 2列配置로 서로 맞보도록 하여야함. 5. 議題는 会議開催日로부터 늦어도 5日前에 美軍側에 伝達하고 미리 附議案件에 対한 委員間의 意見을 調整할것

111

題 目	內 容
	6. 会議参席時는 可能한限 正服을 着用하고 相対方의 議長에 対한 礼儀를 지키며 代表로서의 品位가 損傷됨이 없도록 言•行에 慎重을 期하도록 하여야 할것임 7. 会議의 議長은 主催側委員長이 되며 会議를 進行토록 할것 8. 会議進行上 必要할 境遇에는 通訳官을 配席시켜도 무방함
7. 分任協議会	1. 分任協議会의 委員은 委員長이 委員中에서 事案의 內容에 따라 2 ~ 3 名으로 構成할것 (例) 密輸関係는 税関側委員을, 保健衛生問題는 保健所側委員을 主軸으로 하여 構成할 것 o 分任協議会의 数가 많으면 1人이 数個의 分任協議会委員이 될수있음 (邑面協議会는 設置의 必要가 없을것임) 2. 下級協議会에서 解決되지 못한 事案이 上級協議会에 建議되었을 경우 上級協議会의 美軍側部隊가 地理的으로 遠隔한곳에 位置

112

題 目	內 容
	하였을때에도 分任協議会를 構成하여 解決토록할것
8. 未解決事案의 處理	1. 下級協議会에서 合議되지 못한 事案은 韓美双方의 指揮系統에 따라 順次로 次上級協議会에 建議하고 最終的으로는 韓美合同委員会에 建議토록 할것 2. 이 경우 內務部管理課長参照로 內務部長官에게 報告하면 內務部에서 韓美合同委員会에 建議할것 임 3. 內務部에 報告時는 問題의 発生時点으로부터 現在까지의 処理過程을 明白히한 關係参考書類를 添附할것
9. 参考人의 出席	参考人의 出席이나 資料의 提示要請은 強制할수 없으나 附議案件의 內容에 따라 関係人, 参考人의 出席発言이나 物証提示로서 証拠力과 判断의 正確性을 높여 問題를 円満하게 解決짓기 為한 것이므로 不応함이 없도록 事前에 充分히 説得시킬것

113

題 目	内 容
10. 公報 (発表文)	協議会開催結果를 公表코자할때는 事前에 両側의 合意를 거쳐 発表할것
11. 報 告	1. 内務部에 対한 모든 報告는 参照 管理課長으로 할것 2. 協議会 開催状況報告는 別添書式 (1) 및 (2) 에 의거 報告할것 3. 指揮報告時는 報告後 그要旨를 T.T 로 報告하고 상세한것은 即時 書面으로 할것
12. 既存委員会의 廃 止	이 規程에 依하여 設立되지 아니한 既存의 各種委員会나 類似団体는 全部 本協議会에 統合 또는 廃止시킬것.

-35-

114

(書式 1)　　○○道韓美親善協議会開催状況 (総括)

年　　月分

区分 / 委員会別	開催日字	議題	合意与否	対策및措置状況	備考
○○道 協議会			o 調査後 処理	o 現地警察에서 調査하고 次期会議에 報告키로함	※内容은 例示임
○○郡 協議会			o 次期会議에 再論議		
○○面 協議会			o 上級協議会建議	o 自治団体長의 権限事項이므로 郡協議会에 建議	
			o 合議	o 相互団束을 強化키로함	

作成要領

1. 内容은 簡単히 要約記述할것
2. 委員会를 開催하지 않은 協議会에서는 그 事由를 明記할것
3. 各協議会別로 記述할것

(書式 2)

○○道韓美親善協議会

第 次会議録

1. 開催日時

2. 開催場所

3. 議 題

가.

나.

다.

4. 討議 및 協議事項

(o提案側의 提案説明 및 要望 또는 措置事項을 略述
o相対方의 意見 및 同意与否)

5. 対策 및 措置状況

(o合意与否의 結果에 따른 対策 또는 措置事項을 略述)

6. 特記事項

(其他 参考事項)

-37-

116

(# 別添 3)

韓美親善協議会設置에 関한指示

-38-

117

韓美親善協議会設置에 関한指示 (参考 : 条例準則을 뜻함)

1. '73.4.11의 書信에 对한 回答임. 本人은 그間 地方行政関係 Panel 美側 委員들의 의견청취를 했던바 反応이 대단히 好意的이었음.

2. 4.30日 論議한바와 같이 어떤 特定 KAFC도 新規程의 履行期間동안 中断되지 말아야 함.
여름에 美軍들이 가장 많이 基地村에 쇄도하므로 여름이 닥아올수록 KAFC의 活動은 加重됨.
그래서 軍民間의 効果的인 協調와 協同이 維持되어야 할 必要性이 加重되고 있음.

3. 次期 軍民分科委員会 会議때 内務部 指示 (条例準則을뜻함) 를 軍民分科委員会 委員들에게 알려주기를 要望
이는 確実히 韓美間의 効果的인 軍民関係를 鼓吹시키는데 重要한 단계를 指示하는 것임.

118

HEADQUARTERS, UNITED STATES FORCES, KOREA
APO SAN FRANCISCO 96301
OFFICE OF THE ASSISTANT CHIEF OF STAFF, J5

EJ 14 May 1973

MEMORANDUM FOR: Mr. BAEK Sae Hyun, ROK Chairman, Panel on Local Community and Governmental Relations

SUBJECT: Korean-American Friendship Council Directive

1. To respond to your Memorandum of 11 April 1973, I requested the views and comments of the US members of the Panel on Local Community and Governmental Relations. Their reactions have been most favorable and note with appreciation the proposal to formally recognize the Korean-American Friendship Councils (KAFCs).

2. In line with our conversation on 30 April, I was most pleased to know that you share my concern that local coordination through the several KAFCs should not be interrupted during the period of implementation of the new directive. I believe that KAFC activities assume additional importance as we progress into the summer months. It has been traditional that this season provides the greatest influx of US Forces personnel into the local communities; and, consequently, there is a more urgent need to maintain effective civil-military coordination and cooperation.

3. I recommend that you brief the members of the Ad Hoc Subcommittee on Civil-Military Relations concerning the Ministry of Home Affairs directive at the next Ad Hoc Subcommittee meeting. This certainly represents a major step in enhancing effective Korean-American civil-military relations.

FRANK W. ATKINSON, JR.
LTC, USA
US Chairman
Panel on Local Community and Governmental Relations

119

정/리/보/존/문/서/목/록					
기록물종류	문서-일반공문서철	등록번호	17760 6106	등록일자	2001-06-01
분류번호	729.419	국가코드		주제	
문서철명	SOFA 한·미국 합동위원회 군민관계 임시분과위원회 - 주한미군 기지촌 정화사업, 1973				
생산과	북미2과	생산년도	1973 - 1973	보존기간	영구
담당과(그룹)	미주	안보	서가번호	--	
참조분류					
권차명					
내용목차	* 미군기지 주변에서의 흑백 미국 군인간 충돌사건 계기 * 사진있음				

마/이/크/로/필/름/사/항				
촬영연도	*롤 번호	화일 번호	후레임 번호	보관함 번호
	2007-9/Re-07-10	6	1-252	

대 통 령 비 서 실

대비정 100-2 (75-0031) 1972. 12. 30.

수 신 수신처 참조 외무부

제 목 기지촌 대책 '72 실적 및 '73 계획 제출

'72 기지촌 대책사업 추진 실적과 '73 기지촌 대책 사업 계획을 다음에 의하여 작성 73. 1.12 까지 관계관 지참 제출할 것.

보고 주제관

1회보고 승인

첨 부 : 1. '72 기지촌 대책사업 추진실적보고서 작성요령 1 부

2. '73 기지촌 대책사업 계획보고서 제출요령 1 부 끝.

대 통 령 비 서 실

수신처 : 가. 8. 10. 11. 12. 13. 14. 16. 17. 19. 21.

23. 24. 25. 28. 34. 중앙정보부장

나. 1. 2. 3. 4. 5. 6. 7. 8. 9. 10.

발송 1973. 1. 5 대통령비서실

2

Panel on Local Community
&
Governmental Relations

案　　　　件 (1)

提案者：內務部管理課長 白 世 鉉
BAEK, SE HYUN
ROK Chairman
Panel on Local Community
&
Governmental Relations.

3

目　　次

4

I. 韓美親善委員会 設置規程(案)要旨

5

韓美親善委員会設置規程 " 小題目 "

1 . 目 的

2 . 設置部署

3 . 名 称

4 . 機 能

5 . 構 成

6 . 委員의 辞退

7 . 委員長등의 職務

8 . 節 次

가 . 会 議

나 . 会議主管

다 . 会議開催通報

라 . 小委員会

마 . 未解決事案의 処理

9 . 委員会解散

10 . 参考人의 委員会出席

11 . 報 告

12 . 其他 事項

13 . 既存委員会 廃止

-3-

6

韓美親善委員会設置規程（案）

1．目的： 韓国人과 美軍人間의 理解를 促進하고 関係의 改善으로 相互間의 友誼를 増進하여 親善을 図謀하는데 있다．

2．設置部署： 委員会는 美合衆国의 陸海空軍이 駐屯하고 있는 市，区，邑，面과 이 地域을 管轄하는 特別市，道，郡에 設置한다．

3．名称： 委員会의 名称은 ○○道（特別市，市，郡，邑，面） 韓美親善委員会라 한다．

4．機能： 委員会는 韓美間의 共同関心事와 韓美間에 発生 또는 発生의 憂慮가 있는 아래 事項에 関하여 相互 不詳事의 事前防止 対策을 講究하고 下級委員会에서 建議된 問題를 相互理解와 協調로서 調整하고 解決한다．

가．接客業所의 人種差別 및 서－비스改善策

나．保菌者 및 接待婦의 啓導対策

다．麻薬의 所持，販売 및 団束対策

라．衛生検察対策

마．労使紛糾対策

바．軍票所持와 密輸防止 및 暗市場対策

사．其他 相互間의 権益의 侵害 및 親善沮害 要素에 関한 対策

5．構成： 委員会는 委員長 1人과 委員 5～7人 및 幹事 1人으로 構成한다．

委員長은 地方行政機関의 長 (道知事, 市長, 郡守, 区庁長 및 邑, 面長) 이 되고 委員과 幹事는 委員長이 다음 機関의 代表 또는 構成員中에서 任命 또는 委嘱한다.

가. 司法機関 (検察, 警察 및 税関)

나. 労動行政機関

다. 保健衛生機関

라. ○○諮問委員会 또는 開発委員会

마. 情報機関

바. 観光業体, 遊興 및 料食業協会

사. 業態婦代表

아. 其他 有関機関 또는 住民代表

6. 委員의 辞退 : 委員長은 委員中 다음 事由가 発生하였을 때는 그 職을 辞任케 하고 即時後任者를 交替選任한다.

~~가. 本人이 辞任을 [illegible] 願할때~~

가. 他機関으로 転出되었을 때

나. 会議参席이 微温的이고 委員会運営에 ~~消極的일때~~

다. 韓美親善을 害치는 行為를 하였거나 그러한 行為가 있다고 認定될 때

라. 其他 委員長이 必要하다고 認定될때

7. 委員長등의 職務 : 委員長은 委員会를 代表하고 会議의 議長이 된다. 다만 委員長이 事故가 있을 때에는 委員中에서 委員長이 指定한 者가 그 職務를 代行한다.

委員은 委員長의 命을 받아 委員会에 出席하여 発言하

-5-

며 附議된 案件을 相互協議하고 討論한다.

幹事는 委員長의 命을 받아 委員会에 出席하되 発言할 수 없으며 委員会의 庶務를 処理한다.

8. 節次:

가. 会議……委員会는 每月 1 回 定期的으로 開催하되 日字는 韓美 兩側의 協議로 定한다. 다만 어느 一方의 要求가 있을 때는 随時 開催할 수 있다.

나. 会議主管……定期会는 相互交代로 他方委員을 招請하여 開催하되 招請한 機関이 主管한다. 다만 어느 一方의 要求에 의하여 随時 開催하는 会議에서는 要求機関에서 主管함을 原則으로 한다.

다. 会議開催通報……主管機関은 늦어도 会議開催 5日前에 他方代表에게 아래 事項이 記載된 内容을 書面으로 通知하여야 한다.

(1) 会議開催 日時

(2) 会議開催 場所

(3) 附議案件 또는 開催코자 하는 事由

(4) 招請者와 被招請者의 機関 및 代表名

다만 下級委員会의 未解決 事案을 上級委員会에서 協議코자 할 때에는 兩側의 事前協議로 会議日時와 場所를 따로히 定할 수 있다.

라. 小委員会……委員会의 効率的運営과 附議된 事項을 円滑히 処理하기 為하여 委員会의 協議를 거쳐 小委員会를 構成할 수 있다.

-6-

9

小委員会의 委員은 委員長이 指名하고 委員의 数는 2人 내지 3人으로 한다.

小委員会는 受任받은 事案이 完結되었을 때 自動的으로 解体된다.

마. 未解決事案의 処理……下級委員会에서 合議되지 못한 事案은 韓美 双方의 指揮系統에 따라 漸次 次上級委員会에 建議한다. 이 境遇 上級委員会의 美軍側部隊가 韓国側 行政官署의 管轄地域 外에 所在하고 있을 때에는 小委員会로 하여금 相対方의 委員会와 協議토록 하여 解決한다.

上級委員会에서도 解決되지 못한 事案은 韓美合同委員会에 建議한다.

9. 委員会解散: 被対象機関이 移動하거나 兵営이 廃鎖되는 때는 自動的으로 解体된다. 새로운 部隊가 같은 兵営에 駐屯하게 되거나 前任部隊의 業務를 引受받았을 때는 委員会를 다시 構成한다.

10. 参考人의 委員会出席: 委員会는 必要하다고 認定할 때는 附議된 案件에 関聯되는 関係人, 参考人의 出席発言이나 参考資料의 提示를 要請할 수 있다.

11. 報告: 道知事는 毎月 道와 傘下 市郡邑面의 委員会開催状況을 別紙書式에 의거 翌月 10日까지 内務部長官에게 報告한다.

韓美間의 不詳事나 両側의 親善을 沮害할 要因의 発生 또는 発生의 憂慮가 있는 것은 即刻 内務部長官에게 指揮

10

報告한다.

12. 其他 事項: 委員会運営에 必要한 其他 事項은 委員会의 協議를 거쳐 따로히 定한다.

13. 既存委員会廃止: 既存의 各種 韓美親善組織은 이 委員会에 廃置 統合한다.

//

2. 美八軍例規第 550-5 号 検討

2. 美8軍例規 550-5号에 対한 検討

区分	例規	意見	備考
1. 目的	....委員会의 目的은 美軍人과 韓国人間의 理解를 促進하고 改善하며 大韓民国의 社会的, 経済的 発展에 寄与하는데 있다.	....委員会의 目的은 美軍人과 韓国人間의 理解를 促進하고 関係의 改善으로 相互間의 友誼를 増進하고 親善을 図謀하는데 있다.	委員会의 方向転換 o韓国에 対한 認識感의 刷新 o国威宣揚
4. 定義	다. 地域社会와 関聯된 計劃: 司令部의 機能은..... 및 地域社会의 尊敬과 信義를 받도록 計劃을 作成한다.	다. 地域社会와 関聯된 計劃: 司令部의 機能은.... 및 地域社会의 協調와 親善을 図謀하도록 計劃을 作成한다.	同等한 立場에서의 協調와 親善
6. 指針	라. 対民関係活動(8軍例規 550-1)및 民間活動計劃의 健実한 履行과 着手를 議論하는 委員会로 最大限 活用되어야 한다.	라. 民間活動計劃의 健実한 履行과 着手를 議論하는 委員会로 最大한 活用되어야 한다.	"対民関係活動" 削除
7. 新委員会 設立	나. 新委員会는 特定한 地域 軍部隊長과 計劃된 委員会를 代表하는 地域社会의 地方公務員間의 協定으로 設立된다. 地域軍部隊長은 地方公務員에 対하여 委員会가 任意의, 그리고 諮問的性質 및 委員会의 能力과 限界, 이 委員会의 設立과 運用으로 얻어지는 相互間의 利益에 대하여 分明히 밝혀야 한다.	나. 新委員会는 .... 된다. 地域軍部隊長은 ~~地方公務員에 対하여~~ 委員会가 韓美合同委員会의 協議로 設立되었음과 委員会의 協議事項은 韓美相互間에 信義와 誠実로서 遵守하고 履行할 義務를 지며 이 委員会의 設立과 運用으로 얻어지는 相互間의 利益에 対하여 ~~分明히 밝혀야~~ 周知시켜야 한다.	協議事項의 遵守義務를 明示.

-10-

13

区分	例規	意見	備考
8. 委員会의 解散	가. 部隊의 閉鎖에 関하여(軍保安이 許容하는 内) 承認을 받는대로 地域社会代表에게 通知한다.	가. 部隊의 閉鎖에 関하여(軍保安이 許容하는 内) 承認을 받는대로 韓国側委員会 議長에게 通知한다.	
9. 構成	나. 韓国側 構成員: 韓国側 代表는 地域社会指導者에 依하여 決定된다. 一般的으로 韓国側 委員은 道, 特別市, 郡, 面, 里, 邑, 区 혹은 洞의 最高位者로서 韓国側構成員의 議長이 되며 美軍 構成員에 対한 民間人 相対役이 된다. 高位公務員과 同級이고 그들과 独立된 韓国警察의 代表는 韓国側 構成員에 必須要員이 된다. 代表者는 尊敬받는 部落의 高齡者, 予備軍, 健康, 衛生, 教育関係公務員과 地域事業家, 新聞社代表 및 労動関係公務員이 包含된다.	나. 韓国側 構成員: 韓国側 代表는 地方官署의 長에 依하여 委嘱된다. 一般的으로 韓国側委員長은 特別市, 道, 市, 郡, 区, 邑, 面, 의 最高位者로서 ~~韓国側 構成員의 議長이~~ 되며 美軍側 構成員 ~~에 対한 民間人~~ 相対役이 된다. 韓国側 構成員에는 아래機関의 代表 또는 要員이 包含된다. o 司法機関(検察, 警察, 税関) o 労動行政機関 o 保健衛生機関 o 情報機関 o 諮問委員会 또는 開発委員会 o 観光業体, 遊興業 및 料食業協会 o 菜康婦 代表 o 其他 有関機関 또는 住民代表	委員의 任命権者를 明示하고 構成員도 限定 o 第70次(72.1.28) SOFA 韓美合同委에서 "適切한 水準의 代表"로 構成토록한 바 있음.

-11-

14

区分	例規	意見	備考
11. 節次	가. 会合：会合은 毎月 計劃되어야 한다. 会合을 最小 60日間 開催하지 못한 때는 会合을 가질 수 없는 状況을 書面으로 提出하여야 한다. 将軍이 主宰하는 委員会에서는 위의 条項이 適用되지 아니하며 適当하다고 생각되는 때를 予定할 수 있다.	가. 会合：会合은 毎月 1回 定期的으로 開催하고 一方의 要請이 있을 때는 随時 開催한다. 会合을 最小 60日間 開催하지 못한 때는 会合을 가질 수 없는 状況을 書面으로 提出하여야 한다. 道知事와 将軍이 主宰하는 委員会에서는 위의 条項이 適用되지 아니하며 適当하다고 생각되는 때를 予定할 수 있다.	随時 開催할 수 있는 融通性 賦与
	사. 小委員会의 利用：…… 規模가 큰 委員会에는 安全, 防火, 文化行事, 其他 関心을 불러 일으키는 다른 事項의 常設 小委員会를 두어야 한다. 大部分의 委員会는 軍人의 날, 植木日, 災害救援等 다른 特別活動을 위한 特別 小委員会의 指定을 希望하고 있다.	사. 小委員会의 利用：…… …… 小委員会의 委員은 各各 2名 乃至 3名의 委員으로 構成하고 委員会의 議長이 指名한다.	小委員들의 委員数를 制限

区分	例規	意見	備考
	아. 未解決된 事案 : 下級委員会 水準에서 未解決된 事案은 上級司令部에 移管한다. 委員会에서 解決되지 못한 安全問題는 陸軍性(省) 安全官에게 提出하여야 한다.	아. 未解決된 事案 : .... 이 경우 他方의 上級機関이 地理的으로 遼隔한 곳에 位置하고 있을 때에는 小委員会로 하여금 相対方의 委員会와 接触하고 協議토록 하여 解決한다. 上級司令部에서도 解決되지 못한 事案은 韓美合同委員会(軍民合同委員会)에 建議하여 処理토록 한다. 카. 参考人의 委員会 出席 委員会는 必要한 경우에 附議된 案件에 関聯되는 関係人 参考人의 出席発言이나 参考資料의 提示를 要請할 수 있다.	0 小委員会에서 解決토록하여 委員会開催를 為해 全委員이 他地域으로 出張가는 煩雑을 避하고자 함 (特히 行政区域이 다를경우) 0 協議事項의 円満, 迅速한 解決을 為하여 追加挿入

-13-

16

3 . 韓美親善委員会 階層別構成図 (案)

17

서울特別市

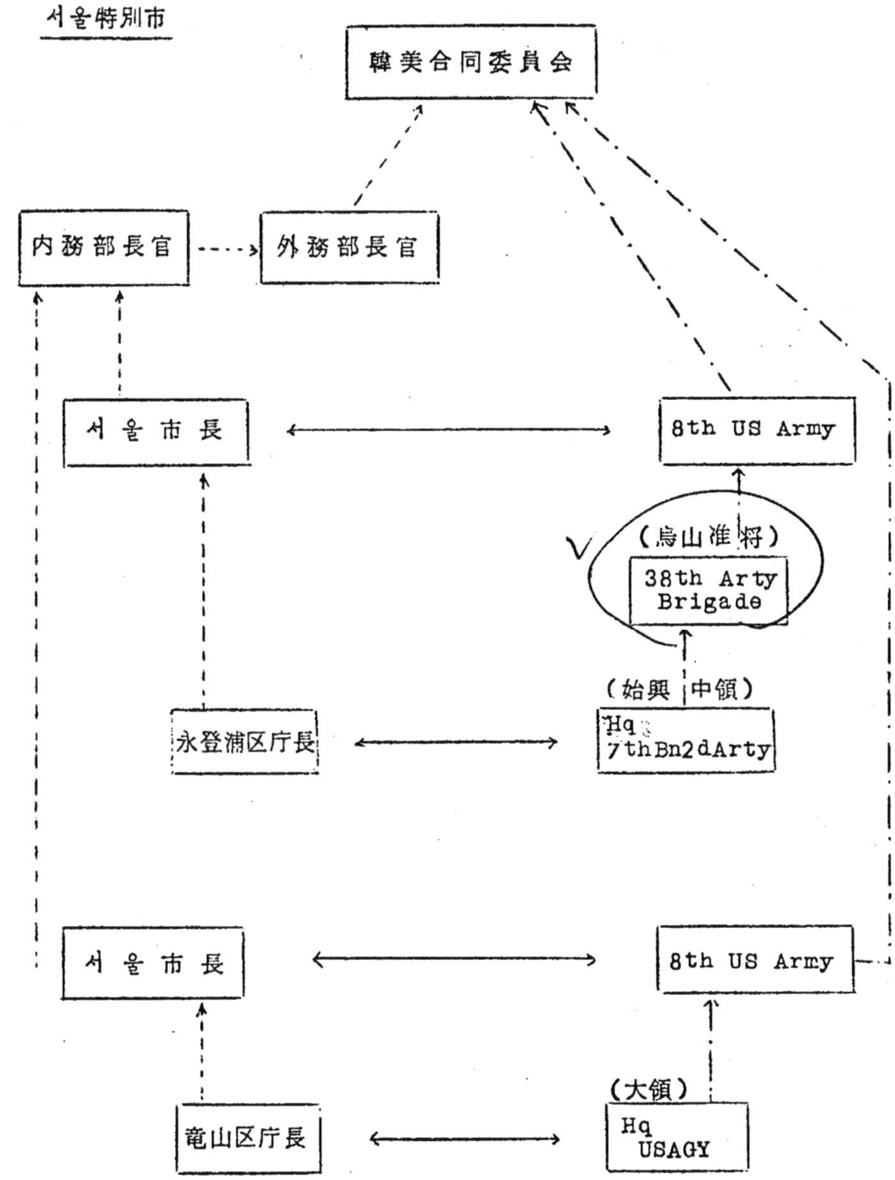
韓美合同委員会
內務部長官
外務部長官
서 울 市 長
8th US Army
(烏山准将)
38th Arty Brigade
(始興 中領)
永登浦区庁長
Hq 7thBn2dArty
서 울 市 長
8th US Army
(大領)
竜山区庁長
Hq USAGY

釜 山 市

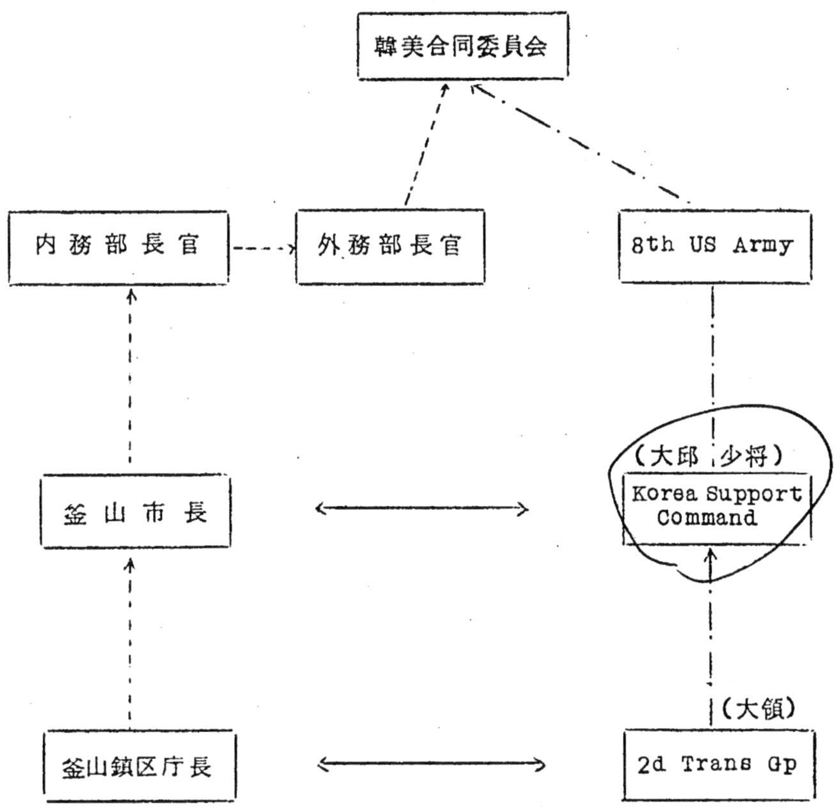
韓美合同委員会
内務部長官
外務部長官
8th US Army
(大邱 少将)
Korea Support Command
釜山市長
(大領)
釜山鎮区庁長
2d Trans Gp

-16-

19

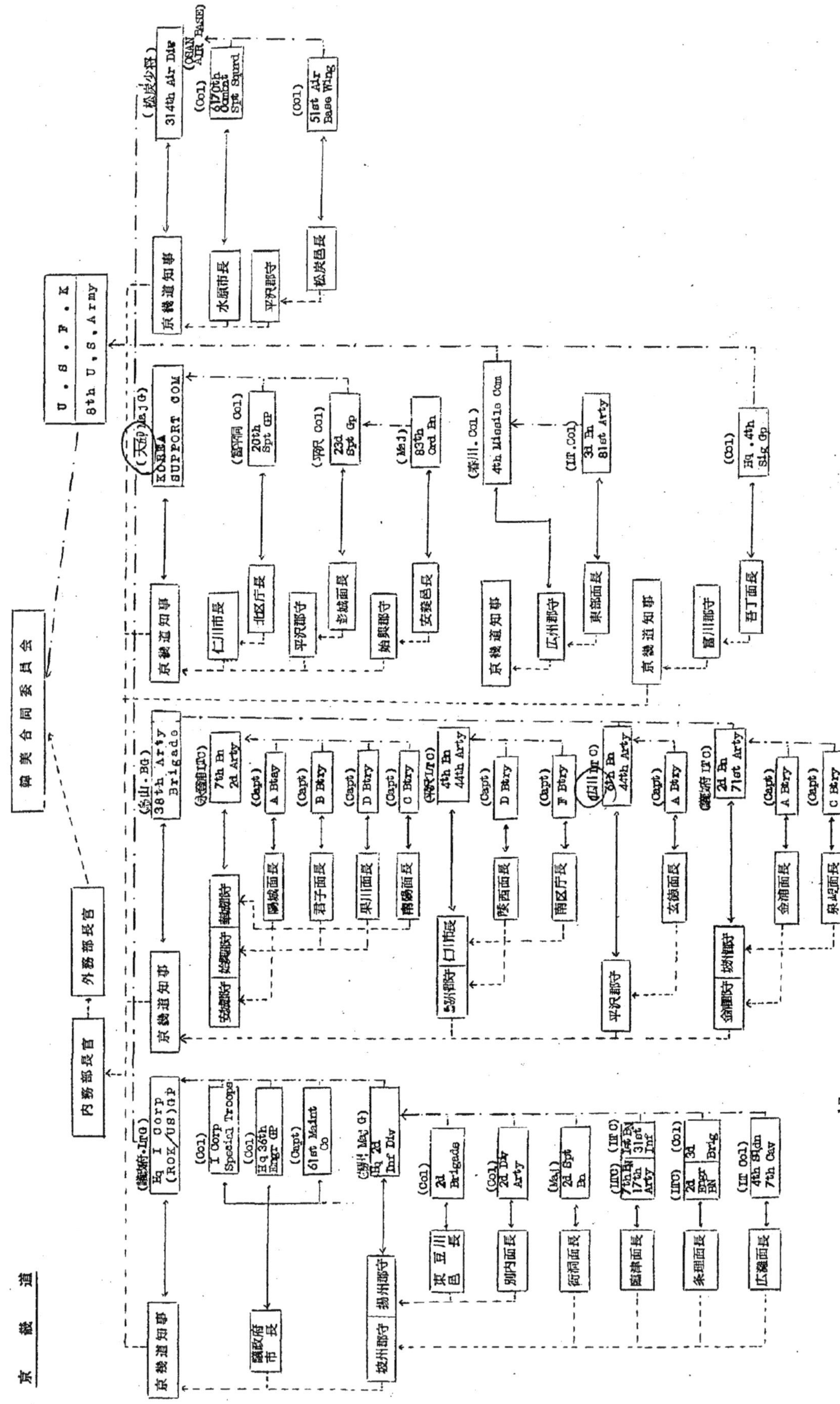

京畿道
韓美合同委員会
外務部長官
内務部長官
U.S.F.K
8th U.S.Army
京畿道知事
Hq I Corp (ROK/US) GP
I Corp Special Troops
Hq 36th Engr GP
61st Maint Co
Hq 2d Inf Div
2d Brigade
2d Div Arty
38th Arty Brigade
7th Bn 2d Arty
A Btry
B Btry
D Btry
C Btry
4th Bn 44th Arty
F Btry
2d Bn 71st Arty
KOREA SUPPORT COM
20th Spt GP
23d Spt Gp
83th Ord Bn
4th Missile Com
3d Bn 81st Arty
Hq. 4th Sig Gp
314th Air Div
6170th Combat Spt Squrd
51st Air Base Wing
水原市長
平沢郡守
松炭邑長
仁川市長
安養邑長
広州郡守
利川郡守

江 原 道

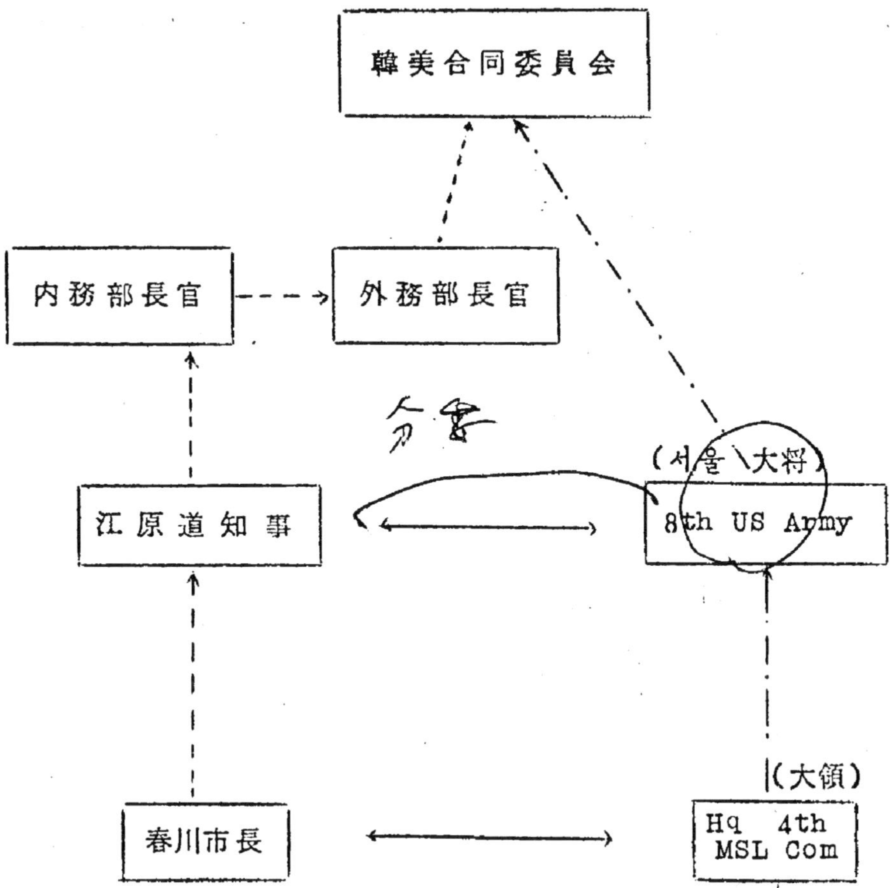
韓美合同委員会
内務部長官
外務部長官
江原道知事
(서울 大将)
8th US Army
(大領)
春川市長
Hq 4th
MSL Com

忠清北道

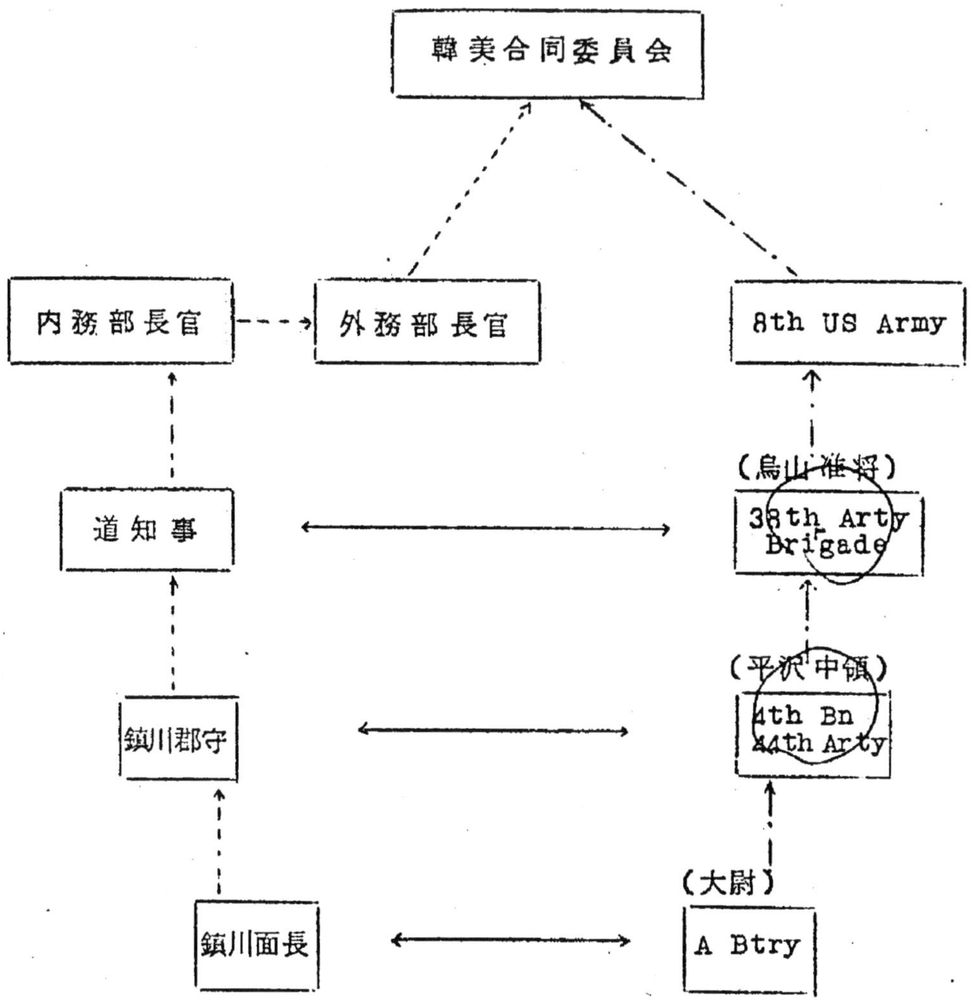
韓美合同委員会
内務部長官
外務部長官
8th US Army
(烏山准将)
38th Arty Brigade
道知事
(平沢中領)
4th Bn 44th Arty
鎮川郡守
(大尉)
鎮川面長
A Btry

22

忠 清 南 道

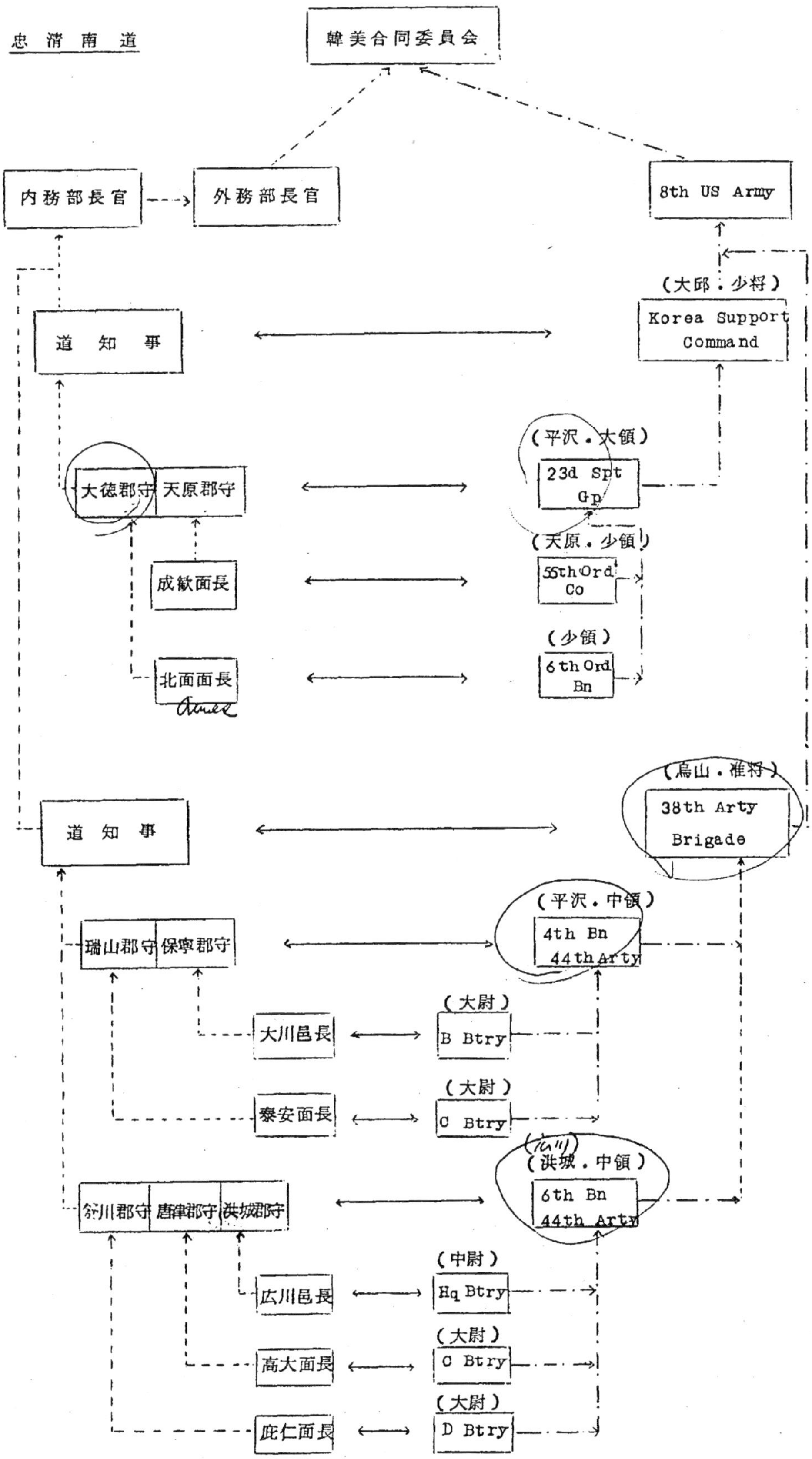
韓美合同委員会
内務部長官
外務部長官
8th US Army
(大邱．少将)
Korea Support Command
道 知 事
(平沢．大領)
23d Spt Gp
大徳郡守
天原郡守
(天原．少領)
55th Ord Co
成歓面長
(少領)
6th Ord Bn
北面面長
(烏山．准将)
38th Arty Brigade
道 知 事
(平沢．中領)
4th Bn 44th Arty
瑞山郡守
保寧郡守
(大尉)
大川邑長
B Btry
(大尉)
泰安面長
C Btry
(洪城．中領)
6th Bn 44th Arty
舒川郡守
唐津郡守
洪城郡守
(中尉)
広川邑長
Hq Btry
(大尉)
高大面長
C Btry
(大尉)
庇仁面長
D Btry

-20-

23

全羅北道

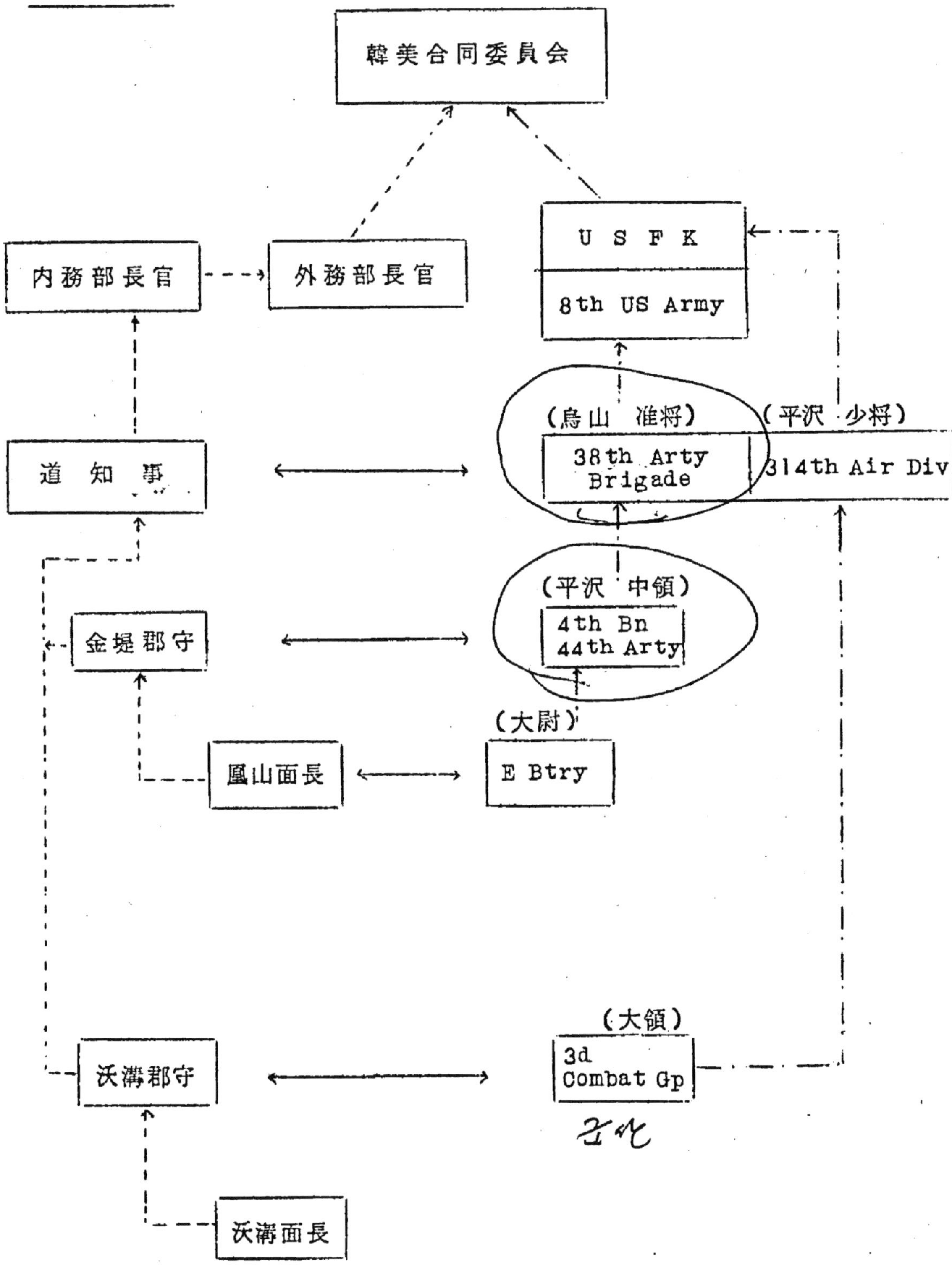
韓美合同委員会
內務部長官
外務部長官
U S F K
8th US Army
(烏山 准將)
38th Arty Brigade
(平沢 少將)
314th Air Div
道 知 事
(平沢 中領)
4th Bn 44th Arty
金堤郡守
(大尉)
E Btry
凰山面長
(大領)
3d Combat Gp
沃溝郡守
沃溝面長

-21-

慶尙北道

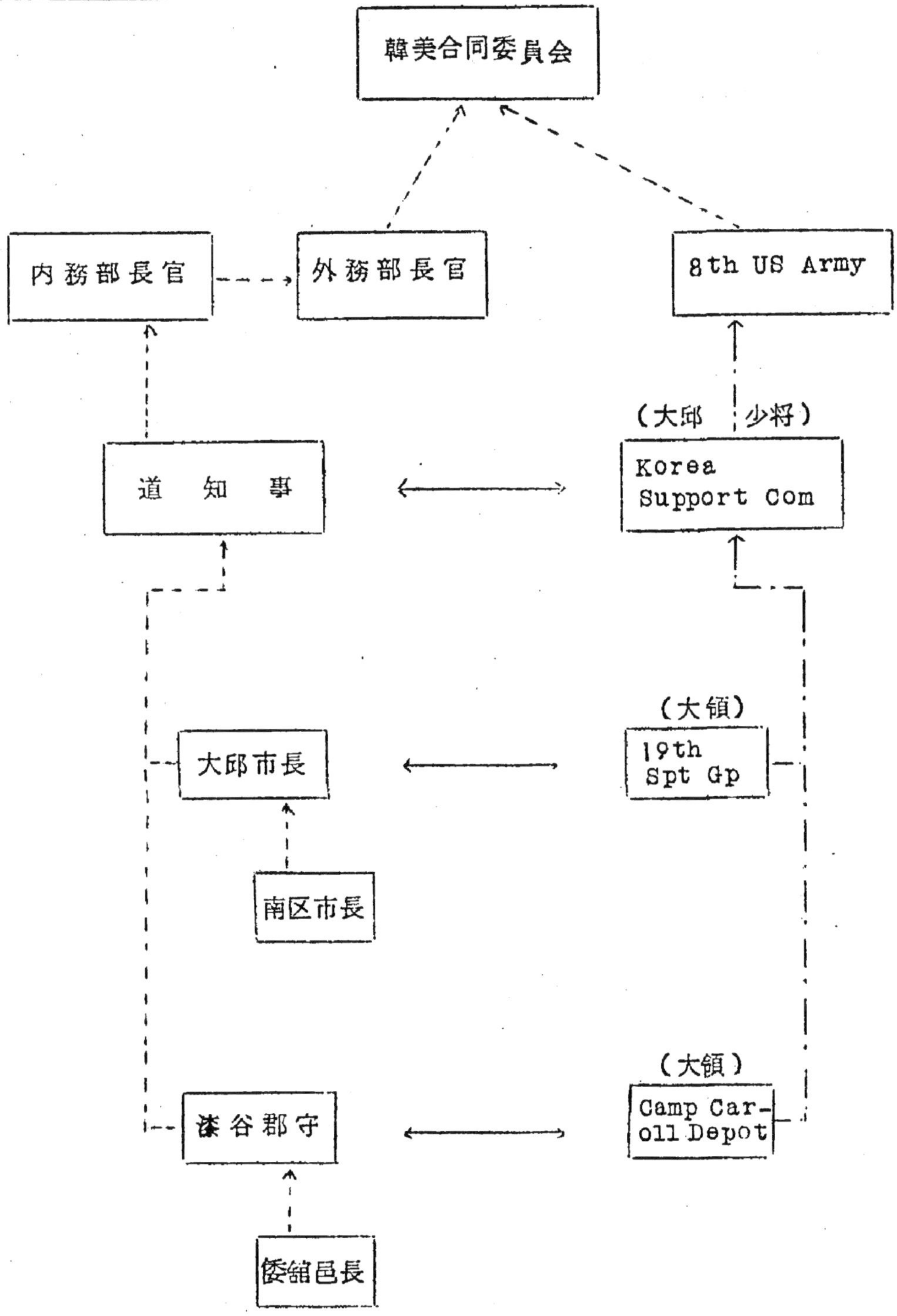

韓美合同委員会
內務部長官
外務部長官
8th US Army
(大邱 少将)
道知事
Korea Support Com
(大領)
大邱市長
19th Spt Gp
南区市長
(大領)
漆谷郡守
Camp Caroll Depot
倭舘邑長

25

慶尚南道

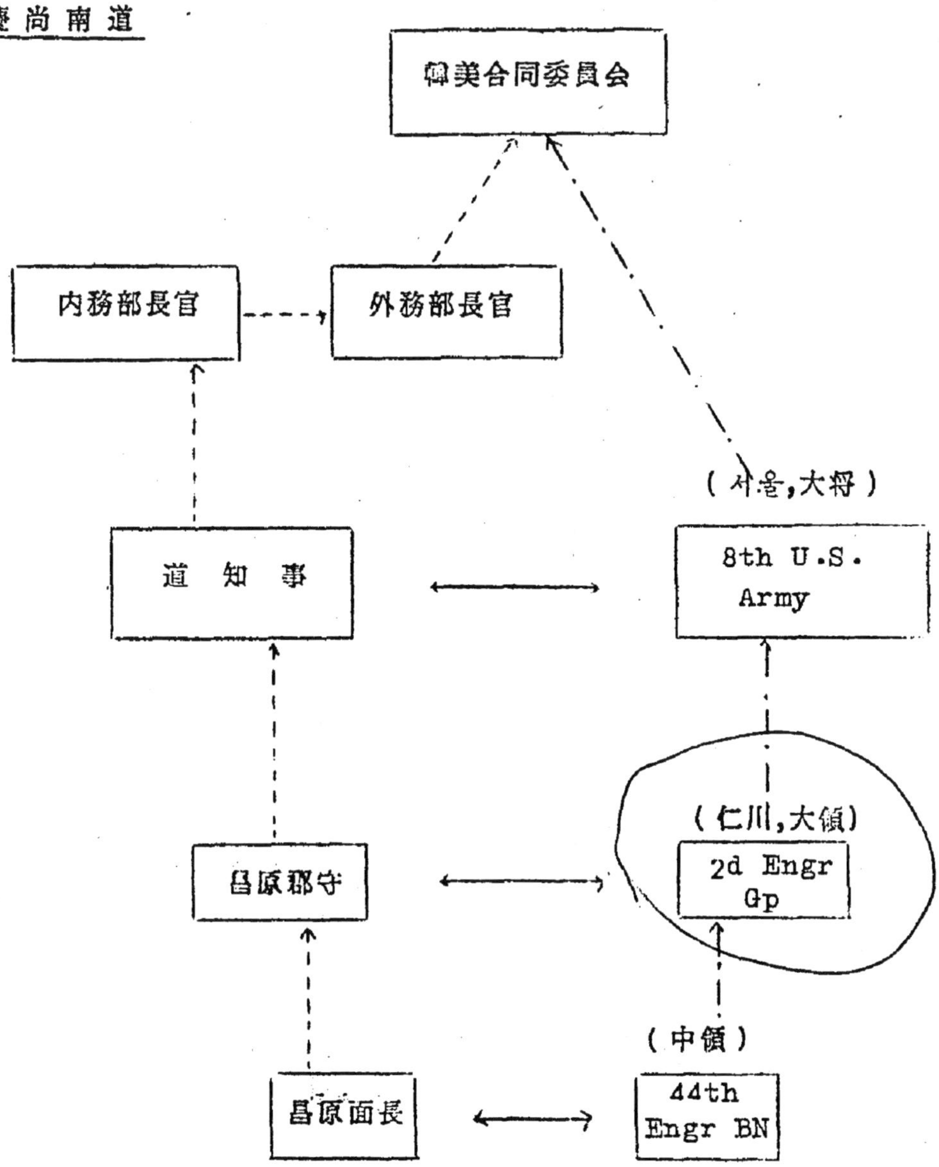

韓美合同委員会
內務部長官
外務部長官
(서울,大將)
道 知 事
8th U.S. Army
(仁川,大領)
昌原郡守
2d Engr Gp
(中領)
昌原面長
44th Engr BN

-23-

26

基地村對策現地確認指導計劃

案件 (2)

內務部

基地村對策現地確認指導計劃

目的

- 基地村對策事業施行促進 ———— 早期目標達成
- 對策事業效率的推進 ———— 事業成果擧揚

期間

72. 7. 15부터 事業終了時까지 (週別 또는 旬期別)

地域

- 72方矣 基地村 21個地域
- 餘他地域中 問題地域으로 判斷되는 地域

方法

- 各部處施策事業 一括確認指導

○ 關係部處公務員으로 確認指導班 構成

(各部處事業이 確定된 後)

— 內務部(治安局包含), 保健社会部, 交通部, 外務部, 文公部, 法務部 關係官 (計劃追后示達)

○ 韓美合同委員会 軍民関係 分科委員의 現地踏査

事 項

○ 事業推進狀況

(1) 事業選定은 基地村의 痼疾的 懸案事項解決을 爲한 根本對策과 關聯하여 適正하게 選定되었는가?

(2) 基地村對策綜合実踐計劃을 뒷받침하는 執行計劃은 樹立되어 있는가?

(3) 內務部가 承認한 實踐計劃事業以外에 別途 自体計劃事業이 있는가

(4) 地区別(基地村別) 事業別 優先順位制度가 一目瞭然하게 運用되고 있는가?

(5) 아직도 着手하지 않은 事業은 없는가?

(6) 年內目標達成이 不可能한 事業은 없으며 그 理由는 무엇인가?

(7) 事業別 推進責任官制는 履行되고 있으며 各 責任官別 分担事項은 明確한가?

(8) 韓美親善委員会의 活動状況은 어떠한가?

(가) 開催 回数

(나) 開催方法

(다) 問題解決実績

(라) 其 他

(9) 事業推進記錄(事業單位別 事業前後 및 中間光景)

을 天然色寫眞 및 스라이드로 保存하고 있는가?

(10) 事業別 現況資料는 整理되고 있는가?

(카-드化 狀況板 其他)

(11) 事業推進上 隘路点은 없는가? 있다면 그 內

容은 무엇인가?

(12) 其他 必要한 事項

○ 豫算支援狀況

(1) 道·市·郡 予算에 事業費를 全額 策定하

였는가?

国 費

道 費

-4-

31

市郡費

(2) 事業費의 予算配定과 資金供給은 適期에 適切하게 이루어 지고 있는가?

-5-

32

軍民関係分科委員會
地方行政関係 Panel 討議

1. 日時 : 1972. 7. 19. 16:00

2. 場所 : 内務部 管理課長室 (綜合廳舍 208号室)

3. 参席範圍 : 軍民関係分科委員會
地方行政関係 Panel 韓國側委員

4. 協議事項

(1) 韓美親善委員會 構成 (案件 1)

- 規程案要旨
- 委員會階層別構成
- 美八軍例規第 550-5号 検討

(2) 基地村 對策 現地確認計劃 (案件 2)

- 確認班 編成
- 確認週期
- 確認 事項

5. 提案者

軍民関係分科委員會
地方行政関係 Panel 韓國側議長
内務部 地方局 管理課長 白 世 鉉

33

기 안 용 지

분류기호 문서번호	미이 723 -	(전화번호)	전결규정 조 항 장관 전결사항
처리기간		전결 자 관	장 관
시행일자	1973. 1. 11.		
보존년한			
보조기관	차관보		협조
	국 장		
	과 장		
기안책임자	권 찬	북미 2 과	
경유 수신 참조	청와대 정무수석비서관 내무 보사담당 비서관	발송 1973. 1. 23 외무부	통제 1973. 1. 15 통제관
제 목	72년 및 73년도 기지촌 정화를 위한 사업실적 및 계획		

대 : 대비정 100 - 2

대호로 요청하신 기지촌 대책 72 실적 및 73 사업계획을 별첨과 같이 송부합니다.

첨부 : 동사업계획 및 실적 1 부. 끝.

정서 관인 발송

공통서식1-2(갑)
1967. 4. 4. 승인

190mm ×268mm (1급인쇄용지70g/m²)
조달청 (500,000매인쇄)

324.

72년 및 73년도 기지촌 정화를 위한

외무부 사업실적 및 계획

1973. 1. 11.

외무부 구미국

김과장 1-15.

35

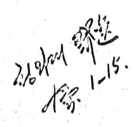

72년 및 73년도 기지촌 정화를 위한 사업실적 및 계획

1973. 1. 10.

I. 72년도 기지촌 대책사업 실적

가. 주요 활동사항

1. 총 15차에 걸친 군.민관계 합동회의를 개최하고 동 분과위원회의 활동사항 및 대정부 건의사항의 집행 진척도를 계속 검검하고 있으며, 한편 동 분과위 산하 7개조 사반에서는 실무자 회의를 계속 진행시키고 있음.

2. 군.민관계 분과위원회는 기지촌 정화를 위한 대책으로 35개의 건의사항을 채택, 통과시키고 이를 관계부처가 집행중에 있음.

3. 총 6차에 걸쳐 (분과위 설치이후 총 16차) 한.미 합동으로 미군기지촌을 시찰, 실정을 파악했음.

나. 구체적인 집행사항

1972년도 SOFA 한.미 합동위원회는 아래사항을 채택, 통과시키고, 이를 관계부처가 집행중에 있음.

1. 성병관리 문제 :

SOFA 제69차 합동회의에서 성병관리 문제에 대해 아래사항을 합의, 채택하였음.

북미2			담당	과장	국장	차관보	차관	장관
			[illegible]	[illegible]	[illegible]			

36

(가) (1) 성병예방을 담당하는 한.미 관계당국은 성병 보균자로 하여금 치료도록하고 완치 될때까지 공중으로부터 격리할것.

(2) 한국 관계당국과 미군당국은 성병의 원인 제거 및 예방에 관한 교육계획을 함께 세울것.

(나) 한국 보건당국은 기지촌 한국 "모텔" 소유자에게 다음과 같은 긴급조치를 취하도록 할것.

(1) 변소의 세척물이 적절히 나오도록 함.

(2) 변소에 수건, 종이등을 비치도록 함.

(3) 변기세척, 청소 및 종이나 수건을 제공하는 사람을 배치도록 함.

2. 마약단속 문제 :

(가) 마약과 습관성 약품의 불법거래 및 매매행위에 대한 통제

(1) 미군 우편시설을 통하여 마약 및 부정약품이 한국에 불법 반입되는것을 방지하기 위하여 미군당국은 우편경로를 통한 약품의 불법 유입을 방지도록 모든노력을 경주할것.

(2) 마약과 부정약품의 상습 복용자에 대하여 아래와 같은 통제를 강구할것 :

317

가) 미군당국은 상습 복용자의 신원을 확인하여 본미치보 및 이들을 우송 시킬것.

나) 한국당국은 마약을 상습 복용하는 위안부들의 영업행위를 금지토록 할것.

(3) 마약거래자와 마약 조기복용자에 대하여 적절한 행정적 또는 형사적 조치를 취할것.

(나) 주한미군에 대한 약품판매 통제

1970.11. 3. 공표한 대통령령 제5378호에 포함되는 약품의 판매는 여하한 경우에도 의사의 처방없이는 미군에게 판매하지 말것.

3. 도난 및 암시장 : (비정부재산 도난)

(가) 도난 및 암거래문제 방지책

(1) 주한미군 당국은 미군장비를 훔쳐서 한국인에게 판매하는 미군인에 대한 처벌결과를 요약형식으로 한국정부에 통보할것.

(2) 주한미군 당국은 한국 관계당국과 협조하여 PX 및 코미써리 (commissary)의 제한품목을 더욱 추가할것이며, 군인 사병이 필요한 적정량 이상의 물품이 흘러나오지 않도록 감시하는 방지책을 더욱 보강할것.

38

4. 한.미 문화의 상호 이해를 위한 활동강화 :

(가) 한.미 친선협의회설치 장려
(나) "Hello Korea" TV 프로그램 추진
(다) 한.미 문화 이해를 위한 자료제작 장려
(마) 가정방문계획 (Home-visit Program) 권장
(마) 국제 친선협회 (PTP)한국지부의 설립승인과
한국내의 친선협의회 설립 장려

5. 효 과 :

(가) 통 계 : SOFA 적용 미군 형사 및 징계사건처리 통계

	69 년	70 년	71 년	72년
1 월	44	40	68	24
2 월	32	44	68	24
3 월	68	52	89	17
4 월	58	56	78	14
5 월	62	53	85	16
6 월	52	42	82	36
7 월	49	35	103	25
8 월	55	41	109	21
9 월	32	18	113	25
10월	44	38	101	20
11월	43	37	113	
12 월	38	27	82	
계	577	483	1,091	222 (10.30. 현재)

39

(나) (1) 청와대 기지촌 정화위원회에 의한 기지촌 정화사업의 계속적인 추진과 군민관계 분과위원회에 의한 한.미 공동 개선활동에 따라 72년도 미군관련 범죄 발생건수 (72. 10. 30. 현재 222건)는 작년도 (71. 12. 31. 현재 1,091건) 대비 약 1/4로 격감됨.

(2) 미군 범죄사건중 강력범 30인에 대하여는 한국의 재판관할권 행사를 결정함.

(3) 10. 17. 비상계엄령 선포에 따라 미군 인등 범죄사건 처리 지침을 작성, 각급 기관에 시달함.

40

II. 73년도 기지촌 사업 계획

가. 한.미 군대지위협정에 의한 한.미간의 기존 "챤넬" 을 통하여 최대로 유효하게 미측과 협조할 것이며,

나. SOFA 합동위원회를 더욱 강화하여 양국간의 어려운 현안문제는 신속히 외계로 제역, 해결할 방침임.

다. 작년도에 한.미 합동으로 시찰한바 있는 미군기지촌 (미군 기지내 및 주변 한국 기지촌 일대)을 재차 시찰하여 그간 1년동안의 개선상태 (the improved situations)와 한.미간의 새로운 협조 사항이 무엇인지를 조사, 건의할 계획임.

라. 한국에 재입국한 미군 제대장병들의 기지촌 일대에서의 많은 비행과 관련하여 당부는 이미 내무부 및 법무부등 관계부처에 강경한 조치를 취하여 줄것을 의뢰한바 있고, 또한 각 재외공관에 대하여도 미군 제대장병의 사증 발급에 있어서 신중을 기하고 신원이 불확실하거나 또는 우범자로 보이는 자들에 대하여는 사증 발급을 억제하는등 가능한 제반조치를 취하도록 훈령하였는바 (72. 11. 25), 외무부는 금년도 기지촌 정화사업의 일환으로 동 제대군인들이 일정한 생계도 없이 기지촌을 배회하면서 마약밀수 및 도난 범죄등을 자행하는 일이 없도록 동 제대군인들의 재입국을 엄격히 규제할 계획임.

41

기 안 용 지

분류기호 문서번호	미이 723 -	(전화번호)	전결규정 조 항 국장 전결사항
처리기간			
시행일자	1973. 1. 23.		
보존년한			국 장
보조기관	과 장		협조
기안책임자	권 찬	북미 2 과	
경유 수신 참조	수신처 참조	발신	통제 1973. 1. 24 통제관
제 목	SOFA 합동위 군민관계 분위의 기지촌 시찰 통보		

1. 1973. 1. 12. 제 16 차 SOFA 한미 합동위 군민관계 임시 분과위 회의에서 합의된바와 같이 1. 30.(화) 의정부 한미 제 1혼성군단 사령부, 2. 5. (월) 평택 미 23 지원단 Camp Humphreys 및 오산 공군기지, 2. 23. (금) 동두천 미 제 2사단 Camp Casey 에 대하여 한미 합동 기지촌 현지 답사를 시행코저 하오니 각 위원들은 필히 참석하시기 바랍니다.

2. 귀부에서 (내무부에서) 현지에 대하여 답사에 필요한 연락과 회의소집등 조치를 취하여 주시기 바랍니다. (취하기로 하였읍니다.)

첨부 : 기지촌 시찰 세부 계획표 1 부.
위원명단 1 부. 끝.

수신처 : 내무부장관 (지방국장, 치안국장), 법무부장관 (검찰국장)
교통부장관, 보건사회부장관, 문화공보부장관

정서 관인 발송

공통서식1-2(갑)
1967. 4. 4. 승인

190mm × 268mm (1급인쇄용지70g/㎡)
조달청 (500,000매인쇄)

42

기지촌 군민관계 분과위원회 위원 명단

1973. 1. 25. 현재

	한 국 측	미 국 측
의장	김기조 외무부 북미 2과장	Chairman Capt. Wallace E. Sharp
간사	권 찬 외무부 사무관	Secretary Mr. Robert A. Kinney
위원	백세현 내무부 관리과장	Member Col. David P. Heekin
"	이병모 치안국 총경	" Col. Garry A. Willard Jr.
"	박보영 치안국 총경	" Col. Bruce T. Coggins
"	현홍주 법무부 검사	" Col. Henry A. Essex
"	박희태 법무부 검사	" Col. George F. Proudfoot
"	김철용 교통부 진흥과장	" Mr. Daniel A. O'Donohue
"	김주환 보사부 만성병담당관	" Maj. Richard G. Toye
"	김명섭 문공부 해외과장	" Mr. Francis K. Cook
"	장석환 청와대 내무.보사담당 비서관	

43

Proposed Itinerary for Trip of Ad Hoc Subcommittee
on Civil-Military Relations to Uijongbu
Tentatively Scheduled for Tuesday, 30 January 1973

*It is proposed that the Ad Hoc Subcommittee on Civil-Military Relations trip to Uijongbu be made on a bus furnished by the Eighth US Army which would leave Yongsan at 1430 hours on Tuesday, 30 January, stop at a point designated by the ROK component to pick up the ROK members at or near the Capitol Building at 1445 hours, and proceed to the I Corps (ROK/US) Group Headquarters, Uijongbu.

The proposed schedule for the Ad Hoc Subcommittee in Uijongbu is as follows:

1445 — ~~start~~ start

~~1530~~-1630 Briefing by the I Corps on the situation relating to civil-military affairs in Uijongbu and I Corps area of responsibility.

1630-1800 Discussion with ROK officials in Uijongbu regarding problems in civil-military relations.

1800-1930 Social Time and dinner at the Officers' Club at I Corps Headquarters.

1930-2100 Visit entertainment areas in Uijongbu.

2100-2200 Return to Seoul by bus.*

*Anyone who prefers to travel in own car, of course, may do so.

Inclosure 3

44

TENTATIVE

Ad Hoc Subcommittee on Civil-Military Relations
Trip to Pyongtaek-gun
Including Osan Air Base (Songtan-eup) and Camp Humphreys (Anjong-ni)
5 February 1973

0900	Leave Yongsan by bus (helicopter?).
1000-1045	Tour Songtan-eup.
1100-1200	Briefing by US officials at Osan Air Base.
1200-1300	Lunch at Osan Officers Club.
1300-1330	Trip to Pyongtaek.
1330-1430	Confer with Rok Officials of Pyongtaek-gun at Pyongtaek.
1445-1515	Tour of Anjong-ni.
1530-1615	Briefing at Camp Humphreys.
1615-1730	Return to Seoul by bus (helicopter?).

Ad Hoc Subcommittee on Civil-Military Relations
Trip to Camp Casey-Tongduchon
~~Tuesday,~~ 23 February 1973

0930	Depart from H-201, Yongsan Helipad.
1000-1045	Tour of Tongduchon.
1100-1200	Briefing by US officials at Camp Casey.
1215-1315	Lunch at Camp Casey.
1330-1500	Discussion with ROK authorities at Tongduchon.
1515	Depart from Camp Casey - R-220.
1600	Arrive H-201, Yongsan Helipad.

45

협 조 문

응신기일

분류기호 및 문서번호	미이 723 - 10
제 목	직원국내출장

수 신 총무과장　　　발신일자 1973. 1. 29.　　　(협조제의)

북미2	안재	73 1 29	담	과	국	차	차	장

발신명의 구미국장

(제 1 의 견)

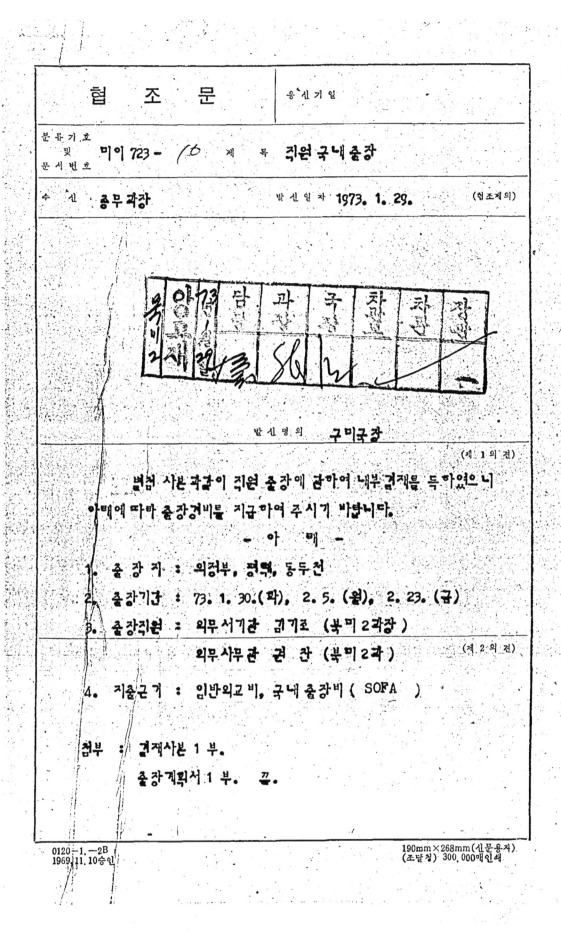

별첨 사본과같이 직원 출장에 관하여 내부결재를 득하였으니 아래에 따라 출장경비를 지급하여 주시기 바랍니다.

- 아 래 -

1. 출 장 지 : 의정부, 평택, 동두천
2. 출장기간 : 73. 1. 30.(화), 2. 5. (월), 2. 23. (금)
3. 출장직원 : 외무서기관 김기조 (북미 2과장)

   외무사무관 권 찬 (북미2과)

(제 2 의 견)

4. 지출근거 : 일반외교비, 국내출장비 (SOFA)

첨부 : 결재사본 1 부.

출장계획서 1 부. 끝.

0120-1.-2B
1969.11.10승인

190mm×268mm(신문용지)
(조달청) 300,000매인쇄

46

기 안 용 지

분류기호 문서번호	미이 723 -	(전화번호)	전결규정 조 항 차관 전결사항
처리기간			
시행일자	1973. 1. 12.	차 관	
보존년한			
보조기관	차관보		협조
	국 장		
	과 장		
기안책임자	권 찬	북미2과	
경유 수신 참조	내부결재	발신	통제
제 목	직원 출장		

한.미 군대지위협정에 의한 한.미 합동위원회는 주한미군 주둔지역 기지주변에서의 한국 민간인과 주둔 미군과의 관계개선을 도울 목적으로 72년 9월에 그 산하에 군.민관계 분과위원회를 설치하여 그동안 활동하여 왔는바, 미측은 동 분과위원회 활동의 일환으로 아래의 미군 기지들을 한.미 합동으로 시찰하여 대책을 건의할것을 제의하여 왔아옵기, 아래와 같이 출장시킬것을 건의합니다.

- 아 래 -

1. 출장직원 : 김기조 북미2과장 (동분과위 한국측 의장)
   권 찬 북미2과 (동분과위 간사)
2. 출 장 지 : (1) 1. 30. (화) : 의정부 한.미 제1혼성군단 사령부
   (2) 2. 5. (월) : 평택 미 23지원단 (Camp Humphreys) 및 오산 공군기지
   (3) 2. 23. (금) : 동두천 미 제2사단 (Camp Casey) 등.

정서 | 관인 | 발송

공동서식1-2(갑)
1967. 4. 4. 승인

190mm ×268mm (1급인쇄용지70g/㎡)
조달청 (500,000매 인쇄)

19

47

출 장 기 획

1. 목 적 지 : 의정부, 평택, 동두천

2. 출장일정 : 73. 1. 29. 서울 출발 - 의정부 도착 (버스)
   1. 30. 의정부출발 - 서울 도착 (")
   2. 4. 서울 출발 - 평택 도착 (")
   2. 5. 평택 출발 - 서울 도착 (")
   2. 22. 서울 출발 - 동두천 도착 (")
   2. 23. 동두천출발 - 서울 도착 (")

48

KOREA HERALD
73. 1. 31

By End of Year 73.1.31.<K.H.>

48 Military Base Towns To Receive Face-Lifting

The Home Ministry will carry out beautification projects for the "base towns" by the end of the year at a total cost of 162,330,000 won, according to the ministry yesterday.

To be remodeled are 48 base towns in 11 districts where there are foreign units larger than a company.

The projects, which are designed to turn the towns into "new ones," include pavement of roads, construction of water supply systems and installation of street lamps.

Also included in the projects are improvement of sewage systems and improvement of houses or building new ones. The 48 base towns are largely those in Seoul, Pusan, Inchon, Uijongbu, Yangju, Pyongtaek and Tongduchon areas, the ministry said.

For effective results, the ministry decided to carry out the projects by grouping the towns into two — 13 for one group and the remaining 35 in another.

Major emphasis in the projects will be given to the 13 towns which are located largely in Yangju and Pyongtaek, both in Kyonggi-do, and Okku in Cholla Pukto and Chilgok in Kyongsang Pukto. For the work in these areas, the ministry will directly involve and supervise them, the ministry added.

The 35 other towns are mainly those in the Seoul, Inchon, Pusan and other city areas where the projects are to be carried out under the programs of the local governments.

49

DEPARTMENT OF THE ARMY
Headquarters 23d Support Group
Humphreys Sub-Area Command
APO 96271

EAKSH-CDR 미제23지원단 험프리스 지역사령부 5 February 1973
1973. 2. 5

US-ROK Ad Hoc Sub-Committee for Civil-Military Relations
한미 행정 협정 군민관계 분과 위원회

Dear Committee Members,
친애하는 위원 여러분

On behalf of the Officers and Men of the Humphreys Sub-Area and the
험프리스 지역 및 23 지원단의 장병을 대신하여 한미 행정 협정
23d Support Group, I wish to convey a most heartfelt "Welcome back" to
합동위원회 군민관계 분과위원 여러분을 진심으로 환영합니다.
you the members of the US-ROK Ad Hoc Sub-Committee for Civil-Military
평택군수 이재창 씨와 평택군 경찰서장 윤조영 총경의
Relations. As a result of the splendid co-operation provided by Governor
훌륭한 협조의 결과로서 여러분의 지난해의 방문이 있은 후
YI, Jae Chang of Pyongtaek-Kun and Senior Superintendent YUN, Jo Yang,
안정리의 모든 면이 안전하고 위생적이고 그리고 인간
Chief of Police in Pyongtaek-Kun, significant progress has been made in
차별이 없는 환경조성에 뜻있는 진보를 해왔읍니다.
providing a safe, sanitary and non-discriminatory enviroment for all in
그러나 아직도 성병관리와 암거래를 위한 험프리스
Anjong-Ni since your last visit. However, problem areas still exist in
영에서의 재산의 절도에 관해서 문제점이 남아있읍니다.
the areas of VD control and larceny of property from Camp Humphreys for
다음 페이지에 있는 도표는 이와같은 문제점을
resale on the Black Market. The charts on the following pages will help
어느정도 더 설명하는데 도움이 될것입니다.
further explain some of these problem areas.
우리는 박정희 대통령 각하와 한국국민이 한국에서의

We most fervently welcome any suggestions you might have as to how
암거래의 제거와 병관리의 개선에 지치지않는 노력에
we can better assist his Excellency PARK, Chung Hee and the people of the
우리가 어떻게 도울수있는가에 관해서 여러분이
Republic in their untiring efforts to eliminate blackmarketing and improve
가질지도 모르는 어떠한 제안이라도 열렬히
sanitation and disease control in the Republic.
환영하는 바입니다.

Sincerely yours,
경구

Frederick W. Best Jr.
FREDERICK W. BEST, JR.
Colonel, Infantry
Commanding
후레데릭 다블. 베스트 2세.
보병 대령
사령관

50

omparative V.D. Rates eb. 1972 ~ Jan. 1973 병 이환율의 비교 72 년 2월 ~ 1973년 1월	EBRUARY 2월	ARCH 3월	PRIL 4월	AY 5월	UNE 6월	ULY 7월	UGUST 8월	EPTEMBER 9월	CTOBER 10월	OVEMBER 11월	ECEMBER 12월	ANUARY 1월
D. Cases in Humphreys S.A. 험프리지구의 성병환자수	198	197	223	312	301	355	313	249	323	251	202	249
umphreys Sub Area Rate 험프리지구의 성병율	518	487	561	745	732	872	752	786	856	684	556	801
SAKORSCOM V.D. Rate 주한지원사령부의 성병율	547	495	612	722	667	688	677	624	657	551	489	—
th Army V.D. Rate 18군 성병율	772	749	701	788	756	776	731	706	669	626	476	—
d INF. DIV. V.D. Rate 제2사단 성병율	1061	1171	1144	1194	1317	1050	940	962	757	675	609	71

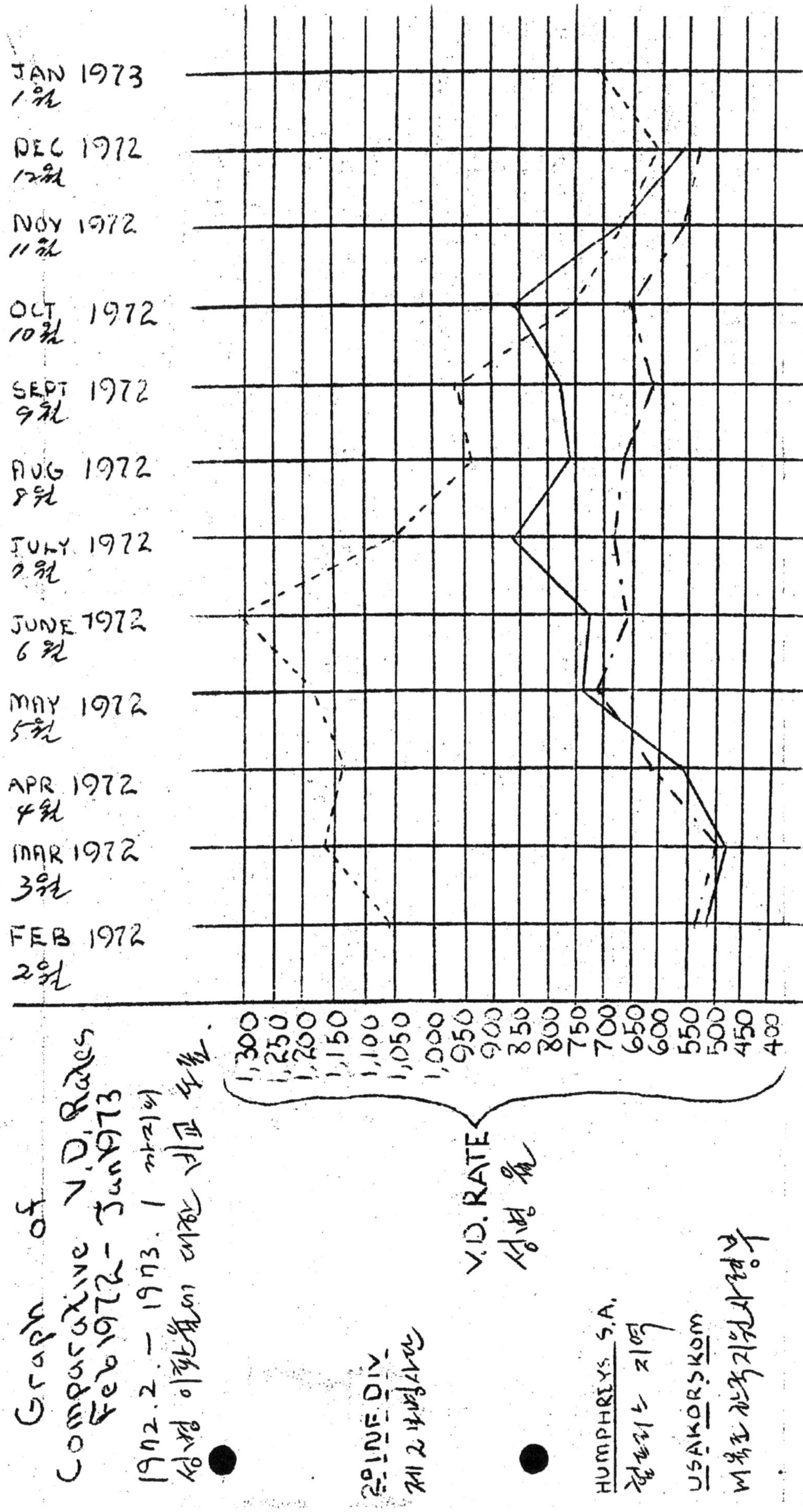
JAN 1973
1월
DEC 1972
12월
NOV 1972
11월
OCT 1972
10월
SEPT 1972
9월
AUG 1972
8월
JULY 1972
7월
JUNE 1972
6월
MAY 1972
5월
APR 1972
4월
MAR 1972
3월
FEB 1972
2월
1,300
1,250
1,200
1,150
1,100
1,050
1,000
950
900
850
800
750
700
650
600
550
500
450
400
Graph of Comparative V.D. Rates Feb 1972 - Jan 1973
1972. 2. - 1973. 1 까지에 성병 이환율에 대한 비교 도표
V.D. RATE
성병 율
2d INF DIV
제2보병사단
HUMPHREYS S.A.
험프리스 지역
USAKORSKOM
미8군 한국지원사령부

Monthly V.D. Cases for Anjong-Ni Clubs
July 1972–January 1973

1972년 7월부터 1973년 1월까지의 안정리 클럽의 월별 성병 환자수

	JULY 7월	AUGUST 8월	SEPTEMBER 9월	OCTOBER 10월	NOVEMBER 11월	DECEMBER 12월	JANUARY 1월
Duffy's 더휘즈	38	39	45	35	42	17	58
Folly 훨리	4	3	7	14	8	6	4
Galaxy 가락시	11	8	8	11	20	18	23
T-Club 티클럽	32	29	25	21	20	12	10
Seven 세븐	11	4	33	33	20	14	21
Maxim 맥심	5	8	18	18	8	12	8
TopHat 탑햇	22	13	3	3	3	3	3
Paradise 파라다이스					2	3	6
Peacock 피콕						5	4

EXPANDED CLUB
V. D. STATISTICS
NOV 1972–JAN 1973

상세한 클럽별
[illegible]병 통계 표
1972. 11 ~ 1973. 1

	NUMBER OF GIRLS ASSIGNED 등록된 여자의 수	NUMBER OF CASES REPORTED 보고된 미군의 환자 수	NUMBER OF GIRLS IDENTIFIED 찾게된 여자의 수	NUMBER OF GIRLS TREATED 치료받은 여자의 수	NUMBER OF GIRLS ASSIGNED 등록된 여자의 수	CLUB V.D. RATE FOR MONTH 클럽별 성병 이환율	NUMBER OF CASES REPORTED 보고된 미군의 환자 수	NUMBER OF GIRLS IDENTIFIED 찾게된 여자의 수	NUMBER OF GIRLS TREATED 치료받은 여자의 수	NUMBER OF GIRLS ASSIGNED 등록된 여자의 수	CLUB V.D. RATE FOR MONTH 클럽별 성병 이환율	NUMBER OF CASES REPORTED 보고된 미군의 환자 수	NUMBER OF GIRLS IDENTIFIED 찾게된 여자의 수	NUMBER OF GIRLS TREATED 치료받은 여자의 수
Duffy's 더휘즈	228	42	19	13	281	720	17	13	10	279	2,454	58	26	20
Folly 훨리	106	8	3	3	121	590	6	4	4	129	366	4	4	2
Galaxy 개랙시	132	20	8	7	155	1,369	18	11	7	139	1,929	23	10	7
T[illegible]lub 티-클럽	135	20	10	8	172	826	12	5	5	121	979	10	6	4
Seven 세븐	127	20	13	6	138	1,192	14	7	6	105	2,360	21	16	9
Maxim 맥심	75	8	4	1	88	1,605	12	7	3	64	1,475	8	5	3
Top Hat 탑햇	35	3	4	1	74	484	3	3	3	45	791	3	1	1
Paradise 파라다이스	2	2	1	0	18	1,971	3	3	2	27	2,620	6	3	3
Peacock 피칵					13	4,531	5	0	0	26	1,817	4	4	2
	MONTH OF NOVEMBER 11월				MONTH OF DECEMBER 12월					MONTH OF JANUARY 1월				

Results of the monthly unannounced club inspection for December 1972 & January 1973

1972년 12월과 1973년 1월달의 클럽에 대한 불시 검열 결과

		NUMBER OF GIRLS PRESENT WHO WERE NOT ASSIGNED TO CLUB 그 크럽에 등록되어 있지않는 여자가 발견된 수.		SERIOUS V.D. CARD VIOLATIONS (NO CARD OR CARD WITH POSITIVE CHECK) 중대한 검진증 위반 (카드 미소지자 또는 보균자로 판명된 카드 소지자)		LESSER V.D CARD VIOLATIONS (EXPIRED CARD OR NOT UP TO DATE ON CHECKS) 가벼운 검진증 위반 (만기된 카드 또는 최근에 검진을 받지않은 카드 소지자)		WERE FAULTS FOUND WITH SANITATION? 위생에 관한 결함 사항이 있었는지?	
Duffy's	더휘즈	2	3	0	0	0	10	YES	NO
Folly	훨리	2	*	0	*	1	*	YES	*
Galaxy	가락시	5	5	0	0	0	0	YES	NO
T-Club	티-크럽	2	1	0	1	1	1	YES	NO
Seven	세븐	3	1	0	2	0	0	YES	NO
Maxim	맥심	6	*	0	*	0	*	YES	*
Top Hat	탑 햇	1	*	1	*	0	*	NO	*
Paradise	파라다이스	2	0	0	0	0	0	YES	NO
Peacock	피컥	7	*	0	*	0	*	YES	*
* CLUB NOT INSPECTED MONTH 검열 받지 않는 크럽		DEC 1월	JAN 2월	DEC 1월	JAN 2월	DEC 1월	JAN 2월	DEC 1월	JAN 2월

CHRONOLOGY OF PROBATION AND OFF LIMITS ACTIONS DIRECTED TOWARDS CLUBS IN ANJONG-NI IN 1972-73

1972년과 1973년간에 경고장(유예기간)과 출입금지 처분을 받은 안정리 클럽.

NAME OF CLUB 클럽 명	PERIOD OF PROBATION OR OFF-LIMITS STATUS 경고기간이나 출입금지기간	REASON 이유
MAXIM 맥심	7 days propation MAY 1972 경고기간 7일 1972. 5	Racial Discrimination 인종차별
FOLLY 훠리	7 days propation MAY 1972 경고기간 7일 1972. 5	Racial Discrimination 인종차별
SEVEN 세븐	7 days propation SEPTEMBER 1972 경고기간 7일 1972. 9	Racial Discrimination 인종차별
FOLLY 훠리	2 weeks propation NOVEMBER 1972 경고기간 2주 1972. 11.	Gambling 도박장소 제공
MAXIM 맥심	OFF LIMITS 4-9 JAN. 1973 출입금지 1973. 1. 4~9	Unsanitary Water 비위생적인 물
PEACOCK 피콕	OFF LIMITS 4-9 JAN. 1973 출입금지 1973. 1. 4~9	Unsanitary Water 비위생적인 물

56

PROPERTY THEFTS ~ C.P. HUMPHREYS
재산 절도 ~ 험프리스 영

MONTH 월	VALUE OF STOLEN GOVERNMENT PROPERTY AT CP HUMPHREYS [illegible] 1972 - JAN. 1973 험프리스 영에서 도난당한 정부재산 의 가치 1972. 8 ~ 1973. 1	VALUE OF PRIVATE PROPERTY STOLEN FROM CAMP HUMPHREYS [illegible] 1972 - JAN. 1973 험프리스 영에서 도난당한 개인 재산 의 가치 1972. 8 ~ 1973. 1
AUGUST 1972 1972. 8	$6,591.00	$2,369.00
SEPTEMBER 1972 1972. 9	$1,846.00	$1,393.00
OCTOBER 1972 1972. 10	$5,356.00	$3,645.00
NOVEMBER 1972 1972. 11	$35,029.00	$2,186.00
DECEMBER 1972 1972. 12	$2,936.00	$5,677.00
JANUARY 1973 1973. 1	$7,039.00	$2,415.00

57

Ad Hoc Subcommittee on Civil-Military Relations
Trip to Camp Casey-Tongduchon
Friday, 23 February 1973

0945	Depart from H-201, Yongsan Helipad.
1030-1130	Arrive at Helipad 221-Briefing by US officials at Camp Casey.
1130-1230	Lunch at Camp Casey.
1230-1400	Tour of New VD Clinic at Soyosan and of Tongduchon
1400-1530	Discussion with ROK authorities at Tongduchon.
1545	Depart from Camp Casey -A-220.
1630	Arrive H-201, Yongsan Helipad.

58

Individuals Traveling to Camp Casey-Tongduchon, 23 February 1973

ROK Component

Mr. KIM Kee Joe
Chief, North American Section II
Bureau of European and American Affairs
Ministry of Foreign Affairs

*Mr. BAEK Se Hyun
Chief, Management Section
Bureau of Local Administration, MOFA

Mr. LEE Byung Mo
Senior Superintendent
National Police Bureau, MOHA

Mr. PARK Hee Tae
Prosecutor, Claims Section
Legal Affairs Office, MOJ

Mr. KIM Chul Yong
Chief, Tourism Promotion Section
Bureau of Tourism, MOT

Mr. KIM Ju Whan
Chronic Disease Officer
Public Health Bureau, MOH & SA

Mr. KIM Myong Sub
Chief, Forcign Press Section
Korean Overseas Information Service
Ministry of Culture and Information

Mr. YANG Sei Hoon
North America Section II
Bureau of European and American Affairs
Ministry of Foreign Affairs

*Will not travel by helicopter.

US Component

Captain W. E. Sharp
United States Navy
Assistant Chief of Staff, J5
US Forces, Korea

Mr. Robert A. Kinney
Chief, International Relations Branch
J5 Division, US Forces, Korea

COL David P. Heekin, USA
Deputy Chief of Staff
Eighth US Army

*COL Garry A. Willard, Jr.
United States Air Force
Vice Commander, 314th
Air Division, Air Forces, Korea

COL Bruce T. Coggins, USA
Staff Judge Advocate
US Forces, Korea/Eighth US Army

COL Henry A. Essex, USA
Surgeon
US Forces, Korea/Eighth US Army

COL George F. Proudfoot, USA
Provost Marshal
US Forces, Korea/Eighth US Army

Mr. Ward Thompson
Political Section
American Embassy

Mr. John Nowell
Civil Relations Division
Public Affairs Office, Eighth US Army

Mr. AN Chang Hun
Interpreter/Translator
J5, UNC/USFK

59

MATERIAL FOR AD HOC SUBCOMMITTEE TRIP
TO CAMP CASEY-TONGDUCHON, 23 FEBRUARY 1973

TONGDUCHON-EUP (Township):

1. Population approximately 56,000, is located about 35 miles north and slightly east of Seoul. The eup-chief, or town mayor, is Mr. YUN Tal Sup; he has 23 ri's or township sub-areas under his jurisdiction. Tongduchon is a part of Yangju-gun (county); the county seat of Yang-ju-gun is Uijongbu-City, where Headquarters, I Corps (ROK/US) Group is located. The County Chief of Yangju-gun, Mr. MIN Chung Kun, is the chief administrative official in the area.

2. Seventeen bars cater to US Forces personnel, one (The Rendezvous) has just been closed, following warning procedures and coordination between local US-ROK officials.

3. Approximately 1,300 special entertainers are registered with clubs; an additional 103 have station registration. The number of free-lance operators has been relatively small since the recent ROKG drive against street walkers.

4. Nearly 50 full-time KNP are available. This includes 29 at the local station, 14 detectives and four on the crime detection team. The police chief, Captain HONG Ung Sam, is responsible directly to the Yangju-County police chief in Uijongbu.

5. Other Key officials include:

a. Prosecutor for SOFA matters in all areas north of Seoul, Mr. PAK Chong Kyu.

b. Chief Prosecutor KIM Tal Hyung, Uijongbu City.

c. CHO Song Chil, Chairman of the local Tongduchon Tourist Association, elected by association members.

60

공　　　란

공　　　란

공 란

공 란

공 란

공　　　란

공　　　란

공 란

공 란

공 란

공 란

공 란

공 란

기 지 촌 사 업 현 황
CAMP-VILLAGE PURIFICATION PROGRAM

동 두 천
DONG DU CHON

1 9 7 3. 2. 2 3.
February 23, 1973

양 주 군
YANG JU GOON

174

목 차

75'

1. 목 표

(1) 조용한 환경조성 — 사 회 대 책

(2) 성병 및 마약근절 — 보 건 대 책

(3) 깨끗한 환경조성 — 환경정화대책

(4) 한국관 개선 — 친선활동대책

(5) 안정된 환경조성 — 생활기반조성대책

2. 방 침

(1) 정화대상기지촌 : 동두천 지구 지역주민 참여에 의한 자조적 정화를 원칙으로 한다.

(2) 한미친선 활동과 협의사항에 의한 강력한 행정으로 사회분규요인을 해소한다.

(3) 접객업소의 흑백차별 대우 근절 및 기존시설의 과감한 개선으로 써비스를 증진시킨다.

(4) 기지촌주변의 불량환경을 정비하고 성병 및 마약의 통제 단속강화를 계속 실시한다.

(5) 외국군 감축에 대비하여 주민의 생활기반책을 강구한다.

(6) 환경정화사업은 주민참여로 새마을사업 실시요령에 준한다.

-2-

76

3. 기지촌 일반현황

기지촌명	주둔부대명	주민실태					미군접객업소		
		계	일반주민	부대 종사자	미군부대 생계자	윤락 여성	계	크럽	기타
계		47,829	38,820	2,530	3,985	2494	192	22	170
보산지구	미제2사단	44,729	37,392	1,820	3,445	2072	138	15	123
광암지구	미제2사단 제2여단	3,100	1,428	710	540	422	54	7	47

4. 72 사업실적

사 업 명	사업건수	진도	중 요 내 역	
총 계	60		총투자 사업비	201, 030천원
사회대책사업	11	100	합동순찰강화	
			관광휴양업소 종사자교육	4 회
			생활상담소 설치운영	1 개소
			윤락여성교육	5 회
			일시보호소설치및윤락여성귀가조치	1 개소 (619명)
보건대책사업	16	100	성병관리소 신축운영	1 동
			낙검자수송용 뻐-스	1 대
			성병치료	23, 707 명
			마약및습관성의약품단속	습 134 마 4
			대용진료소 관리	6 개소
			분뇨차 및 진개차구입운영	4 대
			불량시설개선	14개소
환경정화대책사업	23	100		
			가로 및 뒷골목포장	37, 116㎡
			보안등 및 가로등설치	268등
			하수도설치및소하천개보수	8, 284m
			불량주택개량	주 311동 변소102 〃
			가드레일및가로수식재	7, 860m 1, 350본

-4-

사 업 명	사업 건수	진도	중 요 내 역	
			광압출장소신축	1동 (33평)
			공간록화 및 수벽	1,000본 380m
한미친선유대강화대책사업	4	100	한미회의개최	
			체육대회	
			간행물인쇄배부및광고계시판설치	100부 2개소
생활기반조성	6	100	구호양곡지급	3,348인
			직업보도시설확충	1동 (20평)
			양돈 및 비닐하우스	돈 50두 비닐200개소

19

5. 73 기지촌사업계획

(단위 ; 천원)

사업명	목표	사업비	중요내역
총계		39,702	
사회대책사업	년	386	
	년 4회 250 명	386	윤락여성 선도 (교육 및 귀가조치)
보건대책사업		30,999	
	34,675 명	7,497	성병예방 및 치료 (성병관리소 운영, 성병대행진료소 운영)
		694	마약, 습관성의약품단속 (한미합동전담감시원)
	12 개소	7,500	관광휴양업소위생대책 (불량시설개선, 위생검사 종업원교육)
	1 대	15,308	청소강화 (진개차, 분뇨차 구입및운영)
환경정화대책사업		4,052	
	4,000 m 1 개소	3,060	상수도시설 (간이상수도 포함)
	288 등	992	보안등 및 가로등 유지관리
한미친선활동사업		340	
한미친선활동사업	월 1회	240	회의개최
	년 1회	100	체육대회개최
생활기반조성		3,925	
	1개소 150 명	400	가내공업센타운영 (기능공양성)
	1개소 140 명	2,400	직업훈련
	885 명	1,125	영세민구호

-6-

6. 고질적현안사항 및 대책

기지촌별	고질적현안사항	대 책
	1. 성병예방	ㄱ. 관영 성병관리소 운영
	가) 검진기피	ㄴ. 타지역 유입 억제
	나) 윤락여성의 타지역 유입	ㄷ. 검진기피자 및 미등록자 색출
		ㄹ. 윤락여성 선도강화(귀가조치, 직업보도)
	2. 인종차별	ㄱ. 흑인전용홀 폐쇄
	가) 흑백분규	ㄴ. 한미합동 단속반 편성운영
	나) 마약사범의 근절	ㄷ. 불량배 색출 선도
		ㄹ. 윤락여성 교육강화
		ㅁ. 자율적 신고제 계몽
	3. 도시환경	ㄱ. 뒷골목 및 하수도 포장
		ㄴ. 불량시설 개선
		ㄷ. 보도부럭 설치
		ㄹ. 보안등 및 가로등 시설
		ㅁ. 새마을 가꾸기에 의한 자체정화

81

7. 군민관계문제 및 협의사항

성병대책

1. 윤락여성수 및 유형

총 수						비 고
	자 취	동 거	하 숙	하인상대		
2, 494	797	349	1, 232	116		

2. 성병검진과 낙검현황

구분 / 년도별	등록수	검진수	비율(%)	낙검수	낙검율(%)	비 고
1970	1, 292명	1, 020명	79%	83명	7. 7%	
1971	1, 897	1, 384	78%	216	15%	
1972	2, 600	2, 091	80%	142	7. 2%	
1973	2, 494	2, 069	83%	102	5. 6%	

3. 낙검자 치료현황

구분 / 년도별	치료연인원 (1년)	월평균치료인원	비 고
1972	13, 946명	1, 162 명	
1973	(1개월간) 1, 292		

4. 성병관리소 현황

	시설 및 장비 현황						요 원		
	대지	건평	수용능력	검사기구	배양검사	수송차량	의사	간호원 검사원	기타 종사원
신 성병관리소	2, 171평	200평	150병	2셋트	실시중	1대	2	3	6
구 성병관리소	80〃	60〃	30〃	1셋트			1	2	3

-8-

82

5. 성병근절대책 및 효과

가. 한미간 성병관리 합의사항 계속추진

나. 민들레회원의 소재파악

ㄱ. 민들레회원 카드제실시로 소재파악

ㄴ. 감염자 색출에 흘업주협조로 신속한효과거양

다. 명찰, 명함제 실시

ㄱ. 명찰, 명함, 검진증 미소지자 홀출입금지로 검진기피자 미연방지

미국측도 명찰제시

라. 자체단속반 편성실시

ㄱ. 각홀 기도를 지역별로 구분 분담 가두청객단속으로 거리의 명랑화를 기함

마. 전담반 운영강화

ㄱ. 미검 및 낙검자 청객행위단속

ㄴ. 성병감염자 치료조치

바. 대용성병진료소 지도강화

ㄱ. 매검진일에는 각 진료소에 직원 1명을 파견 현지지도함

ㄴ. 도에 관계의사 순회지도 한다.

사. 환자의 편의제공

ㄱ. 낙검자는 관용대기차량으로 안전수송

ㄴ. 성병관리소의 환경개선

ㄷ. 환자 완전치료에 최선을 다하며 자진입소 의욕고취

C O N T E N T S

1. OBJECTIVES

a. GRACEFUL ENVIRONMENT	SOCIAL AFFAIRS.
b. ERADICATION OF VD & DURG-ABUSE	HEALTH PROMOTION
c. PLEASANT ENVIRONMENT	ENVIRONMENTAL PORIFICATION
d. CREATION OF NEW KOREA IMAGE	FRIENDSHIP ACTIVITIES
e. FORMING OF STABILIZED ENVIRONMENT	PROMOTION OF LIVELIHOOD FOUNDATION

2. POLICIES

a. The Purification Programs will be established under the priniciple of residents self-help with their participation in such area as Tong Du chen where foreign troops are prospected to be stationed continuously.

b. ROK-US friendship & Social confusion will be settled by strong administration.

c. Exterminat of black and white seagregation and improve service.

d. Strict control of drug and arrange poor conditioned camp-villege.

e. Plomotion of residents livelihood foundation Due to decrease U.S. Troops.

f. The purification programs will be established under the principle of community morement assontials.

3. GENERAL STATUS OF CAMP-VILLAGES

Areas	Camps	Type of Residents					Entertain for US Personnal		
		Total	General Residents	Unit Employes	Business for US Personnel	Business Girl	Total	Club	The others
Total		~~47,896~~ 47829	38,820	2,530	3,985	~~2,561~~ 2494	192	22	170
Bo-SAN Area	2nd US Div	~~44,796~~ 44729	37,392	1,820	3,445	~~2,139~~ 2072	138	15	123
Kwan-Am Area	24th US Div	3,100	1,428	710	540	422	54	7	47

4. ACCOMPLISHMENTS IN '72

PROJECTS	NO. OF WORKS	PRO-GRESS	C O N T E N T S
T O T A L	60		
SOCIAL AFFAIRS	11	100%	1. Conduct of strengthened patrols 2. Eduction of club employees 4 time 3. Establish of Livelihood consel 1 place 4. Education of B. Gs 5 time 5. Temporarity protect place 1 place 6. measure Return home 619 persons
HEALTH PROMOTION	16	100	1. Newly-Create of VD clinic 1 2. V.D Treatment 23,707 persons 3. Control of Drug abuse 4. Manegment of privete clinic 6 5. Procurement of trash trucks 4 EA 6. Improvement of poor facilities 14 places
ENVIVONMENT PURIFICATION	23	100	1. Planting of roadside tree 37,116m and side road pavement 2. Street and Security Lights 268 3. Construction of sewers 8,284m 4. Improvement of pool conditioned residence 311 5. Planting of roadside tree 1,350 6. Establishment of Kwang-An branch 1 place
ROK-US FRIENDSHIP ACTIVITIES	4	100	1. ROK-US meetings 2. Atheletic meetings 3. Distribution of publication 100 and Advertisement signs 2
PROMOTION OF LIVELIHOOD FOUNDUTION	6	100	1. Relief food supply 3,348 persons 2. General agency 1 place 3. Hog raising 50

87

5. WORK PLANS OF CAMP-CILLAGES OF 73

DROJECTS	OBJECTIVE	EXPENSES	DETAILS
T O T A L		39,702	
SOCIAL AFFAIRS	year 4 time 250 persons	386	1. Proper guide and Education of BGs
HEALTH PROMOTION		30,999	
	34,675 persons	7,497	1. Prevent of V.D. and treatment (Control of V.D. Clinic and private clinic)
	30 EA	694	Contral habilual drug joint ROK-US supervise team
	12 places	7,500	1 Counter-plans of sanifation (Inprovement of poor facilities Education of Employees)
	1 EA	15,308	1. Control of polish (Procurement of trash truch)
ENVIRON-MENT PURIFICA-TION		4,052	
	400m 1 place	3,060	Water supply
	288	992	Streets and Security Lights.
ROK-US FRIEND-SHIP ACTIVI-TROS		4,052	
	Once month	240	Meetings
	Once year	100	Atheletic meetings
INCRESE OF LIVELIHOOD	1 place 150 persons	3,925 400	Domistic industry center

88

DROJECTS	OBJECTIVE	EXPENSES	DETAILS
	1 place 140 persons	2,400	Vocational training
	885 persons	1,125	Relicf poor people

89

6. CHRONIC PROBLEMS & COUNTER MEASURE

COMP VILLAGE	Chronic Problems	Counter measure
	1. V.P. Prerention a. Med-exam evaders b. Inflow from other area	a. Goverment-management V.D clinic b. Control of inflow from other area c. Search of evaders and non-Registrant d. Proper guidence and education of B.G.
	2. Racial Segregation (Black-white confusion Drug Abuse)	a. Closure of only black Partraning business establishment b. Contant patroling by ROK-US control Team c. Search of hoodlums d. Increased education of BG e. Enlightement of antomous report
	Urban Envirnment	a. Pavement of street and sewers b. Improvement of poor conditioned facilities c. Pavement of Footpath e. Installation of street and security lights. f. Self-Purification of community movement

0

7. PROBLEMS & DISCUSSION ITEM REGARDING TO CIVIL-MILITARY RELATION

1. Countermeasure of V.D.

a. Type of B.G.

Amount	Self-Cook	Steady	Lodger	Korean-mate	Remark
2,494	797	349	1,232	116	

b. Examination status

	NO. of Registered	Examined	Examined %	Rejected	Rejected %
1970	1,292	1,020	79%	83	7.7%
1971	1,897	1,384	78%	216	15%
1972	2,600	2,091	80%	142	7.2%
1973	2,494	2,069	83%	102	5.6%

c. Treatment of Rejected

	No. of Treatment	No. of Averge month
1972	13,946	1,162
1973	1,292	

d. V.D clinic status

	facilities and equipment						Stoff			Remark
	Bulding site	Space	Accom-indation	Utensils	Norsery	Vehecle	Doc	Nurses	Employees	
New VD Clinic	2,171 pyon	200 pyon	150 persons	2 set	Under woking	1 EA	2	3	6	
Old VD Clinic	88 pyon	60 pyon	30 persons	1 set			1	2	3	

e. Extermination V.D. and Effect

(1) Continued propolsion of V.D. manegment of the ROK-US agreement

(2) Seize location of MINDULLE Association members.
a) Cardsystum
b) Searching infected cooperate by UN club runner

(3) Card system
a) Prevention of Mad-exam evader
V.D card and Name plate must be carry.

(4) Organized Self-Control Team
a) Partial charge of UN club maneger.

(5) Strengthen the manegement of take full charge
a) Evader and Rejecter must net call guest
b) Treatment of V.D infectors

92

(6) Guidance of private clinic

a) Mumber of staff will dispatch to private clinic when Mad-exam day

b) Perfessional Doctor will trip Guidance to Private clinic.

(7) Provide for convenience to patient

a) Rejecter will salfy transport by watch and wait vehecle

b) Do best of perfect treat to patients.

c) Improvement of V.D clinic surrounding

Ad Hoc 군민관계

외국군 기지촌 주변 정화를위한 범죄단속 장기계획 및 단속현황

서울지방검찰청 의정부지청

94

외국군기지촌주변정화를위한범죄단속장기계획및단속현황

1. 기지촌 정화반의 설치 연혁

당지청은 관내에 약30개의 주한 미군부대가 주둔하여 주한 미군의 약즐를 수용하고 부대주변은 기지촌을 형성하고 있으며 위안부, 미군부대 종업원 노무자, 군수물자 암거래자, 폭력배 및 마약밀매자등의 발호로 우범지대로 되여있다 따라서 외국군인들의 의곡된 한국관 및 한국에서의 근무 기피현상을 없에며 우리 국가 안전보장에 적극 기여하도록하기 위하여 1971. 12. 21. 가칭 "기지촌 정화 대책 위원회"를 구성하고 동년 12. 23. "청와대 실무자 회의" 및 동년 12. 27. "의정부, 양주지구 기지촌 정화 위원회 회의" 등 진지한 토의와 대검사무 821-329호 (1972. 1. 12) 및 820-1606호 (1972. 2. 7)로 지시된 기지촌 정화를 위한 관련사범 단속계획에 의거하여 기지촌 단속반을 편성하여 단속에 임하게

~1~

95

되였음

2. 목 적

가. 외국군인들의 의곡된 한국관 및 한국에서의 근무 기피 현상을 없에며 우리국가 안전보장에 적극 기여 하도록하기 위하여 주둔지역 주변의 폭력, 보건, 마약사범, 군수품도난사범, 포주등의 착취행위를 단속하며,

나. 외국군 종업원 및 선량한 주민들의 권익을 보호 하기 위하여 인권상담등을 강화함으로서 법질서 확립을 기여한다.

3. 단속기간 및 대상

가. 단속기간

1972 ~ 1975

나. 단속대상지역

의정부, 동두천, 파주등 외국군 주둔 기지촌지역,

~2~

96

다. 대상인물

기지촌 주변의

(1) 폭력배, 치기배, 주거부정자, 무직우범자

(2) 매춘부, 포주

(3) 각종 범죄의 전과자, 유언비어 유포자

(4) 각종 군수물자 및 P.X물자 암거래상과 절도 및 장물거래 우범자

(5) 마약 및 습관성 의약품 암거래상

라. 대상 범죄

(1) 보건범죄

(가) 음료수에 관한 죄

(나) 아편에 관한 죄

(다) 독물 및 극물에 관한 법률위반

(라) 마약법 위반.

(마) 보건범죄에 관한 특별 조치법 위반

(바) 식품위생법 위반

~9~

97

(사) 오물청소법 위반

(아) 전염병 예방법 위반

(자) 습관성 의약품 관리법 위한

(2) 강력사범

(폭력사범)

(가) 상해와 폭행의 죄

(나) 협박의 죄

(다) 체포와 감금의 죄

(라) 공갈의 죄

(마) 폭력행위등 처벌에 관한 법률위반

(흉악범)

(가) 살인의 죄

(나) 강도의 죄

(다) 강도 상해 치사상 죄

(마) 강간죄, 강도강간죄

(3) 경제사범

~4~

98

(가) 관세법 위반

(나) 외국환 관리법 위반

(다) 특정외래품 판매금지법 위반

(라) 기타 이에 준하는 범죄(연초전매법 위반, 조세범 처벌법 위반)

(4) 퇴폐풍조 사범

(가) 음화반포

(나) 음행매개

(다) 공연음란

(라) 윤락행위등 방지법 위반

(5) 군용물자 절도사범

(가) 절도죄

(나) 장물죄

(다) 군용물등 범죄에 관한 특별조치법 위반

4. 상담 및 단속지침

가. 인권상담

~5~

99

(1) 당지청 관내 기지촌주변 인권상담은 전담 검사인 박 전규검사가 월1회 이상 현지 순회상담을 행하며 각 해당 경찰서는 인권상담 대상지역 보고서를 작성 월별 보고하면 전담 검사가 상담 대상의 완급을 구분하여 상담한다.

(2) 각 경찰서장은 외국군인과 주민간의 감정대립을 일으킬만한 사실이 발견되면 즉시 지청장에게 정보보고 한다.

나. 단속지침

(1) 각 경찰서장은 본 단속전담반을 편성하여 본 계획의 실시에 임하는 일방 책임자 1명(경위급이상)을 선정하여 그 명단과 외국인 기지촌 현황을 보고한다.

(2) 각 경찰서장은 본계획에 관련된 일체의 수사사항을 전담 검사의 지휘를 받아 처리한다.

~6~

100

(3) 검거된 사범 피의자의 사건 송치시는 송치기록 우측 상단에 주서로 "기지촌 정화 범죄"라고 표기한다.

(4) 전담 검사가 일제단속을 위하여 수시 일자를 지정 통보할시는 관내 기관의 장은 편성된 인원의 동원에 차질이 없도록 한다.

5. 전담반 편성

가. 반장 검사 박 정 규

나. 폭력, 마약등 단속반

의정부경찰서 형사 제2계장외 17명

파주경찰서 형사계장외 11명

다. 미군수물자 단속반

서울세관의정부출장소 감시계장외 6명

라. 특별단속반

보건사회부 직원등 6명

합계 40명

~7~

101

6. 기지촌 정화대책에 의한 관련사범등 단속현황

당지청 관내는 외국군 부대가 다수 주둔하고 있는 지역적 특수성으로 이에 관련된 사범이 많아 이에 특별한 관심을 갖이고 수차에 미군 당국과의 실무자 회의를 거쳐 기히 대검찰청으로 부터 지시된 단속 지침에 의거 합동 단속반을 편성하여 이를 지휘 중점적인 단속에 임하고 있음.

가. 기지촌 정화시설

(1) 실시기간

(가) 특별단속기간 설정 (1972. 2. 1 ~ 72. 2. 15)

관내 수사과장 회의를 거쳐 각 경찰서 단위로 D데이를 2회씩 설정하여 군수품 P.X유출품으로 장물에 관한죄, 관세법위반, 특정외래품판매금지법위반, 군용물등 범죄에 관한 특별조치법위반, 주세법위반 사범등을 일제히 단속하여 동기간중 103건에 104명을 입건 조치

하였음.

(나) 1972. 2. 16. 이후에는 각 경찰서별로 기지촌 정화단속반을 편성하여 계속실시중에 있음.

(2) 단속 실적 (1972. 1. 1 ~ 12. 31)

(1) 보건범죄 822건 1,080명

(2) 강력사범 1001건 1,867 〃

(3) 경제사범 145건 266 〃

(4) 퇴폐풍조사범 67건 164 〃

(5) 군용물등범죄 731건 1364 〃

합계 2,776건 4,741명.

나. 마약사범등 합동단속

본사범은 당지청에서 특히 집중적으로 합동 단속반을 편성하여 단속하고 있는 사범임.

(1) 단속현황 (1972. 1. 1 ~ 12. 31)

(가) 습관성 의약품관리법 위반

416건 664명 (미군인 173건 286명)

본 사범은 70년 총계 9건 9명 71년 총계 70건 99명에 비하여 급진적으로 증가하고 있는바 본 사범중 한국인에 대하여는 전원 구속기소를 원칙으로 하고 있으며 미군에 대하여는 범증이 극히 악질적인자에 한하여 재판권을 행사 (71년 1건 1명) 하고 있으며 그 외에는 미군측에 증거물을 인도하여 자체에서 처벌하도록 하고 있음

※ 특별 단속기간 설정 (72. 10. 27 ~ 11. 6)

계엄기간중에 특별 단속기간을 설정하여 군, 검, 경 합동 단속반을 편성하여 68건 68명을 구속하고 1건 1명을 불구속 수사하였으며 동 우범자 41명을 즉심에 회부하고 미군인 20명을 소속대에 이첩하여 도합 130명을 단속하였음.

-10-

104

(나) 마약법위반 사범 및 기타 보건범죄

122건 141명

기지촌 주변에 산재하여 국민보건을 해하는 사범으로 습관성의약품관리법위반 사범 단속시 이에 관련하여 단속하였음.

(다) 문 제 점

본 사범단속중 문제점은

(1) 전국 각 농촌에서 광범위하게 재배되는 대마초에 대하여는 규제할수 없는점.

(2) 미군 A.P.O을 통하여 밀수입되는 루-트를 봉쇄할수 없는점 (L.S.D환각제)

(3) 감식장비가 없는점

다. 윤락행위등 방지법위반사범등 단속

기지촌주변에 산재하여 있는 윤락여성 및 그들에게서 기생하는 포주등을 단속하고 이에 파생되는 각종 전염병을 예방하기 위하여 한, 미합동으로

단속을 실시하고 있음

(1) 윤락여정 현황

의정부시	680명
동두천읍	2,100 〃
파 주	1,427 〃
기타지역	24 〃
합계	4,231명

(2) 포주 현황

의정부시	53 명
동두천읍	101 〃
파 주	180 〃
기타지역	91 〃
합 계	425 〃

~12~

106

(3) 단속 현황

윤락행위등방지법위반			전염병 예방법 위반		
1971년	1972년	증감율	1971년	1972년	증감율
758 명	773 명	2%증	787 명	977 명	24.1%증

전기와 같이 윤락행위등 방지법 위반사범은 계속 같이 추세를 유지할 가능성이 있어 포주들의 고리채등 착취행위가 계속될것이 예측되며 이에 따라 본 단속계획이 종료되는 75년도 까지는 이를 완전히 일소하기 위하여 구속을 원칙으로하여 수시 단속을 강화하고 위안부들은 귀가시키고 또는 독립하여 가정을 구성할 수 있도록 교육 및 선도 조치를 취한다.

(4) 문 제 점

(가) 환자 수용시설 부족

현 환자 수용시설능력은 동두천 40명 의정부

~13~

107

17명, 파주 60명 계 117명으로서 현재 낙검율 (한미합동배양검사 결과) 20%를 감안하면 840명 수용시설이 요구되어 723명의 수용시설이 부족되는 현상임

(나) 한국인 상대 창녀촌에 대한 무료검진 및 치료 대책이 없음.

(다) 보건소 지급약품으로 환자에게 적용되는 약품 사용곤란

(라) 혈청검사요원 부족

-14-

108

월별단속현황표

사범별 / 월별	보건범죄	강력사범	경제사범	퇴폐풍조사범	군용물등범죄사범	계
1						
2						
3						
4						
5						
6						
7						
8						
9						
10						
11						
12						

건의사항

1973. 2. 23

1 성병퇴치를 위한 건의

(1) 영내크라브에 특수업태부(윤락여성) 출입제한

영내크라브에 특수업태부가 매일 200명 이상이 출입함으로서

A. 전염병을 유발케하고 미검진자의 도피처로 되고있다

B. 전염병 예방 질서를 파괴한다.

C. 사병교육을 강화할것 (미검진자 및 보상청구등에 응하지 못하도록)

2. 대한민국 법을 준수하기위한 건의

(1) 부대측에 지나친 간섭지양

Report 없음

A. 연대장이 사병에게 명령하듯 부대측이 간섭이 심하다

B. 일방적으로 암행 검열을 하고 결과가 불량하다는 이유로 업소에 미군출입 금지 조치를 하여 주민들에게 큰 위협을 주고 있다

C. 카운타 물적 박스등을 샅샅히 뒤지고 복장, 명찰, 청소 부분까지 지시하는등 간섭이 심하다

D 흑백인에 싸움을 우리에게 책임이 있는양 전가함은 부당하다 (음악이 고르지 않다, 흑인과 춤을 추지 않는다는 등)

3. 검열, 미군 출입금지 조치 등은 한국 기관에 의해서만이 가능해야 한다

관광 휴양업자들의 결의사항

(1) 제1항이 시정되지 않으면 성병 퇴치가 불능함으로 특수업태부를 고용(가칭)치 않고 와이트레스 만을 고용 음료수 판매 사업만을 하겠다 (단 특수업태부의 해결문제는 당국이 책임져야 한다)

(2) 제2항이 관철되지 않으면 미군측의 엄연한 내정간섭 임으로 관철될때까지 산하 22개 관광 휴양업소는 자진 폐업 법질서가 회복될때까지 휴업한다

한국관광휴양업협회 양주지부

110

Report on the implementation of subcommittee recommendations -

US and ROK presentations

1. Recommendations

a. Adequate doses of penicillin, 4.8 million units, in treatment of VD in Korean special entertainers. (1.2 million unics of penicillin is quite inddequate)

b. Emphasis to register all special entertainers.

c. Improvement of sanitary environment in establishments

d. To ban the sale of antibiotics or tetracycline to US military personnel.

2. Implementations

To continue to emphasize forward in the project to clean up the base communities, Government has instructed to the city and provincial government on 17 January 1973 as follows:

a. Treatment

To conform to treat for Korean entertainers with adequate doses, 4.8 million units of penicillin.

b. Registration

In cooperation with the concerned organization,
- to suppress unregistered street walkers and register all special entertainers, and
- to check the VD examination certification card and follow-up the absentees for examination and treatment

c. Sanitation

To improve sanitary environment in facilities and operation of establishment, the establishments for the US military should be taken action for inspection of water and eradication of insects carrying the germs of communicable diseases.

d. Banning the antibiotics sale

On 22 January '73 Government instructed that Korean drug stores should not sell antibiotics and habitforming drugs to the US military personnel and if they disobey the order government will take a strong administrative action.

1. S.O.F.A 제16차 회의 (73.1.12 15:30)에서 건의된 사항을 다음과 같이 조치 하였기 보고합.

가. 건의 제목

1) 유병자에 대한 1.2백만단위 치료요법 시정

2) 미등록자 관리철저

3) 수질검사 철저

4) 항생제 판매금지

나. 조치사항

73년 1월 17자 기지주변 성병관리 철저를 기하기 위한 대책으로 다음과 같이 각시,도지사에게 강력히 지시 하였음.

1) 치료

유병자에 대하여 페니실린 4.8백만단위 치료요법을 철저히 준수할것을 지시.

2) 등록관리 철저

등록기피, 검진기피, 치료 기피자를 입소하기 위하여 관계기관의 협조를 얻어 강력히 단속토록 지시 하였음.

3) 음료수 수질개선

가) 73.1.18자로 기지촌지역 특수 유흥음식점에 대하여 수질검사 철저, 매기곤충 근접, 환경위생개선, 조치토록 지시 하였음.

4) 항생제 판매금지

73.1.22자로 의약품 판매업소에서 미군에게 항생제 판매금지토록 하였으며, 만약 위반업소는 강력한 행정조치를 취할것을 아울러 지시 하였음.

112

기 안 용 지

분류기호 문서번호	미이 723 -	(전화번호)	전결규정 조 항 국장 전결사항
처리기간			
시행일자	1973. 3. 19.		
보존년한		국 장	
보조기관	과 장		협조
기안책임자	양세훈	북미 2 과	
경유 수신 참조	내무부장관	발송	통제
제목	SOFA 합동위 군민관계 분과위 기지촌 시찰		

73. 3. 22. (목) 실시키로된 SOFA 군민관계 분과위의 미 8군사령부 및 이태원 일원 시찰과 관련하여, 귀부에서 현지에 대하여 답사에 필요한 제반 조치를 취하여 주시기 바라며, 아래와 같은 해당 지방관서의 관계관을 필히 참석시키도록 조치하여 주시기 바랍니다.

~~1. 서울시장~~

1. ~~2.~~ 용산구청장
2. ~~3.~~ 용산경찰서장
3. ~~4.~~ (용산관할) 보건소장 끝.

정서 관인 발송

공통서식 1-2(갑) 1967. 4. 4. 승인

190mm × 268mm (1급인쇄용지 70g/m²) 조달청 (500,000매인쇄)

113

기 안 용 지

분류기호 문서번호	미이 723 -	(전화번호)	전결규정 조 항 국장 전결사항
처리기간			
시행일자	1973. 3. 19.		
보존년한			국 장
보조기관	과 장		협조
기안책임자	양세훈	북미 2 과	
경 유 수 신 참 조	수신처 참조	발신 1973. 3. 20 외무부	통제 1973. 3. 20
제 목	SOFA 합동위 군민관계 분위의 기지촌 시찰 통보		

73. 3. 16. 제 18차 SOFA 한미 합동위 군민관계 임시 분과위 회의에서의 합의에 따라 다음과 같이 한미합동 기지촌 현지 답사를 실시키로 하였으니, 각 위원들은 필히 참석하시기 바랍니다.

1. 일 시 : 73. 3. 22. (목) 1700 - 2100
2. 장 소 : 서울 용산소재 미 8군사령부 및 이태원 일원
3. 집합장소 : 8th Army Officers' Club
4. 비 고 : 당일 1700 시부터 미측의 브리핑에 이어 한미 양측 간에 의견교환이 있으니 필요한 자료를 준비하여 주시고, 브리핑 시작 5분전까지 필히 도착하여 주시기 바람.

첨부 : 1. 일정표 1 부.
2. 위원명단 1 부. 끝.

정서 / 관인 / 발송

공통서식1-2(갑) 1967. 4. 4. 승인 190mm×268mm(1급인쇄용지70g/㎡) 조달청 (500,000매인쇄)

114

수신처 : 내무부장관 (지방국장, 치안국장)

법무부장관 (검찰국장)

교통부장관

보건사회부장관

문화공보부장관

청와대 정무수석비서관 (내무.보사담당 비서관)

115

분류 지급

기 안 용 지

분류기호 문서번호	미이 723 -	(전화번호)	전결규정 조 항 국장 전결사항
처리기간			
시행일자	1973. 3. 21.		
보존년한			국 장
보조기관	과 장		협조
기안책임자	양세훈	북미 2 과	
경유 수신 참조	서울특별시장	발신 1973. 3. 21	통제 검열 1973 3 21
제 목	SOFA 합동위 군민관계 분위의 기지촌 시찰에 따른 협조		

1. 제 18차 SOFA 한미 합동위원회 군민관계 분과위 회의에서의 합의에 따라 한미합동 기지촌 현지답사를 별첨과 같이 실시키로 되었읍니다.

2. 금반 시찰은 주한미군 주둔지역 주변의 환경 정화사업의 일환으로 한미 양측 관계위원들 (별첨 명단)이 현지답사를 행하는 것인바, 아래와 같은 해당 지방관서의 관계관의 참석이 요망되오니 필히 참석토록 조치하여 주시기 바랍니다.

가. 용산구청장

나. 용산경찰서장

다. 용산 관할 보건소장

첨부 : 1. 시찰계획 1 부.

2. 위원명단 1 부. 끝.

정서 / 관인 / 발송

공통서식1-2(갑)
1967. 4. 4. 승인

190mm × 268mm (1급인쇄용지70g/m²)
조달청 (500,000매 인쇄)

116

Proposed Schedule for Ad Hoc Subcommittee Trip
to Yongsan Garrison-Itaewon
Thursday, 22 March 1973

1700-1830	Discussion with US and ROK Authorities at Yongsan.
1830-1930	Dinner at Yongsan.
1930-2100	Tour of Itaewon Club Area.

117

Schedule for Ad Hoc Subcommittee Trip
to Yongsan Garrison-Itaewon
Thursday, 22 March 1973

1700-1830	Discussion with US and ROK Authorities at Yongsan.
1830-1930	Dinner at Yongsan.
1930-2100	Tour of Itaewon Club Area.

118

SOFA 군민관계 분과위원회 위원명단

의장	이상훈	외무부	북미 2과장
위원	백세현	내무부	관리과장
"	이병모	치안국	총경
"	이해구	"	"
"	현홍주	법무부	검사
"	박회대	"	"
"	김철용	교통부	진흥과장
"	김주환	보사부	만성병담당관
"	김명섭	문공부	해외공보관 외보과장
"	장석환	청와대	내무.보사담당 비서관
간사	양세훈	외무부	북미 2과 서기관

119

기 안 용 지

분류기호 문서번호	미이 723 -	(전화번호)	전결규정 조 항 국장 전결사항
처리기간			
시행일자	1973. 4. 2.		
보존년한			국 장
보조기관	과 장		협 조
기안책임자	양세훈	북미 2 과	
경유 수신 참조	수신처 참조	발신	통제
제 목	기지촌 군민관계에 관한 진정		

1102
1973 4. 3
외무부

(제 1안)

한국 관광유양업협회 (서울시 중구 을지로 4가 310번지 소재)는 별첨과 같이 동두천지역 미군부대 처사의 부당성과 이의 시정을 건의하여 왔으므로 조회하오니 검토후 귀견을 회신하여 주시기 바랍니다.

첨부 : 건의서 사본 1통. 끝.

수신처 : 내무부장관 (지방국장, 치안국장)
법무부장관 (검찰국장)
교통부장관 (관광국장)
보사부장관 (보건국장)

(제 2안)

수신 : 한국 관광유양업 협회 회장

제목 : 건의서 처리 회신

정서 | 관인 | 발송

공통서식1-2(갑)
1967. 4. 4. 승인

190mm ×268mm (1급인쇄용지70g/m²)
조달청 (300,000매인쇄)

120

:대 : 관유협 제46호 및 제46 - 1호

:귀 협회가 제출하신 동두천지역 미군부대 처사에 관한 건의서는

당부 및 관계부처에서 검토중이오며, 동 검토가 끝나는대로 조치내용을

알려드리고저 하오니 양지하시기 바랍니다. 끝.

121

기결 ⑫ 3/31.

한 국 관 광 휴 양 업 협 회

서울시 중구 을지로 4가 310번지

삼풍 빌딩816호실

관휴협제 46호 (26-1181-9의 372번) 1973. 3. 23

수 신 한미 합동군민 관계 분과위원회(SAHA)

제 목 건의서

기지촌 정화를 위하여 주야로 노고하시는 귀 위원회에 대하여 깊은 감사를 드립니다.

당협회 산하 회원은 미군 기지촌에서 주한유엔군 전용의 관광휴양업을 경영하고 있으며 유엔군의 휴양에 손색이 없는 시설과 각종 주류를 염가로 제공하여 최대의 써-비스로서 봉사하고 있읍니다. 그런데 요즘 동두천 지역 미군부대에서 다음과 같은 부당한 처사를 하고 있어 이의 시정을 건의하오니 빠른 시일내에 시정조치하여 주시옵기 간절히 바라나이다.

다 음

1. 한국인 윤락여성을 영내 크라부에 대거 유치하고 있읍니다.

숙녀를 영내에 초청한다는 이유로 매일 저녁 윤락여성 200여명을 버스 또는 도보로 영내 크라부에 유치하고 있는바

영내에는 방역당국의 단속이 미치지 못하고있어 검진 미필자의 도피처가 됨으로 성병 전염자가 많이 발생하게 될것이며 또한 해피스모크등 마약 판매의 안전 루-트가 되고 있읍니다.

그럼에도 성병에 걸리면 그책임을 우리휴양업자에게 전가시켜 출입금지등 부당한 조치를 취하고 있읍니다.

122

외 무 부	30 MAR '73 13:39
접수일시	197
번호	10981
처리과	
담당자	
결	. . 까지 처리할것

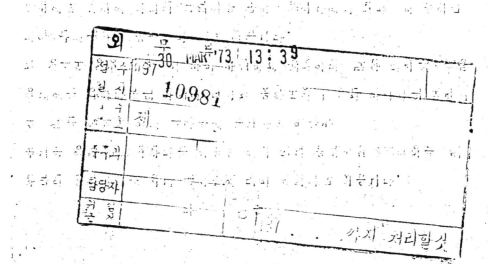

2. 관광휴양업소에 대하여 지나친 간섭

가. 관광휴양업소에 대하여 수시로 암행 검열을 하고 있으며 한국기관 이나 우리업자의 허명도 듣지 않고 일반적으로 미군출입 금지조치 를 취하고 있읍니다.

나. MP、CP、 들이 수시로 업소에 들어와 종업원의 패스 명찰등을 조사하고 카운타 바 뮤-직 박스를 샅사치 뒤지고 있읍니다. 끝.

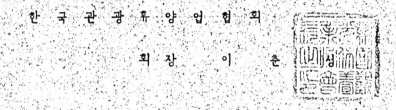

한 국 관 광 휴 양 업 협 회

회 장 이 춘

(23

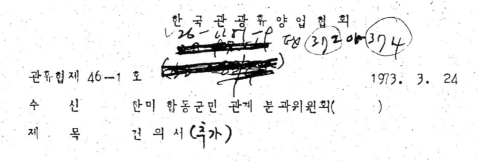

한 국 관 광 휴 양 업 협 회

[redacted] 대 312 에 374

관휴협제 46―1 호 [redacted] 1973. 3. 24

수　　신　　한미 합동군민 관계 분과위원회(　　)

제　　목　　건 의 서 (추가)

관휴협제 46호(73. 3. 23) 로 제출한바 있는 건의서에 대한 보완자료로서 사실을 증명할수 있는 현장사진을 추가로 제출합니다.　끝.

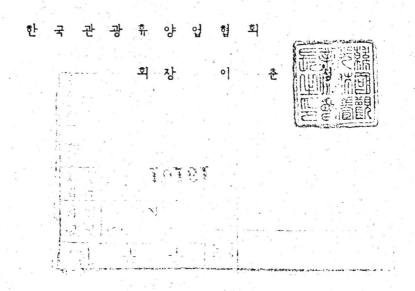

한 국 관 광 휴 양 업 협 회

회 장　　이　　춘

124

외 무 부		결재	
접수 일시	19 . . . 시 분	기	
접수 번호	10161		
주무			
협조			
공람			

[illegible]

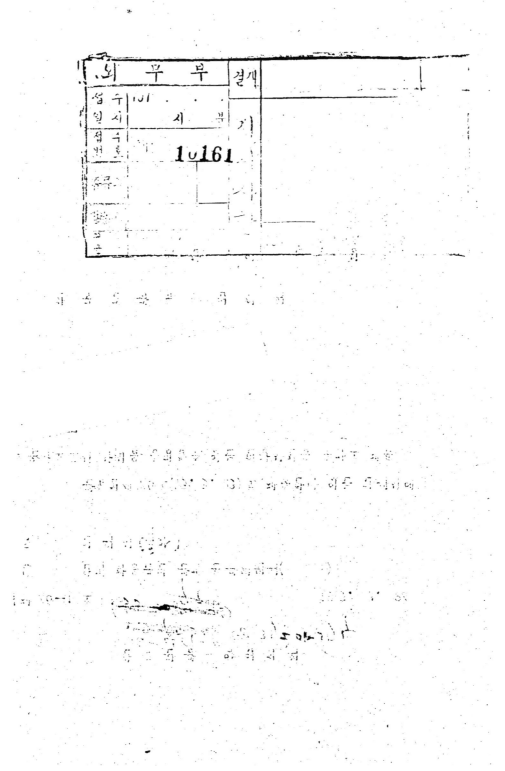

윤락 여성 단체 사무실 앞에서 크라브 차량에 윤락 여성들을 대거 싣고 있다.

125 윤락여성들이 도보로 영내 크라브로 들어가고 있다.

윤락 여성 단체 사무실 앞에서 크라브 차량에 윤락 여성들을 대거 싣고 있다.

125 윤락여성들이 도보로 영내 크라브로 들어가고 있다.

3213

한 국 관 광 휴 양 업 협 회

서울시 중구을지로4가 310번지

삼풍빌딩 816호실

28 6288

관휴협제 46 호 (26-1181-9의 372번) 1973. 3. 30

수 신 한미합동군민 관계 분과위원회( )

제 목 건 의 서

기지촌 정화를 위하여 수야로 노고하시는 귀 위원회에 대하여 깊은 감사를 드립니다.

당협회 산하 회원은 미군 기지촌에서 주한유엔군 전용의 관광휴양업을 경영하고 있으며 유엔군의 휴양에 손색이 없는 시설과 각종 주류를 염가로 제공하여 최대의 써-비스로서 봉사하고 있읍니다. 그런데 동두천 및 부평지역 미군부대에서 다음과 같은 부당한 처사를 하고 있어 이의 시정을 건의 하오니 빠른 시일내에 시정조치하여 주시옵기 간절히 바라나이다.

다 음

1. 동두천 지역

가. 한국인 윤락여성을 영내 크라부에 대거 유치하고 있읍니다.

숙녀를 영내에 초청한다는 이유로 매일 저녁 윤락여성 200여명을 뻐스 또는 도보로 영내 크라부에 유치하고 있는바

영내에서는 방역당국의 단속이 미치지 못하고 있어 검진 미필자의 도피처가 됨으로 성병 전염자가 많이 발생하게 될것이며 또한 해피스모크등 마약 판매의 안전 루-트가 되고 있읍니다.

그럼에도 성병에 걸리면 그책임을 우리휴양업자에게 전가시켜 출입금지등 부당한 조치를 취하고 있읍니다.

126

외 무 부	
번 수	137
일 시	6 APR '73 16:28
	11925
주무	
담당자	

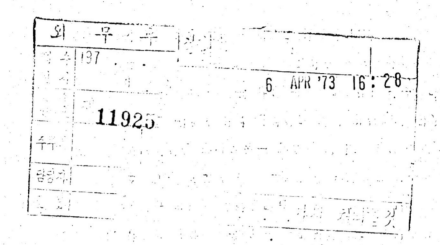

나. 관광휴양업소에 대하여 지나친 간섭

(1) 관광휴양업소에 대하여 수시로 암행 검열을 하고 있으며 한국기관이나 우리업자의 해명도 듣지 않고 일반적으로 미군출입 금지조치를 취하고 있읍니다.

(2) MP-cp. 들이 수시로 업소에 들어와 종업원의 패스 명찰등을 조사하고 카운타 뮤-직 박스를 샅샅치 뒤지고 있읍니다. 끝.

2. 부평지역

각업소마다 cp. 2명씩 고정배치하여 (부대와 직통 전화도 가설해 놓고있음) 미군의 출입을 제한 또는 감시하고 있읍니다. 끝.

한 국 관 광 휴 양 업 협 회

회 장 이 춘

북미2과	공람	73년 4월 9일	담당	과장	국장	참관	차관	장관
			(서명)	(서명)				

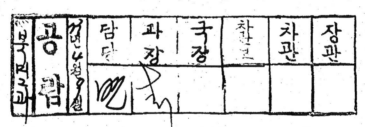

3.23자 동일 내용의 진정서 接受하여, 關係部處에 意見問議하였으며 陳情業所에 對하여도 一次 回信하였음. 4/9 (서명)

1217

Mr. Jang

내 무 부

외사 2068 - 2422 1973. 4. 10.

수신 외무부 장관

제목 기지촌 군민관계에 관한 진정

미이 723-11024 (73. 4. 3.) 기지촌 군민관계에 관한 진정과 관련된것으로서 동두천지역 미군부대 처사의 부당성과 시정건의사항은 관계부처 (교통부, 보사부) 에서 처리함이 타당하다고 사료됩니다.

끝.

내 무 부 장 관

정부공문서규정제27조 제2항의규정에의하여 외사과장 김봉곤 전결

발송 No. 1973. 4. 10. 내무부

128

접수 일시	197 . . APR '73 14:00
접수 번호	12933
주무	

지급

기 안 용 지

분류기호 문서번호	미이 723 -	(전화번호)	전결규정 9 조 2 항 국장 전결사항
처리기간			
시행일자	1973. 5. 4.	국 장	
보존년한			
보조기관	과 장		협조
기안책임자	양세훈	북미 2 과	
경유 수신 참조	수신처 참조	발신 1973 5. 4 15494	통제 검열 1973 5 4
제목	SOFA 군민관계 분과위의 긴급 현지답사		

최근 송탄읍 소재 미군기지 주변에서의 폭행사건 및 미군당국의 일부 지역에 대한 출입금지 조치등 (별첨 참조)과 관련하여, SOFA 군민관계 임시분과위 미국측 의장은 사실조사 및 대책강구를 위한 긴급 현지답사를 제의하여 왔으므로 양측 협의끝에 아래와 같이 실시키로 되었으니 귀부소속 위원들로 하여금 필히 참가토록 조치하여 주시기 바랍니다.

1. 일 시 : 73. 5. 8 (화) 09:30 시 출발
2. 장 소 : 경기도 평택군 송탄읍
3. 집합장소 : 동일 08:50시까지 중앙청 동편광장 관용주차장

(내무부) 상기답사와 관련하여 현지 관계관의 참석등 필요한 제반 조치를 취하여 주시기 바랍니다.

첨부 : 미군당국 서한 사본 1통. 끝.

수신처 : 내무부장관 (지방국장, 치안국장)

정서 / 관인 / 발송

공통서식1-2(갑) 1967. 4. 4. 승인

190mm×268mm (1급인쇄용지70g/㎡) 조달청 (500,000매인쇄)

129

법무부장관 (~~법무실장~~, 검찰국장, ~~출입국관리국장~~)

보건사회부장관 (보건국장)

교통부장관 (관광국장)

문화공보부장관 (공보국장)

청와대 정무수석비서관 (내무.보사담당 비서관)

130

DEPARTMENT OF THE AIR FORCE
HEADQUARTERS AIR FORCES KOREA/314TH AIR DIVISION
APO SAN FRANCISCO 96570

MEMO FROM THE OFFICE OF
THE COMMANDER

TO: DATE:

Gen Smith:

It is my personal goal to force the ROK to accept their responsibility for providing security. I feel that the quantity and professional quality of the KNP in (Chiri Vill) leaves a lot to be desired. Would appreciate any help you could give.

T. R. McNEIL
Brig General USAF

Mac

HEADQUARTERS AIR FORCES KOREA
UNITED NATIONS COMMAND
APO SAN FRANCISCO 96570

26 April 1973
1973. 4. 26

REPLY TO ATTN OF: SS 사안공

SUBJECT: Security and Protection - Songtan-Up, Korea
송 탄 읍 내 에서 보 안 과 보 호

TO: Superintendent Yun, Cho Yung
총 경 윤 조 영 서 장

Over the past several months, I have become increasingly concerned
과거 수개월간에 걸쳐서 본인은 평택군 송탄읍 (쉬 콜) 내에서
about the numerous assaults and other criminal acts directed towards
수 많은 폭행사건과 기타 각종의 범죄행위가 미국 군인들에게 가하여
United States Armed Forces personnel in Songtan-Up (Chicol Ville),
지는 사실에 대하여 깊은 관심을 가지게 되었읍니다. 예를 들면
Korea. Last week, for example, that section of Chicol Ville known as
지난 주일에 송탄읍 쉬콜에 소재한 소위 파파죠 라고 불리지는 골목
Papa Joe Alley was declared off-limits to all Armed Forces personnel
구역 일대에 앞으로 30 일간을 모든 미국 군인들에게 그 구역의 출입
for a period of thirty (30) days because of the high risk of harm to those
을 금지하도록 공포하였읍니다. 그 이유는 동구역에 출입하는 자들은 피
entering that section. It is quite possible that other areas or business
해를 받을 위험이 있기때문입니다. 앞으로 다른 구역이나 또는 관광접객
establishments will be similarly placed off-limits in the future.
업소에도 출입금지령을 내릴 가능성은 다분히 있는것입니다.
Unless Chicol Ville is kept a safe place for United States servicemen
송탄읍내가 미국 군인들이 안심하고 출입할수있는 장소로 계속 유지않는
to visit, I shall have no option but to forbid my men from entering the
다면 본인은 모든 미군들의 송탄읍 출입을 전적으로 금지하는 방법외에
village altogether.
다른 도리가 없읍니다.

132

I am particularly concerned that inadequate lighting conditions exist
본인은 송탄읍내의 가로등 시설이 불충분하여 특히 관광 접객업소가
throughout the village, especially in the alleys near the nightclubs.
위치한 부근 골목길의 보안등에 특히 관계되는 것입니다. 거의 매일
Almost daily I learn that many of the street lights are not functioning
본인은 많은 가로등이 제대로 작동을 하지 않고 있는것을 알고있읍니다.
because bulbs have not been replaced after local officials have been
그 사유는 적시에. 본인의 휘하 헌병들이 관계 지방 관공서원에 그 사
timely advised by my military policemen. I also find that bar owners
실을 통보하여도 전구를 갈아 끼우지 않는데 있읍니다. 그리고 또 관
provide no security or protection for the safety of patrons, and, when an
광업소의 주인들이 고객의 안전을 위하여 보안이나 또는 보호조치를 하지
assault or affray occurs, no assistance to innocent victims is rendered.
않으며 폭행사건 또는 난동이 발생시에 선의의 피해자를 도와주지 않는다는
I cannot and will not condone such action in the future.
사실을 알았으며 이러한 행위는 앞으로 본인이 묵과 하지않을것입니다.

Most seriously, I believe that there are too few Korean National Police-
본인이 가장 심각하게 생각하는것은 송탄읍 주민 50,000 명이 넘는 도시에
men allotted to this village of over 50,000 inhabitants. My officials have
너무나 적은 경찰병력을 배정하였다고 믿고 있읍니다. 본인 휘하의 관계
repeatedly requested added protection. To date, the response has not
관이 계속하여 보다더 좋은 보호를 요청하였읍니다. 오늘 현재까지 그에
been satisfactory.
대한 조치는 만족하지 못하였읍니다.

I have always enjoyed working with you for the betterment of the Chicol'
본인은 항상 오산기지와 송탄읍의 공동사회의 향상을 위하여 즐거이
Ville-Osan Air Base community. I have the deepest personal respect for
일을 하여왔읍니다. 본인은 귀하가 본인 휘하의 군인들이 귀관하에 있음

2

1335

your desire to protect my servicemen while in your area, but we must
때 그들을 보호하려고 노력하는데 대하여 개인적으로 깊이 존경하고 있읍니다
now increase efforts to institute protective measures and assure safety
그러나 우리들은 지금 보다많은보호조치를 수립실시하여 송탄읍내의 안전을
in Chicol Ville.
확보하여만 되겠읍니다.

I regard the situation as serious. I hope that the drastic step of for-
본인은 현상태가 심각하다고 사료합니다. 본인은 미국 군인들이 송탄읍내
bidding my servicemen from entering the village will not occur.
에 출입금지하는 강력한 조치가 다시 없기를 바라는 바입니다.

I would be pleased to learn what additional steps are being taken by
본인은 송탄읍에서 추가적으로 취한 조치와 귀하의 경찰이 송탄읍내를
the Korean community and your personnel to make Chicol Ville a safer
보다더 안전하게 하기위하여 실시한 사항이 있으면 알려주시면 감사히 여기
place.
겠읍니다.

Sincerely
경 구

T. R. MCNEIL, Brig Gen, USAF
Commander
사 단 장
미공군준장 티. 알. 맥 닐

Copy to:
CINCUNC/USFK
APO 96301

134

PAGE 2 RUADMBA0033 UNCLAS

RUYNWGA/CTU 75.4.1

RUWTEJA/USAFSS/DOC

RUEOIAA/DIRNSA ATTN: RNI

BT

UNCLAS JPCCO/JOPREP JIFFY/PINNACLE/001/314ADCP/

OPREP-3/001

H. ASSULT

H1. VOICE 02/1616/MAY 73
H2. 02/1455/MAY/1973

H3. N/A

H4. AT 2355I A CAUC AIRMAN ASSIGNED TO 51ST AIR POLICE WAS STABED IN THE STOMACH AT THE ALOHA CLUB CHICOL VILLAGE, HE WAS ASSULTED BY MALE KOREAN NATIONAL. VICTOM IN USAF HOSP OSAN BEING TRANS TO YONGSAN HOSP. POSSIBLE STOMACH LINING PUNCTURE. 3 KOREAN WITNESS AND 2 AMERICAN WITNESS WITH DESCRIPTION. KNP AND OSI INVESTIGATING ALL FURTHER REPORTS THROUGH THE CHANNELS.

(007 WAS LAST NBR OF MONTH OF APR 73)

Z. 02/1615Z

BT

#0033

TOR-1646

05-0802

135

협 조 문

용신기일

분류기호 및 문서번호	미이 723 - 45	제 목	직원 국내 출장
수 신	총무과장	발신일자	1973. 5. 5. (협조제의)

북미2과	[illegible] 고재	73년 5월 일	담당	과장	국장	차관보	차관	장관

발신명의 미주국장

(제 1 의 견)

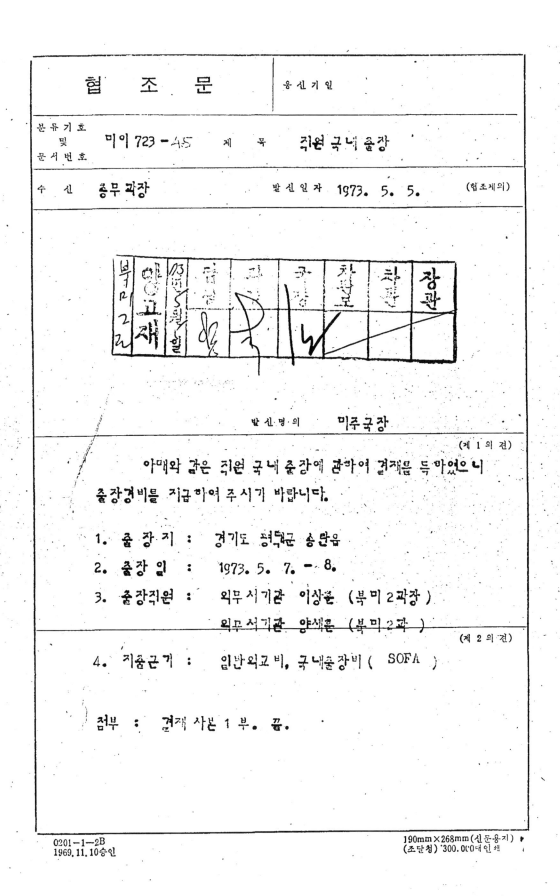

아래와 같은 직원 국내 출장에 관하여 결재를 득하였으니 출장경비를 지급하여 주시기 바랍니다.

1. 출 장 지 : 경기도 평택군 송탄읍
2. 출 장 일 : 1973. 5. 7. - 8.
3. 출장직원 : 외무사기관 이상훈 (북미 2과장)
   외무서기관 양세훈 (북미 2과)

(제 2 의 견)

4. 지출근거 : 일반외교비, 국내출장비 (SOFA)

첨부 : 결재 사본 1 부. 끝.

0201-1-2B
1969.11.10승인

190mm×268mm(신문용지)
(조달청) 300,0?0매인쇄

136

기 안 용 지

분류기호 문서번호	미이 723 -	(전화번호)	전결규정 조 항 자관 전결사항
처리기간			
시행일자	1973. 5. 5.		
보존년한		차관	

보조기관	차관보		협조	동무과장
	국 장			
	과 장			
기안책임자	양세훈	북미 2 과		

경유 수신 참조	내부결재	발신		통제	
제 목	직원 출장				

최근 송탄읍 소재 미군기지 주변에서 발생한 폭행사건 및 미군 당국의 일부지역 출입금지 조치등 기지촌에서의 불상사와 관련하여, SOFA 군민관계 분과위원회 미국측 의장은 사실조사 및 대책강구를 위한 긴급 현지답사 실시를 제의하여 왔으므로, 아래와 같이 관계직원을 출장시킬것을 건의합니다.

1. 출장직원 : 이상훈 북미 2과장 (동 분위 한국측 의장)
   양세훈 서기관 (동 분위 간사)
2. 출장일시 : 1973. 5. 7. (월) - 8. (화)
3. 출 장 지 : 경기도 평택군 송탄읍

참고 : 동 분과위원회는 현재까지 총 20회에 걸쳐 기지촌 시찰을 실시한바 있으며, 한국측으로서는 관계부처 관계위원 및 현지 관계관들이 참석하여 왔음.

정서 / 관인 / 발송

1375

공통서식1-2(갑) 1967. 4. 4. 승인

190mm×268mm (1급인쇄용지70g/㎡) 조달청 (500,000매 인쇄)

1375

참 고 사 항

1. 5. 2. 송탄읍의 관광업소 클럽에서 한국인에 의하여 미 공군 헌병이 복부 자상, 현 한미 합동으로 조사 진행중.

2. 미군당국은 30일간 미군인의 일부지역 출입금지 조치 및 차후 전지역 금지조치 경고.

3. 오산기지 주둔 미군당국 서한에서 제시된 문제점

(1) 과거 수개월간 미군인에 대한 수많은 폭행사건 및 범죄행위 발생

(2) 가로등 시설 불충분

(3) 수차 통고에도 불구하고 보안등 정비불량

(4) 관광업소의 고객 안전 조치 전무

(5) 송탄읍 주민 5만에 비하여 한국 경찰 병력 소수 배치

(6) 미군인에 대한 보호 조치 촉구하였으나 만족한 조치 전무

(7) 경찰당국의 실시사항 통보 요망

138

한.미 합동 기지촌 시찰

1.	1971. 9. 10.	동두천	Camp Casey
2.	1971. 9. 13.	평택군 안정리	Camp Humphreys
3.	1971. 9. 24.	평택군 송탄읍	Osan Air Base
4.	1971. 9. 28.	대구	Camp Henry Walker
5.	1971. 9. 30.	부평	ASCOM
6.	1971. 10. 7.	군산	Kunsan Air Base
7.	1971. 10. 28.	이태원, 용산	
8.	1971. 11. 14. - 15.	부산	Hialeah Compound
9.	1971. 11. 30.	파주군	
10.	1971. 12. 3.	대전	Camp Ames
11.	1972. 2. 25.	평택군 안정리	Camp Humphreys
12.	1972. 3. 30.	동두천	Camp Casey
13.	1972. 5. 1.	부평	ASCOM
14.	1972. 5. 10.	춘천	Camp Page
15.	1972. 6. 2.	왜관	Camp Carroll
16.	1972. 6. 9.	진해, 마산	44th Eng Bn
17.	1973. 1. 30.	의정부	
18.	1973. 2. 5.	평택	Camp Humphreys
19.	1973. 2. 5.	송탄읍	Osan Air Base
20.	1973. 2. 23.	동두천	Camp Casey
21.	1973. 3. 22.	이태원, 용산	
22.	1973. 5. 7.	평택군 송탄읍	Osan Air Base

오산 미 공군기지 주변 군.민 관계

[1973.5.7]

가. 문제의 제기

(1) 오산기지 관광업소 근처의 각종 범죄증가와 흑백 인종 차별로 인한 충돌 빈번으로 사태 악화 경향.

(2) 5. 2. 오산기지 (송탄읍)주변 관광업소 클럽에서 한국인 (군인)과 미공군 헌병이 충돌, 미공군 헌병이 복부자상, 현 한.미 합동조사중.

(3) 미군당국은 30일간 미군인의 일부지역 출입금지 조치 및 차후 전지역 금지조치 경고.

나. 한.미 합동 현지답사

5. 7. SOFA 군.민관계 분과위원회의 현지답사 및 미측 요구에 대한 일차적 조치

(1) 경찰관 증원 (현 33 + 6 = 39)

(2) 가로등 증설 (현 123 + 169 = 292)

(3) 관광업소내 경찰관 고정배치 강구

(4) 현 업소들의 위치이전, 신규업소 허가억제, 송탄읍의 시승격등 미측 요구사항에 대한 연구 검토.

140

다. 문 제 점

(1) 미군인 자신들의 흑백 분규에 한국인 관광업소 및 개인이 개재.

(2) 미하원 외무위 아시아.태평양지역 분과위원장인 Robert N. C. Nix (흑인)는 72년 평택에서의 한국인과 흑인 충돌사건과 관련, 한국이 흑인에 대한 인종차별을 한다는 인식을 가진바 있어, 사태의 재발은 군원심의에도 악영향 우려.

라. 대 책

(1) 사태 악화전에 수습 필요

(2) 주요 조치방안 :

(가) 송탄읍의 행정강화를 위한 시승격 조치 요망

(나) 관광업소 소재 주변의 도로망 확장

(다) 송탄읍 관광업소 신규허가시의 위치등 환경조건 참작 요망

(141)

Feb 73 Assaults 5-7 / 3 KNP >

Courtesy Patrol Teams

Steps taken (Letter to Senior Supt. Yun — KNP added temporarily

Results of Uniform Policy **참 고 사 항**

~~Mad~~ Reduced Population

Behave Better

Discrimination

1. 5. 2. 송탄읍의 관광업소 골목에서 한국인에 의하여 미 공군 헌병이 부부 자상, 현 한미 합동으로 조사 진행중.

2. 미군당국은 30일간 미군인의 일부지역 출입금지 조치 및 차후 전지역 금지조치 경고.

3. 오산기지 주둔 미군당국 서한에서 제시된 문제점

(1) 과거 수개월간 미군인에 대한 수많은 폭행사건 및 범죄 행위 발생

(2) 가로등 시설 불충분 Lighting conditions

(3) 수차 통고에도 불구하고 보안등 정비불량 street lights not functioning

(4) 관광업소의 고객 안전 조치 전무 security or protection provide

(5) 송탄읍 주민 5만에 비하여 한국 경찰 병력 소수 배치 KNP allotted to over 50,000 inhabitants

(6) 미군인에 대한 보호 조치 촉구하였으나 만족한 조치 전무 repeatedly requested added protection

(7) 경찰당국의 실시사항 통보 요망

		GI&KN	GI
Number Assaults (72.7-73.5)	101	44	57

Western Village — 뒷골목, 폭행사건 유발 — Club 허가문제

Papa Joe Alley — perpetrators impossible to catch

Discrimination (72.11.2. 사건) not satisfactory to our standard

142

한.미 합동 기지촌 시찰

1.	1971. 9. 10.	동두천	Camp Casey
2.	1971. 9. 13.	평택군 안정리	Camp Humphreys
3.	1971. 9. 24.	평택군 송탄읍	Osan Air Base
4.	1971. 9. 28.	대구	Camp Henry Walker
5.	1971. 9. 30.	부평	ASCOM
6.	1971. 10. 7.	군산	Kunsan Air Base
7.	1971. 10. 28.	이태원, 용산	
8.	1971. 11. 14 - 15.	부산	Hialeah Compound
9.	1971. 11. 30.	파주군	
10.	1971. 12. 3.	대전	Camp Ames
11.	1972. 2. 25.	평택군 안정리	Camp Humphreys
12.	1972. 3. 30.	동두천	Camp Casey
13.	1972. 5. 1.	부평	ASCOM
14.	1972. 5. 10.	춘천	Camp Page
15.	1972. 6. 2.	왜관	Camp Carroll
16.	1972. 6. 9.	진해, 마산	44th Eng Bn
17.	1973. 1. 30.	의정부	
18.	1973. 2. 5.	평택	Camp Humphreys
19.	1973. 2. 5.	송탄읍	Osan Air Base
20.	1973. 2. 23.	동두천	Camp Casey

143

1973. 5.

케이-55 기지촌 주변 환경 정화 대책

명 택 경 찰 서 장

144

1. 현황

가. 기지촌 실태

순위	구분	현황	비고
1	인구	53,548	
2	세대수	7,031	
3	주둔미군인	4,500	
4	한국군인	1,887	
5	미군부대종업원	1,925	
6	위안부	1,043	
7	우범자	65	
8	관광홀	12	
9	여관	28	
10	하숙옥	11	
11	극장	3	
12	다방	15	
13	당구장	8	
14	고물상	80	

145

케이-55 [illegible]촌 72. 73. 년도 범죄 발[illegible] 현황

죄종별	년도별	계	월누계	1	2	3	4	5	6	7	8	9	10	11	12
계	72	1696	1439	342	415	362	320	403	382	379	363	388	392	511	439
	73		1387	398	353	346	290								
	대비		-52	+56	-62	-16	-30								
강력	72	6	2		1	1		1	1		1		1		
	73		1	1											
	대비		-1	±1	≐1	-1									
폭력	72	309	128	22	39	39	28	25	31	18	29	13	25	21	19
	73		54	15	16	9	24								
	대비		-74	-7	-23	-30	-4								
도범	72	172	62	20	14	13	15	11	11	16	10	12	17	19	14
	73		53	15	18	10	10								
	대비		-9	-5	+4	-3	-5								
한미	72	99	20	4	7	3	6	12	9	11	13	16	7	6	5
	73		26	5	5	6	10								
	대비		+6	+1	-2	*3	+4								
마약	72	39	7	3	2	1	1	6		2	4	3	8	4	5
	73		8	4	1	2	1								
	대비		+1	+1	-1	+1									
기타	72	361	119	29	26	36	28	47	26	21	47	19	22	29	31
	73		109	37	27	21	24								
	대비		=10	+8	+1	-15	-4								
특별	72	3710	1101	264	326	269	242	301	304	311	259	326	312	432	315
	73		1136	321	286	298	231								
	대비		+35	+57	-40	+29	-11								

46

3. 대책

항목	세부 실천 사항	비 고
가. 경찰관증원	(1) 현재경찰관 배치수 송탄지서 24명	현원 24명
	(2) 증원요망(경위1.순경5)6명증원 30명으로	증원6명
	(3) 전담반 5.오에스아이 2. 엠피2	총계 39명.
나. 순찰강화	(1) 기존2개 순찰선 정선 순찰을	심야뒷골목난선
	(2) 1개선 증설 3개선으로 재책정 난선순찰로	순찰위주
	(3) 방범 싸이카 2대배치 우범지역기동순찰	3회를 5회로
	(4) 심야 기동 순찰 강화 실시	
다. 고정배치	(1) 사고빈발 우범지역 6개소 선정	바바죠 삼성 금강
	(2) 정복 경찰 2인1조 6개조 편성	아로아 카네기 오비
	(3) 매월 19시부터 24시까지 고정배치	2인1조 계 12명.
라. 방범대원활용	(1) 기존 대원 11명을 3명증원 계 14명	기존 대원 11명.
	(2) 경찰관 합동 근무	증원 3 명.
		계 14명.
마. 방범등 증설	(1) 기존시설 123 신설 69현재 192 개소 인바 증설 100개예정	계 292
바 방범시책 강화	(1) 방범위원회 개최 매월 1회 (송탄지서 주관)	협의
	(2) 위안부 교양계도 실시 매월 1회)송탄지서 주관)	보건소
	(3) 관광업자 회의 매월 1회(송탄지서 주관)	보안과 군 사회과
사. 집중단속	(1) 케이-55 기지촌 우범지역에 대한 집중 단속 실시	본서원 갑을부편성
	(2) 검문검색 입검 우범자 전과자 동태파악단속	2부제로 실시 19시30분 송탄집결

147

항 목	세부 실천 사항	비고
	(3) 단속 대상 가. 폭력사범 치기배 나. 부량아 및 우범분자 다. 윤락 및 청객 뗌프 행위자 라. 악질 포주 업자 마. 타락행위자 및 유흥업소 바. 퇴폐풍조 사범 사. 통금 위반자 아. 기타 보안사범.	
무허가 주점단속	(1) 삼성 바바조홀 주변에 산재한 무허가 주점	8개소
	(2) 기타 홀 주변에도 계속 단속	

148

List of Participants

√ LEE Sang Hoon

√ BAEK Se Hyun

√ HYUN Hong Joo √ Shin Hong On

~~PARK Hee Tae~~

√ KIM Chul Yong

~~KIM Ju Whan~~

√ ~~MYUNG Joong Sup~~ (for Superintendent LEE Byung Mo)

√ YOO Myung Doo

√ YANG Sei Hoon

이재창 도경찰국장

도경찰국 경찰서장

신 경기도경 형사과장

149

Trip to Osan Air Base-Songtan-Eup
7 May 1973

ROK Component

Mr. LEE Sang Hoon
Chief, North America Division II
American Affairs Bureau
Ministry of Foreign Affairs

Mr. BAEK Se Hyun
Chief, Management Section
Bureau of Local Administration
Ministry of Home Affairs

Mr. ~~PARK Hee Taeg~~ Shin Chang On
~~Prosecutor, Claims Section~~
~~Legal Affairs Office, MOJ~~

Mr. HYUN Hong Joo
Prosecutor, Prosecution Section
Bureau of Prosecution, MOJ

Mr. KIM Chul Yong
Chief, Tourism Promotion Section
Bureau of Tourism, MOT

Mr. ~~KIM Ju Whan~~ Yoo Myung Doo
~~Chronic Disease Officer~~ MOHA
~~Public Health Bureau, MOH&SA~~

Mr. ~~KIM Myong Sub~~ Myung Joong Sup MOHA
Chief, Foreign Press Section
Korean Overseas Information Service
MOC&IA

Mr. YANG Sei Hoon
North America Division II
American Affairs Bureau
Ministry of Foreign Affairs

US Component

Captain Wallace E. Sharp
Assistant Chief of Staff, J5, USFK

COL David P. Heekin
Deputy Chief of Staff, EUSA

COL Garry A. Willard, Jr.
Vice Commander, 314th Air Division

COL Bruce T. Coggins
Judge Advocate, USFK/UNC

COL Henry A. Essex
Surgeon, USFK

COL George F. Proudfoot
Provost Marshal, USFK

COL William W. Woodside
Public Affairs Officer, USFK

Mr. Robert A. Kinney
Chief, International Relations Branch, J5

Mr. Jack Leonard
Political Section, US Embassy

Observer

Major Richard G. Toye
J5 Division, USFK

150

MATERIALS FOR US COMPONENT - AD HOC SUBCOMMITTEE TRIP TO OSAN AIR BASE - SONGTAN-EUP, 6 ~~FEBRUARY 1973~~ 7 March 1973

SONGTAN-EUP:

1. Population of Songtan-eup's 12 villages was approximately 51,000 at the time of the last census (October 1972). "Chicol Village" is the term loosely applied to three of these villages (Shinjang-ri, Suhjon-ri, and Chisan-ri) whose population of roughly 42,000 shows a female majority. Chicol Village area extends from the Osan Air Base main gate to the MSR.

2. The local, lowest-level, government appointed civil administrator is the Songtan-eup township chief, Mr. YI Chong Sub. He administers government affairs for the 12 villages in Songtan-eup; the village chiefs are not government employees, but village leaders. The village office is located in Suhjon-ri, a few minutes from Osan Air Base's main gate.

3. Twelve bars cater to US Forces personnel; ~~all are on limits.~~ four are now off-limits

4. Approximately 1,200 special entertainers, most of them registered with the local women's association. (This is about 500 less than reported last year.)

5. Eighteen full-time Korean National Police under jurisdiction of the Songtan-eup police captain, Mr. CHOE Ki Ho; three on joint US-ROK patrol, four in the village area. There are two additional investigator-detectives assigned from Pyongtaek County.

6. US Military population roughly 4,600 (including the 38th Brigade).

PAGE 2 RUADMBA0C33 UNCLAS

RUYNWGA/CTU 75.4.1

RUWTEJA/USAFSS/DOC

RUEOIAA/DIRNSA ATTN: RNI

BT

UNCLAS JPCCO/JOPREP JIFFY/PINNACLE/001/314ADCP/

TDR-1646

OPREP-3/001

H. ASSULT

H1. VOICE 02/1616/MAY 73
H2. 02/1455/MAY/1973

CS-0802

H3. N/A

H4. AT 2355I A CAUC AIRMAN ASSIGNED TO 51ST AIR POLICE WAS STABED IN THE STOMACH AT THE ALOHA CLUB CHICOL VILLAGE, HE WAS ASSULTED BY MALE KOREAN NATIONAL, VICTOM IN USAF HOSP OSAN BEING TRANS TO YONGSAN HOSP, POSSIBLE STOMACH LINING PUNCTURE, 3 KOREAN WITNESS AND 2 AMERICAN WITNESS WITH DESCRIPTION, KNP AND OSI INVESTIGATING ALL FURTHER REPORTS THROUGH THE CHANNELS;

(007 WAS LAST NBR OF MONTH OF APR 73)

Z. 02/1615Z

BT

#0033

152

DEPARTMENT OF THE AIR FORCE
HEADQUARTERS AIR FORCES KOREA/314TH AIR DIVISION
APO SAN FRANCISCO 96570

MEMO FROM THE OFFICE OF
THE COMMANDER

TO: DATE:

Gen Smith:

It is my personal goal to force the ROK to accept their responsibility for providing security. I feel that the quantity and professional quality of the KNP. in (Civilian Duty) leaves a lot to be desired. Would appreciate any help you could give.

Mac

T. R. McNEIL
Brig General USAF

26 April 1973

1973. 4. 26

CC

Security and Protection - Songtan-Up, Korea

송 탄 읍 [illegible] 치 보 안 [illegible] 요 소

Superintendent Yun, Cho Yun:

총 경 윤 조 영 서 장

Over the past several months, I have become increasingly concerned
과거 수개월간에 걸쳐서 본인은 한국군 송탄읍 (치 콜) 내에서
about the numerous assaults and other criminal acts directed towards
수 없는 폭행사건과 기타 다수의 범죄행위가 미국 군인들에게 가하여
United States Armed Forces personnel in Songtan-Up (Chicol Ville),
지는 사실에 대하여 깊은 관심을 가지게 되었습니다. 예를 들면
Korea. Last week, for example, that section of Chicol Ville known as
지난 주일에 송탄읍 치콜에 소재한 소위 파파조 라고 불리어지는 골목
Papa Joe Alley was declared off-limits to all Armed Forces personnel
구역 일대에 앞으로 30 일간을 모든 미국 군인들에게 그 구역의 출입
for a period of thirty (30) days because of the high risk of harm to those
을 금지하도록 공포하였습니다. 그 이유는 동구역에 출입하는 자들은 위
entering that section. It is quite possible that other areas or business
해를 받을 위험이 있기때문입니다. 앞으로 다른 구역이나 또는 관광업소
establishments will be similarly placed off-limits in the future.
업소에도 출입금지령을 내릴 가능성은 다분히 있는것입니다.
Unless Chicol Ville is kept a safe place for United States servicemen
송탄읍내가 미국 군인들이 안심하고 출입할수있는 장소로 계속 유지안는
to visit, I shall have no option but to forbid my men from entering the
다면 본인은 모든 미군들의 송탄내 출입을 전적으로 금지하는 방법외에
village altogether.
다른 도리가 없습니다.

Mr. Leonard
desegrate forced policy - not so good.

New Recommendation of Ad Hoc.

Letter.
Briefing
준수
강화

Move Clubs to MSR —

1555

I am particularly concerned that inadequate lighting conditions exist
본인은 송탄읍내의 가로등 시설이 부적당하여 특히 관광 음식점소가
throughout the village, especially in the alleys near the nightclubs.
위치한 부근 골목길의 조명등에 특히 관계되는 것입니다. 거의 매일
Almost daily I learn that many of the street lights are not functioning
본인은 많은 가로등이 작동도 노후된 켜지 않고 있는것을 알고있읍니다.
because bulbs have not been replaced after local officials have been
그 사유는 제시에 본인의 휘하 헌병들이 관계 지방 관공서원에 그 사
timely advised by my military policemen. I also find that bar owners
실을 통보하여도 전구를 갈아 끼우지 않는데 있읍니다. 그리고 또 관
provide no security or protection for the safety of patrons, and, when an
광업소의 주인들이 고객의 안전을 위하여 보안이나 또는 보호조치를 하지
assault or affray occurs, no assistance to innocent victims is rendered.
않으며 폭행사건 또는 언쟁이 발생시에 선의의 피해자를 도와주지 않는다는
I cannot and will not condone such action in the future.
사실을 알았으며 이러한 행위는 앞으로 본인이 묵과 하지않을것입니다.

Most seriously, I believe that there are too few Korean National Police-
본인이 가장 심각하게 생각하는것은 송탄읍 주민 50,000 명이 넘는 도시에
men allotted to this village of over 50,000 inhabitants. My officials have
너무나 적은 경찰병력을 배정하였다고 믿고 있읍니다. 본인 휘하의 관계
repeatedly requested added protection. To date, the response has not
관이 계속하여 보다더 좋은 보호를 요청하였읍니다. 오늘 현재까지 그에
been satisfactory.
대한 조치는 만족하지 못하였읍니다.

I have always enjoyed working with you for the betterment of the Chicol
본인은 항상 오산기지와 송탄읍의 공동사회의 향상을 위하여 즐거이
Ville-Osan Air Base community. I have the deepest personal respect for
일을 하여왔읍니다. 본인은 귀하가 본인 휘하의 군인들이 귀관하여 있음

2

156

Countermeasures taken

- Publicity ~~A~~ Campaign
  "Defender"
  Osan in perspective
- Camp Town Purification Program.

Answers

① May 4 Letter to Commander McNall
  If any further request,
② Legal jurisdiction No. But act.

평택군수 Briefing

1. Number of ~~Crime Of~~ Occurrence. — 3년치 같은.

Western Village

55 beds
night club
fire proof
quality of construction — good
Shopping Center.

157

your desire to protect my servicemen while in your area, but we must
며, 그들을 보호하려고 노력하신데 대하여 개인적으로 깊이 감사하고 있읍니다
now increase efforts to institute protective measures and assure safety
그러나 우리들은 지금 보다 안전보호조치를 수립실시하여 송탄읍내의 안전을
in Chicol Ville.
확보하여야 하겠읍니다.

I regard the situation as serious. I hope that the drastic step of for-
본인은 사태가 심각하다고 봅니다. 본인은 미국 군인들이 송탄읍내
bidding my servicemen from entering the village will not occur.
에 출입금지하는 강력한 조치가 다시 없기를 바라는 바입니다.
I would be pleased to learn what additional steps are being taken by
본인은 송탄읍에서 추가적으로 취한 조치와 귀하의 경찰이 송탄읍내를
the Korean community and your personnel to make Chicol Ville a safer
보다더 안전하게 하기위하여 취하신 사항이 있으면 알려주시면 감사히 여기겠
place.
읍니다.

Sincerely
경 구

T. R. McNEIL, Brig Gen, USAF
Commander
사 령 관
미공군준장 티. 알. 맥 닐

Copy to:
CINCUNC/USFK
APO 96301

158

③ April 19 Assault at Big Heart.
Papa Joe Alley Off Limits
Letter from General McNeil
Meeting with Supt. Yun/General Park 경기도경찰청
May 1 May 3.
Aloha incident -- 2 May
Air
ROK Soldiers stabbed GI Police

Papa Joe 83%. Black people's world.
Safe Environment required
Street lights — Composition of Streets.

Requirements

	33	Today Add	39
∨ ○ Additional KNPs	26	6	~~32~~
	(+9) plainclothes		
∨∨ ○ Uniformed police			5.5.
○ Additional Lighting	~~4~~ 23	69	→ 192
			+100 (in May
○ Civic Responsibility Education			292

○ ∨ ○ More Clubs To MSR — Main Stream.
- (돈 문제) ○ Western Village ~~License~~ Governor — 내부허가
Registration — MOT.
군수 ○ ∨ - ○ Incorporated City Gov't. — ~~AA~~ 국회법률 → 건합.
시 전환 — Pyong Taik
? Gen. Bennett to Mr. Ambassador.

459

Report of Osan Base Commander at USFK Civil Affairs Conference - 2 March 1973

COL J. H. ALLISON, USAF (COMMANDER, 51ST AIR BASE WING, OSAN)

My presentation this morning will cover four areas of mutual interest in our relations with the local community, especially Songtan-eup, or, as it is known to most Americans, Chicol Ville. These areas are: Community Relations Activities, Venereal Disease, Criminal Activities, and Race Relations.

We at Osan believe we pursue a vigorous community relations program, both on an official and personal level. I would like to briefly mention a few examples of our efforts to improve US-ROK relations. First, we have an active Korean American Friendship Council (KAFC) which is designed to provide an effective two-way channel of communication to identify existing or potential areas of mutual concern, and to foster better understanding between the personnel of Osan Air Base and the local community. The membership of the KAFC includes the mayor of Suwon City, the chiefs of Pyongtaek and Hwasung Counties, the Chief Prosecutor of Suwon District, and the police chiefs of Pyongtaek and Suwon. USAF members are heads of agencies or sections which serve as counterparts to the Korean members. The Council meets quarterly and is alternately hosted by Osan Air Base and Korean counterparts. An agenda is drawn up in advance for each meeting and minutes are provided afterwards. Discussion usually centers on matters of such mutual concern as public health, sanitation, traffic safety, venereal diseases, larceny and people-to-people programs. However, any topic of mutual concern is suitable for discussion.

Frankly, the usefulness of the council is somewhat limited. As the map shows, Osan Air Base borders Songtan-eup. Yet, since Songtan does not have city status and has no recognized local governing officials, Songtan-eup is not directly represented on our council. Consequently, we deal with diverse county and city officials with differing interests. We attempt to overcome this limitation by working on a very close personal basis with the appropriate local official on a case-by-case basis and have very close and cordial relationships with these officials. We understand that Songtan-eup may become an incorporated city during 1973. We, of course, are delighted over this prospect since we feel that the absence of an official local government hampers our problem-solving abilities.

This council is by no means the only way of getting involved in community affairs, for Osan is involved in a wide variety of civic action activities. For example, the Civil Engineer Squadron continually assists in community improvement programs by providing volunteer workers and equipment. Some of these projects involve road paving and land levelling which have provided needed recreational areas at local orphanages and schools. Our hospital

TAB D.

has a Mobile Sick Call jeep, which visits local orphanages weekly and administers to the immediate medical needs of the children.

Osan was deeply involved in the rescue of 763 Korean civilians during the August floods. Our rescue assistance has also resulted in the evacuation of a wounded seaman from a Korean destroyer, rescue of eight fishermen who were stranded on a rock off Pigum Island and the evacuation of another seaman who had suffered a skull fracture in an accident aborad ship.

Our formal support of orphanages is handled through the Chin Mok Association, established here on Osan to centralize orphanage sponsorship by base units. Although orphanages are still sponsored by individual units, Chin Mok provides a means for these groups to collect and distribute funds and goods to the orphanages. Currently, there are seven orphanages sponsored by Chin Mok. One example of this organization's effectiveness as a central collection agency is the annual radio marathon. Last October, this marathon raised $9,200 for distribution and assistance to the orphanages.

Another Chin Mok project is known as "Dad for a Day", an annual Christmas event which pairs orphans with GI's who spend the entire day together attending a wide variety of events. The activities culminate in a traditional Christmas dinner served at our dining halls. Chin Mok also assists in individual efforts. Recently, a sergeant with the aid of his wife back in the States, collected over 1,000 pounds of clothing and toys for the orphans. Chin Mok assisted in the distribution of these items.

Beyond the formal support given to the orphanages, most squadrons and many individuals provide direct assistance to the orphanages on a unilateral basis. For example, last November, an estimated 250 local orphans celebrated Thanksgiving Day thanks to the almost spontaneous efforts of 56 Osan Air Base men and women.

Another important subject of command-community interest at Osan Air Base is the area of environmental control. We have established an Environmental Protection Committee to investigate and alleviate pollution problems, particularly those which adversely effect the local community. Environmental protection is an area of increasing concern here at Osan and we are working hard on well-rounded pollution abatement activities.

I think it important to note that mutual assistance is working both ways. We are most happy with the many community improvement projects underway in Songtan-eup which make Osan a better place to live and work. For example, recent street paving and widening projects have been implemented, including the addition of wider sidewalks along the main street. We are most appreciative of these efforts to improve conditions in the village.

You may be interested to know that although personnel are assigned to Osan unaccompanied, that is, without their families, we do have approximately 1,200 dependents residing in the local village. We are concerned, of course, with their safety, health and security, so we particularly welcome the community improvement projects underway.

Despite the positive efforts made by American and Korean personnel, problems do exist which detract from our mutual efforts. Among these problems are:

1. Venereal Disease. Gonorrhea is our most prevalent venereal disease; fortunately, there has been very little syphilis. To give you some idea of the scope of the problem, there are 12 night clubs in Chicol Ville and approximately 1,200 registered special entertainers. There are an additional 200 or so unregistered entertainers who compound the problem.

Osan's VD rate for CY-72 averaged out at 1.30 (Formula: Number of cases per month times 1,000, divided by the number of days in the month times the average base strength, gives the number of cases per thousand per day). Our VD rate seems to have stabilized but we are not complacent.

Noting that our monthly recurrent rate ranged between 10-15% of total monthly cases, in November 1972 we raised our standard treatment for gonorrhea of 4.8 million units of penicilin to include 1 gram of oral probenecide 30 minutes prior to the penicilin shot. Although too soon to evaluate the current program, the recurrent rate of 7% for December 1972 is encouraging.

Osan has qualified health personnel assigned to inverview VD patients to obtain information on sex contacts. To enable patients to report these sex contacts, a registration and identification system is used in all off-base entertainer establishments. This involves assigning each girl a numbered badge to wear, the issue by the doorman of a contact slip bearing her registration number to the male escort, and maintaining photo files at the base hospital to confirm identification. This contact information is then forwarded to local Korean health officials.

At the present time, the bulk of the treatment of female contacts is being done at the base hospital. The girls are treated here every Monday, Wednesday and Friday. Since we are unable to follow-up on these cases, we are looking forward to the opening of the new Korean hospital in Pyongtaek as a great stride toward effectively controlling VD.

I might add here that the clinics in the community use the smear method to detect the presence of VD. We feel that the culture method is much more reliable, and we would recommend that this procedure be instituted as a more effective means of controlling VD.

I'd like to discuss a few of the programs underway at Osan to control VD. At our weekly newcomers' briefing, a doctor briefs all personnel on the VD problem. Emphasis is placed on the control measures employed here.

Despite this, the cooperation received from our personnel is somewhat discouraging. Too often our people forget to obtain the girl's contact slip number, do not remember her name, and cannot identify her from our photo file.

Some of the other measures we take include:

Reporting monthly VD statistics to Squadron Commanders.

Forwarding periodic "emphasis letters" to all squadrons soliciting support in helping to reduce VD.

Preparing bilingual handouts to inform local entertainers of the medical programs and control measures relative to VD.

Holding periodic discussions with local club owners on VD problems within their establishments and making routine medical inspection during hours of highest patronage to detect and correct violations.

Forwarding monthly statistical reports to local health officials outlining data on female contacts.

A joint US-ROK health and sanitation inspection of the various clubs has been proposed and meetings have been set to coordinate efforts. Agreement has already been reached that upon completion of the new Pyongtaek hospital, ROK health officials will treat all entertainers identified as VD contacts.

We recognize and appreciate the increased emphasis by ROK officials in controlling VD since our military public health staff does not have the independent capability to control it.

We will continue to seek close cooperation and coordination of VD control efforts in an effort to eliminate this problem. Regarding VD control by Korean authorities, we favor an orderly, planned approach which concentrates on the registered and unregistered entertainers.

Active participation by Korean Health Officials and KNP in monitoring the clubs and streetwalker compounds is of paramount importance. We recommend that, where necessary, these officials should impose their authority to close offending establishments.

4

163

2. Sanitation. I would like to briefly mention a potential problem in the off-base clubs in the serving of food. A snack bar providing sandwich service was recently opened in one of the local club.. If the snack bar is financially successful, we anticipate that other clubs will quickly follow suit. We realize that other eating establishments exist outside of club facilities; however, the relative density of our personnel in the clubs focuses our prime concern upon them.

We view the presence of such snack bars as a potentially serious health problem. Food can transmit numerous communicable diseases. To prevent or break the chain of transmission requires complete control over food handlers, food preparation and approved sources. We feel that the rigid standards normally enforced in the United States, including procurement from an approved source, may not be maintained.

To correct this problem, we have taken several steps. Besides contacting club owners in an effort to persuade them to accept our point of view, we have been in touch with Eighth Army officials. Our recommendation to them is to revise the policy document governing clubs to preclude the operation of eating facilities within the clubs.

3. Criminal Activity. Another subject of great concern to us in our relations with the community is crime. Here, I would like to briefly mention the areas of larceny, assaults, narcotics, and blackmarketing.

Larceny: Between 1 July - 31 December 1972, Osan Air Base reported the loss of $77,300 in government and private property. Our loss rate is unacceptable and we look to increased vigilance on the part of our security police in conjunction with the local Korean National Police in an effort to reduce our losses to a minimum.

We have a grave theft problem in Chicol Ville and in its back alleys. In addition, our people are constantly harassed when they leave the main gate by streetwalkers and beggar boys. We need some vigorous law enforcement action in these areas.

Assaults: Osan Air Base reported a total of 70 off-base assaults between 1 July 1972 - 31 January 1973; 39 of these involved US personnel only, 31 involved US personnel and Korean Nationals. Thirty-four assaults took place in dark or poorly-lit areas.

Recently, Osan AB donated 40 lights and poles to Songtan-eup to illuminate dark areas in an effort to help prevent criminal activities, particularly assaults. This is in addition to several lights provided in the past.

We are experiencing a problem involving taxis off-base. Briefly, some of our people try to avoid paying the fare. A related problem concerns the practice of taxi drivers overcharging or not returning change to the passenger. This often leads to arguments and fights. We are working with the local KNP in this matter.

We want to assure you that we move quickly in taking appropriate disciplinary action against offenders and remove them from Korea when such action is in our best mutual interests.

Blackmarket: We recognize that we have a problem primarily involving the illegal sale of such high-interest items as small electric appliances and alcoholic beverages. However, with the recently instituted stricter ration control on alcoholic beverages and increased vigilance and emphasis on controlling such illegal activities, we believe that we are making strides in reducing blackmarketing.

Drugs: As you know, drugs are readily available in Korea. Marijuana is the most popular, accounting for the majority of US subject investigations at Osan. Barbiturates would probably be second in popularity, with amphetamines following behind. Heroin is the fourth most popular drug, although indications are that the availability of this drug is rising.

We currently have nine cases involving the criminal use of drugs under investigation, six of these involving marijuana. Since the termination of martial law, we have noted an increase in activity by drug sellers. However, the local police are aware of the situation and have increased their efforts to identify and arrest Korean dealers.

Another aspect of the drug situation is the Osan Air Base Drug Abuse Monitoring Program. This program applies to all Air Force active duty personnel under 29 years of age. The majority of personnel are tested by the "random sample" method. This is a random selection of personnel by social security number. Personnel may also be tested by Commander direction, unit, or the Limited Privilege Communication Program.

Urine samples are collected at the hospital and forwarded to Japan for analysis. Personnel having positive urine samples are interviewed by a physician and upon his recommendation are placed into a five-phase rehabilitation program. During rehabilitation, the individual is required to submit urine samples at frequent intervals. Between 1 August 1972 - 31 January 1973, 1,021 persons were tested. Of these, 23 lab tests were positive with four of them subsequently confirmed positive by the physician.

Race Relations: In an effort to eliminate racial problems, the Base Commander has met with the club owners to discuss discrimination and make it clear that he will recommend that any club continuing to practice discrimination will be placed off-limits. The Base Equal Opportunity and Treatment Office staff has contacted club owners individually when blatant incidents of discrimination were observed.

We send "Salt and Pepper" teams on frequent visits to the clubs during business hours. The team's purpose is to observe the operation of the clubs for evidence or signs of a discriminatory nature. Since late November 1972, 70 such inspection visits were made by the "Salt and Pepper" teams and 16 incidents reported.

A campaign was begun last month to acquaint bar owners and business girls with racial differences. The film, "Black and White Uptight" with a Korean soundtrack is being shown and to date, 670 business girls have seen it. The film is also being shown to Korean base employees.

We recognize that a good portion of the discriminatory practices by club owners and business girls can be attributed to economics. Nevertheless, the Air Force is dedicated to the principles of fair and equal treatment for all and we cannot tolerate discrimination.

It is clear that discrimination only strains US-ROK relations and we are actively seeking the cooperation and understanding of all Koreans in helping us to deal with this problem.

기 안 용 지

분류기호 문서번호	미이 723 -	(전화번호)	전결규정 조 항 차관 전결사항
처리기간			
시행일자	1973. 5. 22.		
보존년한		차 관	
보조기관	차관보		협조
	국 장		
	과 장		
기안책임자	양세훈	북미 2 과	

경유 수신 참조	수신처 참조	발신		통제	
제 목	SOFA 군민관계 분과위원회 현지시찰				

1. 한국 관광 휴양업 협회 및 동협회 양주 지부는 별첨(1) 과 같이 미군당국의 윤락여성 영내 유치, 미군출입 간판등의 부착, 관광 휴양업소에 대한 검열등 행위의 부당성을 지적하고 이를 시정 조치 하여 달라고 진정하여 왔읍니다.

2. 한편, 미 8군사령부 당국은 동협회측에 대하여 별첨 (2) 과 같이 여성의 영내출입이 강력히 통제되고 있고 미군당국이 관광 휴양업소에 대한 검열을 단독으로 실시한 예가 없다고 회답하고, 이와같은 문제는 SOFA 군민관계 분과위원회에서 적절히 처리되는 문제임을 지적하였읍니다.

3. 이상 문제점들이 한미 양측 간에 계속 확대되어 사태가 점차 악화되기 이전에 현지의 진상을 조사하고 적절한 대책을 강구하기 위하여 다음과 같이 SOFA 군민관계 분과위 한국측 위원들의 현지 답사를 실시코저 하오니 필히 참가하여 주시기 바랍니다.

정서 관인 발송

폐안" 전통으로 조치. 현지답사 완료 5/25

664

공통서식1-2(갑) 1967. 4. 4. 승인

190mm×268mm(1급인쇄용지70g/m²) 조달청 (500,000매 인쇄)

가. 일 시 : 1973. 5. 25. (금) 1400 출발

나. 장 소 : 동두천지역

다. 집합장소 : 동일 1400시 까지 중앙청 동편 정문앞

바. 교통편 : 자동차편

첨부 : 1. 교통부 공한 및 관광유양협회측 공한 사본 각 1통.

2. 미군당국 서한 사본 1통. 끝.

수신처 : 내무부장관 (지방국장, 치안국장 (외사과, 수사지도과))

법무부장관 (법무실장, 검찰국장)

보사부장관 (보건국장)

교통부장관 (관광국장)

문공부장관 (공보국장)

청와대 정무수석비서관 (내무 보사담당 비서관)

166-2

(부내 참고)

1. 주무부처 관계관들 (교통부 진흥과장, 내무부 관리과장)은 미군당국뿐만 아니라 해당 협회 본부와 지부간에도 각기 상이한 주장을 하고있어, 우선 한국측 위원들의 현지답사가 필요하다고 말함. (73. 5. 22. 11:00 회합)

2. 현지답사에 필요한 제반 조치는 관계부처가 행할것임.

3. 당부에서는 다음과 같이 관계관이 참석코저 함.

이상훈 북미 2과장 (SOFA 군민관계분위 위원장)
양세훈 북미 2과 서기관 (SOFA 군민관계분위 간사)

167

기 안 용 지

분류기호 문서번호	미이 723 - 337	(전화번호)	전결규정 조 항 차관 전결사항
처리기간			
시행일자	1973. 5. 30.		
보존년한		차 관	
보조기관	차관보		협
	국 장		
	과 장		
기안책임자	양세훈	북미 2 과	
경유 수신 참조	수신처 참조	발신	발송 1973. 6 2. 외무부
제 목	SOFA 군민관계 분과위원회 현지답사		

1. 5. 22. 11:30경 경기도 시흥군 소재 미군부대 소속 미군병사들이 공무집행중인 전매청 수원지청 소속 공무원들에게 집단 폭행을 가하여 이중 1명이 사망하고 3명이 중상을 입는 불상사가 발생하였읍니다.

2. 당부는 이와같은 미군들에 의한 공무집행 방해 및 집단 폭행 치사상 사건이 특히 P.X. 물품 부정유출 및 암거래 방지를 위한 단속중에 발생하였다는 점에서 매우 중요시되므로, 이 사건에 관련된 피의자들에 대한 형사적 처리와는 별개의 문제로서 SOFA 합동위원회 및 군민관계 임시분과위원회가 이 문제를 취급하여 주한미군 주둔에 따른 군민관계의 원만한 해결과 기지촌 정화등 한미간의 대책강구가 필요하다고 사료됩니다.

3. 이와같은 대책의 일환으로 SOFA 군민관계 임시분위 한국측 의장의 제의에 따라 한미 양측은 다음과 같이 현지답사를 실시하고 문제점을 검토키로 하였으니 귀부소속 위원들이 필히 참가토록 조치하여 주시기 바랍니다.

정서 | 관인 | 발송

168

공통서식 1—2 (갑) 190mm×268mm (1급인쇄용지70g/m²)
1967.4.4 승 인 조 달 청 (500,000매 인 쇄)

가. 일시 : 1973. 6. 8. (금) 9:30 - 12:00

나. 장소 : 경기도 시흥군 군자면

다. 세부일정 : 별첨

라. 집합장소 : 9:20 까지 용산 헬리콥터장

첨부 : 일정표 1 부. 끝.

수신처 : 내무부장관 (관리과장, 외사과장, 수사지도 과장)
법무부장관 (송무 과장, 검찰과장)
교통부장관 (관광국 진흥 과장)
보건사회부장관 (만성병담당관, 마약과장)
문화공보부장관 (해외공보관 외보 과장)
청와대 정무수석비서관 (내무.보사담당비서관)

(부내 참고) : 당부 참가자
이상훈 북미 2과장 (군민관계분위 의장)
양세훈 북미 2과 서기관 (군민관계분위 간사)

169

Schedule for Trip to Gunja-Myun, Shiheung

09:30	Leave Yongsan Helipad
09:45-11:45	Briefings and Discussions
12:00	Arrive Yongsan Helipad

170

지급

기 안 용 지

분류기호 문서번호	미이 723 -	(전화번호)	전결규정 9 조 2 항 국장 전결사항
처리기간			
시행일자	1973. 6. 7.		
보존년한		국 장	
보조기관	과 장		협조
기안책임자	양세훈	북미 2과	
경유 수신 참조	내무부장관 치안국 수사지도 과장	발신	1973. 6. 7. 외무부
제목	SOFA 군민관계 분과위 현지답사		

연 : 미이 723 - 337

연호 SOFA 군민관계 분과위원회의 시흥군 군자면 현지 답사와 관련하여 현지 관계관이 참석할 수 있도록 조치하여 주시기 바랍니다.

첨부 : 세부 일정표 1통. 끝.

정서 | 관인 | 발송

공통서식 1—2 (갑)
1967.4.4 승 인

190mm×268mm (1급인쇄용지70g/m²)
조 달 청 (500,000매 인 쇄)

세부 일정

73. 6. 8. (금)	0915	중앙청 동편광장 출발 (뻐스편)
	1100	미 제38대공포부대 (Battery B 본부 도착)
	1100 - 1230	한미 양측 브리핑 및 토의
	1230 - 1330	오 찬
	1300 - 1500	귀 임

172

동두천 지역 군민 관계

1. 73. 5. 3. 한국 관광 휴양업 협회 진정 (별첨 1)

한국 관광 휴양업협회 및 동 협회 양주지부의 하기 미군당국의 부당성 시정 조치 진정

(1) 윤락여성 영내 유치

(2) 최저기준 간판 부착

(3) 관광 휴양업소에 대한 일방 암행 검열

2. 73. 5. 15. 협회에 대한 미군당국 서한내용 (별첨 2)

(1) 여성 영내 출입 엄격 통제

(2) 일방 암행검열 실시 부인

(3) 협회 양주지부장의 진정 사실 부인으로 협회 진정내용의 신빙성 결여를 지적

(4) SOFA 군민관계 분과위에서 적절히 처리되는 문제임을 지적

3. 73. 5.22. SOFA 군민관계 주무부처 관계관 회의

(1) 참석자 : 교통부 진흥과장, 내무부 관리과장, 외무부 북미 2과장

(2) 합의사항 : 미군당국, 협회본부 및 지부가 각기 상이한 주장을 하고 있어 우선 한국측 위원들의 현지 답사가 필요하다고 합의

173

4. 73. 5. 25. 군민관계 한국측 위원-현지답사

(1) 참석자 : 교통부 진흥과장 김철용
내무부 관리과장 백세현
외무부 북미 2과장 이상훈
외무부 북미 2과 서기관 양세훈
보사부 만성병 담당관실 황홍석
내무부 치안국 황 경위

(2) 조사내용 :

(가) 윤락여성 영내유치

1) 관광협회 양주 지부장 이건차 및 동두천지구 윤락여성 단체 민들레회 (회원 2,359명) 총회장 김상수는 매일 1700 - 1800 사이 2-3회씩 미군차량으로 윤락여성 (대부분 민들레회 회원)들이 영내로 들어가며, 영내 출입수가 점차 증가하여 최근에는 매일 약 2-300명으로 추산된다고 진술함.

2) 이들 진술에 의하면, 미군영내 클럽측이 윤락여성들의 주민등록증과 검진증을 확인한후 승차시킨다 함.

3) 군민관계 한국측 위원들은 매일 2-300명이라는 숫자를 확인할 수는 없었으나 별첨 (3)과 같이 미군 차량에 의한 영내 출입을 확인함. 위원들이 목격한 차량번호는 USFK Vehicle 7 이었으며, 차체에 CCA

174

NCOOM We give a damn   이라고 쓰여 있었음.

이밖에 다른 차량도 목격되었음.

(나) 미군당국의 최저기준 간판 부착

1) 관광 휴양업소뿐만 아니라 동두천지역 전역에 걸쳐 각종 상점에 미군간판이 부착되어 있음이 확인됨.(별첨 4)

2) 협회측은 이와같은 미측 처사가 사실상 미군상대 영업을 위한 허가권의 구실을 하고있어 영업행위에 대한 부당한 간섭이라고 주장함.

(다) 관광 휴양업소에 대한 미측의 일방 암행 검열

1) 미군당국이 73. 1. 18.부터 미측 관계관들로만 구성된 암행 검열을 실시하고 있음이 확인됨. (별첨 5)

2) 또한 73. 2. 21.자로 미군당국과 동두천읍 당국간에 관광 휴양업소의 운영기준에 대한 합의 서명이 있었음. (별첨 6)

(라) 미군당국 서한에서 지적한 협회 양주 지부장의 진정사실 부인

협회 양주 지부장이 73. 5. 3.자로 교체되었음으로 진정 사실 자체 부인은 신, 구 지부장간의 알력 또는 미측과의 언어장애 때문인것으로 추측됨.

5. 대 책

SOFA 군민관계 분과위원회에 이 문제를 정식으로 제기.

부미22	공람	73. 6. 8일	담당	과장	국장	차관보	차관	장관

175

교 통 부

시설 1535 182 1973. 5. 3

수신 외무부 장관

참조 미주 국장

제목 기지촌 군민관계에 대한 사항

1. 미이 723-11024 (73. 4. 3)의 관련임

2. 기지촌 주변 관광휴양업체 (바)는 주한 유엔군에 대한 편의 제공으로 한미친선의 유대를 강화하는 반면 국가 시책인 외화획득 사업체로 서의 임익을 담당하고 있는바

3. 별첨과 같은 관광 휴양업협회의 시정요구 사항을 통보 하오니 조치있기 바랍니다.

첨부 : 한국관광휴양업협회 건의서 (사본) 1부.

발송 No. 1973. 5. 3 교통부

교 통 부 장 관

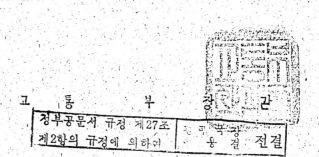

정부공문서 규정 제27조 제2항의 규정에 의하여	관리국장 응결 전결

176

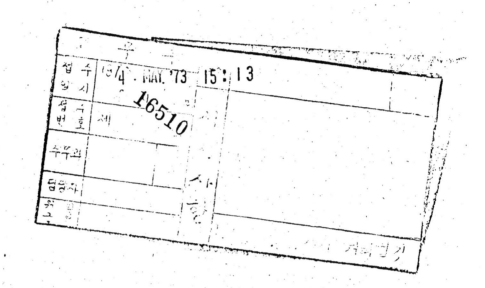

접수일시	4. MAY. '73 15:13
접수번호	제 16510
주무과	
담당자	

한국관광휴양업협회

관휴협 제49-1호 (26-1181-9 의 372번) 1973. 4. 9.

수신 교통부 장관

제목 건의서

동두천 및 부평지역 미군부대에서 다음과 같은 부당한 처사를 하고 있어 이의 시정을 건의하오니 빠른 시일내에 시정조치하여 주시옵기 간절히 바라나이다.

다 음

1. 동두천 지역

가. 한국인 윤락여성을 영내 크라부에 대거 유치하고 있읍니다.

숙녀를 영내에 초청한다는 이유로 매일저녁 윤락여성 200여명을 버스 또는 도보로 영내 크라부에 유치하고 있는바 영내에서는 방역당국의 단속이 미치지 못하고 있어 검진미필자의 도피처가 됨으로 성병전염자가 많이 발생하게 될것이며 또한 해피스모크등 마약 판매의 안전 루-트가 되고 있읍니다. 그럼에도 성병에 걸리면 그 책임을 우리 휴양업자에게 전가시켜 출입금지등 부당한 조치를 취하고 있읍니다.

나. 관광휴양업소에 대하여 지나친 간섭

(1) 관광휴양업소에 대하여 수시로 암행 검열을 하고 있으며 한국기관이나 우리업자의 해명도 듣지않고 일반적으로 미군 출입 금지조치를 취하고 있읍니다.

(2) MP. CP 들이 수시로 업소에 들어와 종업원의 패스 명찰등을 조사하고 카운타 뮤-직 박스를 샅샅치 뒤지고 있읍니다.

1177

2. 부평 지역

각 업소마다 2명씩 고정배치하여 (부대와 직통전화로 가설해 놓고 있음) 미군의 출입을 제한 또는 감시하고 있읍니다. 끝.

첨부 : 미군의 부당한 처사에 대한 구체적인 내역. 1부. 끝.

한국관광휴양업협회

회장 이 춘 성

1178

공　　란

공 란

OSAN AB ASSAULT STATISTICS (OFF BASE)

1 JULY 72 - 5 MAY 73

MONTH	TOTAL ASS.	GIs & KNs	GIs
JUL 72	13	8	5
AUG 72	12	5	7
SEP 72	8	4	4
OCT 72	8	2	6
NOV 72	14	5	9
DEC 72	11	4	7
JAN 73	11	4	7
FEB 73	8	3	5
MAR 73	10	5	5
APR 73	5	3	2
MAY 73	1	1	0
TOTALS	101	44	57

181

공 란

CHRONOLOGY OF EVENTS

- NOVEMBER 2nd DISTURBANCE
- MEETING WITH CLUB OWNERS--10 NOV
- MEETING WITH CLUB OWNERS--16 JAN

1887

STEPS TAKEN

- COURTESY PATROL TEAMS
- LETTER TO SENIOR SUPT. YUN
- A-FRAME OFF LIMITS--31 MARCH
- UNIFORM POLICY--31 MARCH
- PJ ALLEY OPENED--31 MARCH

184

RESULTS OF UNIFORM POLICY

- REDUCED POPULATION IN VILLE
- PERSONNEL LOOK & BEHAVE BETTER
- LESS DISCRIMINATION

CHRONOLOGY (CONT'D)

- MEETINGS WITH GOVERNOR LEE/CLUB OWNERS
- APRIL 19 ASSAULT AT BIG HOUSE:
  PAPA JOE ALLEY OFF LIMITS
  LETTER FROM GENERAL McNEIL
- MEETINGS WITH SUPT. YUN/GENERAL PARK
- ALOHA INCIDENT -- 2 MAY

0.8

MAP OF PAPA JOE ALLEY

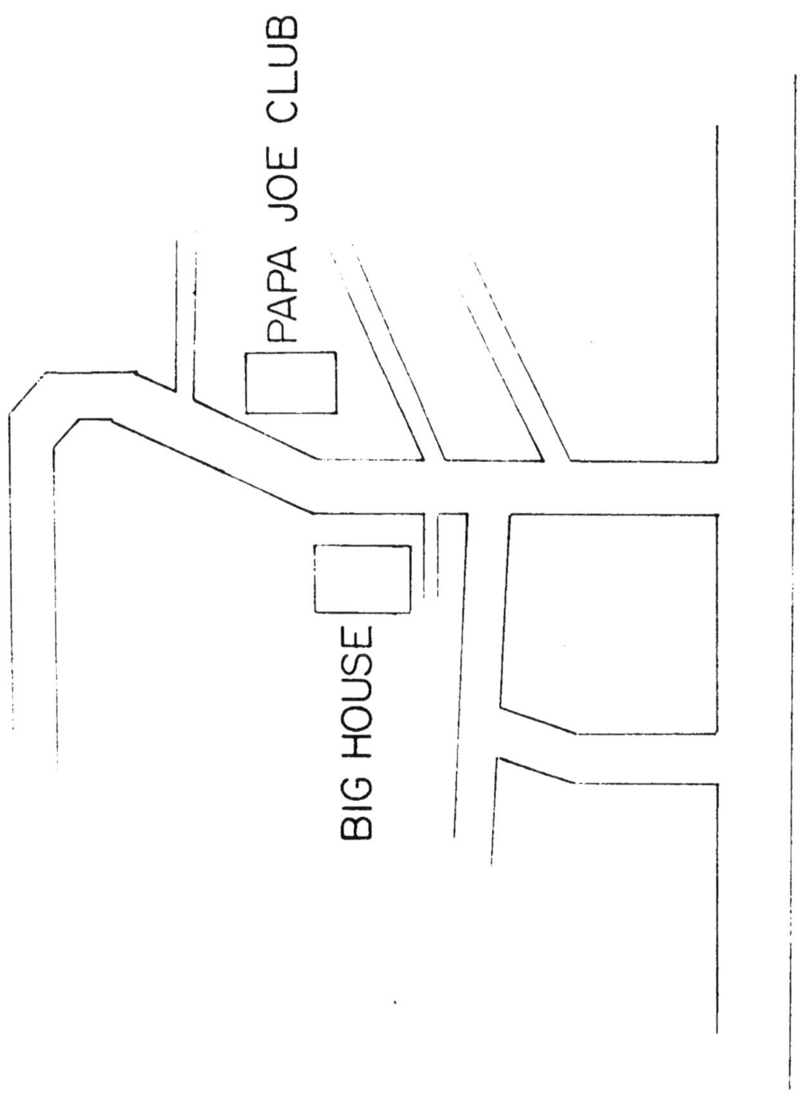

REQUIREMENTS

- ADDITIONAL KNPs
- UNIFORMED POLICE
- ADDITIONAL LIGHTING
- CIVIC RESPONSIBILITY
- MOVE CLUBS TO MSR
- INCORPORATED CITY GOVERNMENT

1886

COUNTERMEASURES TAKEN

- PUBLICITY CAMPAIGN:
  - DEFENDER
  - OSAN IN PERSPECTIVE
- CAMP TOWN PURIFICATION PROGRAM

77. 5. 25 일촬영

별첨 3.

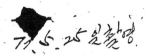

한여자가 여자들의 패스를 거두어서 크라브책임자 미군에게 패스를 넘겨주고있다.

크라브차량에 여자들이 대거승차하고있다.

190

73. 5. 25 일 촬영

별첨 3.

한 여자가, 여자들의 패스를 거두어서 크라브책임자 미군에게 패스를 넘겨주고있다.

크라브차량에 여자들이 대거승차하고있다.

190

73. [illegible] 25일 촬영

크라브차량을대기시켜 놓고, 여자들이승차하기를기다린다.

크라브차량에 여자들이승차하고있다.

191

73. 5. 25일 촬영

크라브차량을대기시켜 놓고. 여자들이승차하기를기다린다.

크라브차량에 여자들이승차하고있다.

191

별첨 4

73. 5. 25 일촬영

시중 하층상점에까지도 부대에서 발행한 미군 출입허가용 간판이 부착되여있다.

192

73. 5. 25 일촬영

별첨 4

시중 각종상점까지도 부대에서 발행한 미군 출입허가 간판이 부착되여 있다.

192

한국관광휴양업협회 양주지부

관휴양제 69 호 1973. 5. 17

수 신 교통부장관

참 조 관광국장

제 목 "미군 출입간판" 철거건의

1. 한국 정부의 제반 허가증이 있어도 미군측에서 발행한 미군 출입간판(발전사진)이 있어야 미군 출입이 허용되고 따라서 영업도 가능하게 됨으로 미군측에서 실질적인 영업 허가권을 행사하고 있음으로

2. 이는 독선적이고 횡포이며 엄연한 내정 간섭으로 간주 이에 시정을 강력히 요구한바 일체에 간섭을 지양하고 행정 조치도 한국 기관만이 할수 있다고 부대측에서 답변해 놓고도 미군측에 간섭과 횡포는 시정되지 않고 있읍니다.

3. 실예로는 미군측에서 한국 행정 당국에 요청을 해서 한국 행정 당국으로 하여금 "아자수" 홀에 지난 4월 2일부터 4월 20일까지 영업정지 처분을 하여 그 시효가 만료 되었는데도 부대측에서는 미군 출입 간판을 돌려 주지 않으며 계속 미군 출입 금지 조치를 해제치 않고 있어 영업을 못하고 폐문 하고 있읍니다.

4. 미군 출입 간판이 상존하는한 미군측에 월권과 간섭에 소재가 남아 있으니 철거토록 조치하여 주시기를 건의 합니다. 끝

한국관광휴양업협회양주지부

지부장 이 건

193

"미군 출입간판" 원본

This Establishment
Meets Acceptable Standards
FOR. U.S Patronage.

이 시설물은 미군을
고객으로 채용 될 만한
기준에 도달하고 있음.

194

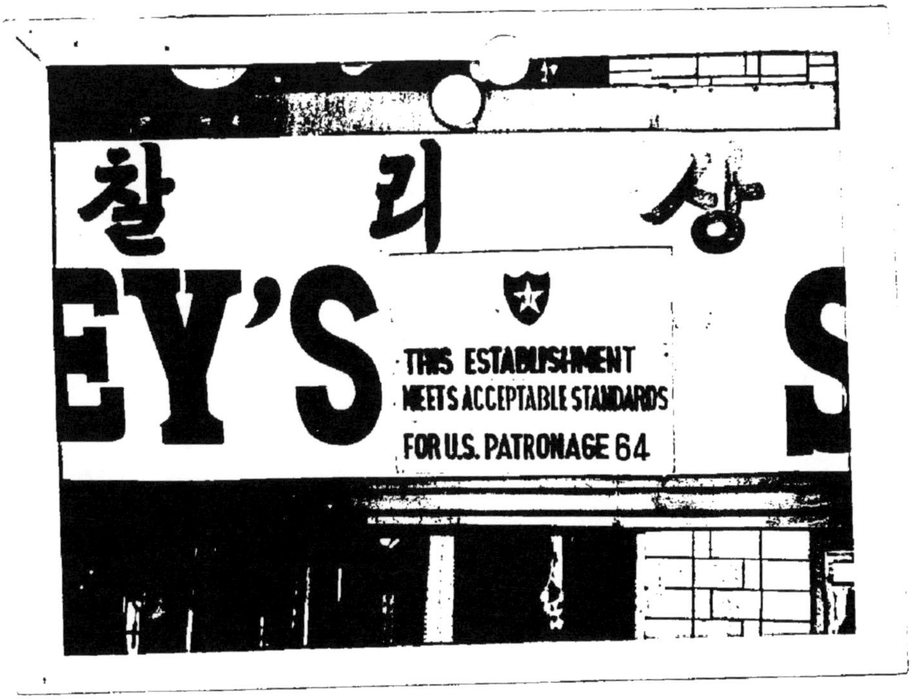

일반상점

휴양업소

195

찰리상
EY'S
THIS ESTABLISHMENT
MEETS ACCEPTABLE STANDARDS
FOR U.S. PATRONAGE 64

일반상점

THIS ESTABLISHMENT
MEETS ACCEPTABLE STANDARDS
FOR U.S. PATRONAGE 2
LUCKY CLUB

휴양업소

별첨 5

DEPARTMENT OF THE ARMY
Headquarters 2d Infantry Division
Office of the Assistant Chief of Staff, G5
APO San Francisco 96224
미 제2보병사단 민사참모부 민사처

JIMGO

SUBJECT: On Limits Actions
제 목: 미군 출입

18 January 1973
1973년 1월 18일

Mayor Chi, Tok Un
Tongduchon, Yangju-gun

지 덕 운 읍장님
양주군, 동두천읍

Dear Mayor Chi:
친애하는 지읍장님:

1. The following three Tongduchon clubs will be placed on limits to
1. 다음 동두천의 세(3) 크라브에는 미제2사단 군인들이 출입할수 있는
Second Division soldiers and issued MINIMUM STANDARDS signs:
출입최저기준 간판을 받을 것입니다:

a. Las Vegas Club effective 19 January 1973.
1973년 1월 19일에는 라스베가스 크라브.

b. Starlight Club effective 3 February 1973.
1973년 2월 3일에는 성광운.

c. New Korea Club effective 5 February 1973.
1973년 2월 5일에는 뉴코리아크라브.

2. All TDC clubs are now under a system of daily unannounced inspections
2. 앞으로 동두천에 있는 모든 크라브는 매일과 같이 사전에 통고없이
by commanders, ROT, G-5, Provost Marshal, C.I.D., Preventative Medicine
지휘관들, 휴네스검실, 민사참모, 헌병참모, 씨아이디, 예방의학관
and Inspector General representatives. These inspections will quickly
그리고 감찰부 대표자들이 검열을 하는 제도 아래 있게됩니다. 이 검열들은
bring to light any discrepancies and shortcomings and you will receive
어떠한 상위된 점과 미비점을 그 즉시로 노출시키게되며 귀하께서

Bravo Club

380

196

EAJ-GG [illegible] On Limits Actions　　　　18 January 1973

제 목 : 미군 출입　　　　1973년 1월 18일

a written copy of all such inspection results.

그와같은 검열 결과를 서면으로 받게 될것입니다.

3. In addition to black market, discrimination, narcotics and sanitation areas, we are placing continuous emphasis on the venereal disease problem and expect all officials and clubs to cooperate with the new control measures and elimination of streetwalkers. For example, two reasons for placing clubs off limits would be:

3. 우리들은 앞으로 계속적으로 성병문제 해결을 두며 이에 암거래, 인종차별, 마약 그리고 위생문제등에 주력을 계속함으로 이에 관계되는 당국과 클럽들은 성병단속, 새방침이 행과 노정기 행위자 제거에 협조를 기대합니다. 클럽에 출입금지를 취하는 그 두(2)가지 이유로서의 예는 :

a. Girls present in a club without name tag, business cards and a valid V.D. card and doorkeeper checking each girl.

명찰 나부에있는 여자로서, 명찰, 명함, 계급 및 검진증이 없고 그리고 기도가 각 여자들을 조사를 하지 않을때.

b. Streetwalkers observed from now on will cause the clubs to be placed off limits. Girls will NOT solicit in the streets, only in the on limits clubs.

지금으로부터 허가된 노정행위 여자는 그 클럽에 출입금지를 받을 원인으로 될 것입니다. 여자들은 길가에서는 유흥행위를 못하도록 하며 다만 출입 클럽에서만 하도록 한다.

PETER D. BURRIS　피터 디. 브리스
LTC, GS　미 육군, 중령
ACofS, G-5　민사 참모부

Copies: Each club owner
　　Kinqullae

사본 배포 : 미군클럽 주인
　　민원처

2

197

별첨 6

JOINT STATEMENT OF AGREED STANDARDS FOR TDC CLUBS
동두천지역 크라브에 대한 합의된 기본·합동서명

1. This statement of agreed standards for Tongduchon clubs is promulgated
크라브에 대한 합의된기본의 본서명은 크라브의 모든 고객들의 복리를
for the welfare of all club customers. The Mayor of TDC and the Commanding
위하여 공포되여지다. 동두천읍장, 사단장은 이 기본
General agree to these standards. Each club will have a full time manager on
기준에 합의하다. 각 크라브는 여기 기본기준의 전 사항을
duty who will enforce all provisions of these standards. The manager will
이행하도록 지배인은 완전 근무태세에 있어야한다. 지배인은
immediately contact appropriate authorities for assistance whenever required
언제라도 도움이 필요할때 즉시 경찰관 및 미헌병과 같은 당국에 연락을
such as KNP and Military Police.
취한다.

2. All patrons are welcome without regard to race, creed or color.
모든 고객은 인종, 종교나 피부색과 관계없이 접대를 받는다.
Discrimination of any kind is forbidden. All types of music will be available
어떠한 종류의 인종차별이라도 금지된다. 모든 종류의 음악이 가능하며
and played on a rotational basis.
기본적으로 음악이 고루고루 들리어져야함.

3. Service will be denied to rowdy, obscene or intoxicated soldiers.
난폭하던지, 상스럽던지 또는 술에 만취된자에게는 서비스를 거절한다.
Open bottles or cups will not be carried into or out of the club. No drinks
뚜껑이 열린 병이나 컵을 크라브 밖 또는 안으로 가지고 들어가지못하게한다.
will be served in bottles.
병채로 음주 서비스를 하지못하게한다. (도움이 필요할 때는 미헌병을 호출한다)

4. M.P.C. and U.S. currency or coins will not be accepted. Only Korean Won
미군표, 미본토불 또는 주화를 받지 아니한다. 한국돈만이
will be used. No credit can be extended. Ration control plates and
사용된다. 외상거래를 하지않는다. 피엑스 물품증 및 군인 신분증은
indentification cards will not be accepted for any reason. No gambling will
어떠한 경우라도 받지않는다. 도박은 허용
be allowed.
되지않는다.

198

5. All girls in clubs will be required to be registered and to have a valid
크다브 에있는 모든 여자들은 반듯이 등록되어야하며 제대로된 검진증과
VD card and business cards and to wear a name tag. The doorman will refuse
명함을 소지하며 이름표를 달고있어야합니다. 기도는 이 세가지를 구비
entry to any girl without all three items. Girls are required to show VD
하지 않은 여자는 출입못하도록한다. 여자들은 어떠한 손님이라도
cards on request of any patron and will give a business card to any patron
제시 요구시는 검진증을 보이며 그리고 그 여자와 관계가 있을 때는 명함을
with whom she does business. Patrons are encouraged to obtain business
손님에게 제공한다. 손님들은 앞으로 그 여자의 소재를 확인하기
cards from girls for future identification purposes. Name tags will be worn
위하여 여자들로부터 명함을 받도록 권유된다. 이름표는 가슴위에
over heart.
붙인다.

6. Sale, use or possession of drugs is prohibited. Club employees will
마약판매, 사용 또는 소지는 엄금이다. 크다브 종업원들은
report any drug or black market activity to the KNP and Military Police
어떠한 마약 또는 암거래 행위에 대하여서라도 즉시 경찰관 및 헌병에게
immediately.
신고한다.

7. Last call for serving drinks will be 2325 hours. Club will be closed
술은 마지막으로 청구할 시간은 2325시로 한다. 크다브는 2330시에는
and must be vacated by 2330 hours.
문을 닫고 사람이 없어야한다.

8. Food will not be prepared or eaten on the premises. All prices will be
음식은 시설물내에서 준비 또 먹어서는 안된다. 모든 가격표는
prominently posted. Only disposable cups will be used and they must be
명백하게 표시되여야한다. 처분될수있는 컵들만 사용되어야하며 재사용을
crushed after use to prevent reuse. Only ice tested and approved by medical
못하도록 사용후 부숴버려야한다. 의무당국에서 시험하고 인정한 얼음에
authorities will be used in drinks.
한하여 음료주에 사용된다.

9. Latrines will be kept clean and functional with water, paper towels,
화장실은 깨끗이 청결되며, 물이흐르며, 종이수건, 비누 및 변소휴지가
soap and toilet paper. Club will be kept clean at all times with floors
구비되여 제대로 가동되여야함. 크다브는 항상 정상적으로 입구 낭하 및 홀

swept regularly, to include sidewalks and streets outside. Spilled drinks
밖에있는 도로등을 포함하여 바닥을 깨끗히한다. 음료수가 엎지러

will be mopped up immediately.
졌을 때 즉시 마포질한다.

10. Fire laws limit the capacity of this club to ____ total persons.
이 크라브의 화재법규상 수용인원수는 ___명으로 제한되어있음.

Adequate lighting and fire extinguishers must be provided. Congestion
적절한 조명과 소방기구가 구비되어야한다. 출구에 밀집되어

near exits will not be permitted to include loitering by patrons.
있거나 손님들이 출구근처에서 서성거리지 못하게한다(도움이 필요할 때한 병을부른다

11. Girls will not solicit in the street, and unregistered street girls and
여자들은 노상에서 청객행위를 못하게하며 미등록 노상행위 여자들 및 펨프들

pimps will be promptly reported by club owners to the appropriate authorities.
은 즉시 크라브업주로 하여금 관계당국에 신고한다.

WE AGREE TO THE ABOVE STANDARDS
상기 기본기준에 대하여 합의한다.

Peter D. Booras Peter D. Booras LTC, GS AC of S, G-5 민사참모부	윤길섭 Mayor of TDC 읍장
21 Feb 73 Date 1973. 2월 21일	조성칠 Chairman, KTA 관광협회 지부장

I AGREE TO ABIDE BY THE ABOVE STANDARDS
본인은 상기한 기본기준을 준수함을 동의한다.

NAME of Club 업소명	Owner Signature 업주 서명
Witness 증인	Date 날자

200

3

Report on Situation in Tongduchon

1. The Korean Tourist Recreation Service Association and its Yangjugun District Office have submitted to the Ministry of Transportation a petition in which the Ministry is requested to take necessary measures to correct injudicious actions taken by the US military authorities in Tongduchon area.

2. The actions the Association describes injudicious are as follows:

   a. Over 200 business girls are taken by bus or on foot every evening to the clubs in the camps. This provides a safe route to drug traffickers and a good shelter to unregistered business girls.

   b. Unannounced inspections by US military authorities are conducted to the Korean recreation service establishments and off-limits are placed for US military personnel by unilateral actions taken by US authorities. Passess and ID cards of employees are checked and service counters, music boxes and other facilities in these establishments are searched by US MPs and CPs.

201

c. The US authorities issues to Korean stores a plate for US patronage which is regarded as an actual license for business despite the authorization given by the Korean Government authorities.

3. Based upon the petition, the authorities concerned conducted an investigation for fact-finding and the findings are as follows:

a. It is noted that business girls are gathered in group on the roads adjacent to the US military compound, and taken into the compound by a USFK vehicle. The transportation to and from the compound is in service three times from 1700 to 1800 hours. Exact number of girls taken into the compound a day cannot be verified. According to the statements made by residents in that area, the estimate of number of girls are more than 200 a day. (Photos are attached.)

b. The Association has provided us with a letter of the US military authorities dated 18 January 1973 as an evidence that all clubs in Tongduchon

202

are under a system of daily unannounced inspections by US commanders, EOT, G-5, Provost Marshal, CID, Preventative Medicine and Inspector General representatives.

c. It is found that the plate for US patronage is hung at the entrances of Korean stores in Tongduchon area. The plate reads: "This establishment meets acceptable standards for US patronage." (Photos are attached.)

4. What I recommend here to this Ad Hoc Subcommittee is to consider these situations and draw a certain conclusion in the spirit of mutual cooperation and friendship.

a. Inviting ladies to the compound is entirely the independent business of US military authorities. However, bringing business girls into the camps every day in such a large scale indicates a different nature from inviting ladies for social occasions.

203

This kind of action, it is feared, might hamper the joint ROK-US efforts to deal effectively with the chronic problems existing in base areas, namely, drug abuse, VD control and black-market and larceny and, worse yet, might eventually result in destroying the very purpose of this Subcommittee; that is to improve civil-military relations in camp village areas. It is also said that such actions by the US base authorities might adversely affect the business activities in the community and the existing cooperation between the US base and the Korean community in that area. Since the inception of this Subcommittee the ROK Government with US cooperation made maximum efforts to improve the environmental conditions of the base areas, particularly that of sanitary and health conditions of the recreationary establishments for the US personnel. In many cases such efforts paid off because local community leaders were more than willing to cooperate with the Government

204

authorities for better facilities and services. Such being the case, if local communities are to be deprived of their business in its entirety they will have little incentive to cooperate with the authorities for better conditions. Admittedly, the US rights to escort in ladies for social occasions and recreations for its troops are not questioned. But for the best interest of ROK-US joint efforts it is suggested that both sides excercise moderate approaches to this problem and refrain from daily busing a large number of business girls into the military compound.

205

b. It is needless to say that there is only good intension on the part of the US authorities in conducting unannounced inspections on Korean business establishments and placing the said plates. It is also known that such practices are being accepted in part by the authorities of the local community and by individual business owners. Nevertheless, there is no denying that such actions by the US authorities are causing considerable ill-feelings on the part of majority of local community. Particularly, placing of plates mentioned in effect constitute double licencing of business; one by Korean authority and the other by US authority. As for the unannounced inspection, the US authorities should entrust those aspects of inspections to proper Korean authorities and when the conditions are found to be unfit to US personnel US authorities should take it up with the Korean authorities for necessary remedial actions. In my view, these problems should have been handled at the local level and need not have been brought up at this Subcommittee in the first place.

206

In any event, the problems were brought to our attention and putting aside legal aspects of the problems in question we should in all sincerity find ways to resolve these problems based on the spirit of mutual cooperation which is the back-bone of this Subcommittee.

207

기 안 용 지

분류기호 문서번호	미이 723 -	(전화번호)	전결규정 9 조 2 항 국장 전결사항
처리기간			
시행일자	1973. 5. 14.		
보존년한			국 장
보조기관	과 장		협조
기안책임자	양세훈	북미 2 과	
경유 수신 참조	수신처 참조		통제
제 목	SOFA 군민관계 분과위 제 19차 회의		

1973. 5. 15

외무부

검열 1973 5 15

연 : 미이 723 - 15494 및 16567

연호 SOFA 군민관계 분과위원회의 송탄읍 현지답사시 미군 당국이 브리핑한 자료를 별첨 송부하오니 참고하시기 바랍니다.

첨부 : 자료 1통. 끝.

수신처 : 내무부장관 (지방국장, 치안국장 (외사과, 수사지도과))

법무부장관 (법무실장, 검찰국장)

교통부장관 (관광국장)

보건사회부장관 (보건국장)

문화공보부장관 (공보국장)

청와대 정무수석비서관 (내무.보사담당비서관)

정서

관인

반송

1381

공통서식1-2(갑)
1967. 4. 4. 승인

190mm × 268mm (1급인쇄용지70g/m²)
조달청 (500,000매 인쇄)

208

Send copy to Prondfoot

1. GOOD MORNING, GENTLEMEN. ON BEHALF OF THE 314TH AIR DIVISION AND THE 51ST AIR BASE WING, I'D LIKE TO WELCOME YOU ONCE AGAIN TO OSAN AIR BASE.

THE PURPOSE OF MY PRESENTATION THIS MORNING IS TO DISCUSS OUR MUTUAL PROBLEM REGARDING SONGTAN-UP, OR AS IT IS KNOWN TO AMERICANS, CHICOL VILLE. OVER THE PAST SEVERAL MONTHS WE HAVE BECOME INCREASINGLY CONCERNED ABOUT THE NUMEROUS ASSAULTS AND OTHER FORMS OF VIOLENCE INVOLVING U.S. FORCES PERSONNEL IN TOWN.

2. FIRST, PERMIT ME TO SET THE SCENE. THIS CHART DEPICTS THE NUMBER OF SERIOUS ASSAULTS INVOLVING U.S. FORCES PERSONNEL WHICH HAVE OCCURRED IN CHICOL VILLE SINCE JULY, 1972. AS YOU CAN SEE, WE HAVE A PROBLEM. ALMOST 50% INVOLVE KN'S, EITHER AS VICTIMS OR PERPETRATORS

3. HERE IS A MAP OF CHICOL VILLE INDICATING THE LOCATION OF THE TWELVE CLUBS. AS YOU CAN SEE, MANY OF THEM ARE AWAY FROM THE MSR. (TALK TO ALLEYS - TALK TO WESTERN VILLAGE.)

209

4. THIS NEXT CHART GIVES YOU AN INDICATION OF WHERE THESE INCIDENTS ARE OCCURING. NOTE THAT OUR PROBLEM IS CONCENTRATED IN THE BACK ALLEYS LEADING TO AND FROM THE CLUBS. (DISCUSS 33 NOT ON CHART IN VARIOUS COMPOUNDS, ETC.)

AT THIS POINT I WOULD LIKE TO GIVE YOU A BRIEF CHRONOLOGY OF EVENTS LEADING TO OUR PRESENT SITUATION.

5. YOU MAY RECALL THAT ON NOVEMBER 2ND OF LAST YEAR, A DISTURBANCE OCCURRED IN CHICOL VILLE INVOLVING AMERICAN SERVICEMEN AND KOREAN NATIONALS. THIS LED TO A COUPLE OF MEETINGS THE NEXT DAY BETWEEN BASE PERSONNEL, PREDOMINATLY BLACKS, AND BASE OFFICIALS, INCLUDING THE DIVISION COMMANDER, GENERAL MCNEIL, IN WHICH MANY GRIEVANCES WERE AIRED. FOREMOST AMOUNG THESE GRIEVANCES WERE CHARGES OF DISCRIMINATION AGAINST BLACKS AND OTHER MINORITIES IN THE CLUBS IN CHICOL VILLE - - A DEFINITE CONTRIBUTING FACTOR TO OUR ASSAULT RATE.

A MEETING WAS HELD WITH ALL THE CLUB OWNERS ON 10 NOVEMBER TO DISCUSS THE PROBLEM AND TO SOLICIT THEIR COOPERATION IN ELIMINATING DISCRIMINATORY PRACTICES. THIS SAME SUBJECT WAS DISCUSSED A FEW DAY EARLIER (NOVEMBER 8) WITH MAJOR GENERAL BANG, WHO AT THE TIME WAS KYONGGI PROVINCE MARTIAL LAW COMMANDER.

210

THE SITUATION IMPROVED SOMEWHAT AND ON JANUARY 16TH ANOTHER MEETING WAS HELD WITH THE CLUB OWNERS TO REVIEW OUR PROGRESS. AT THAT TIME WE STATED THAT IT WAS NOT OUR DESIRE TO PUT ANY CLUB OFF LIMITS, BUT THAT WE WOULD HAVE NO ALTERNATIVE IF MORE DEFINITE PROGRESS TOWARD ELIMINATING DISCRIMINATION AND CURBING VIOLENCE WAS NOT MADE.

THEN CAME FEBRUARY AND MARCH - - BAD MONTHS. A SERIES OF BRUTAL ASSAULTS IN THE VARIOUS ALLEYS NEAR THE CLUBS PLUS DOCUMENTED CASES OF DISCRIMINATION IN THE A-FRAME LEAD US TO TAKE A SERIES OF STEPS. WE HAD A PARTICULARLY BAD WEEKEND, 9 - 11 FEBRUARY WHEN 4 ASSULTS OCCURED.

6. ON FEBRUARY 13TH A PROGRAM OF COURTESY PATROL TEAMS WAS INITIATED. THESE WERE TEN TWO-MAN TEAMS COMPOSED OF OFFICERS AND SENIOR NCOs IN UNIFORM. THEIR PURPOSE WAS TO CIRCULATE AMONG THE CLUBS AND IN THE VILLE GENERALLY SO AS TO DETER ANY ACTS OF VIOLENCE. THE PROGRAM WAS ONLY MODERATELY SUCCESSFUL. AT THE SAME TIME IT WAS ANNOUNCED TO OUR PEOPLE THAT CONTINUATION OF THE ASSAULTS WOULD RESULT IN A REQUIREMENT FOR UNIFORMS IN THE VILLAGE.

ALSO, IN MID-FEBRUARY WE SENT A LETTER TO SENIOR SUPERINTENDENT YUN, CHIEF OF PYONGTAEK POLICE STATION, OUTLINING OUR PROBLEMS AND REQUESTING

211

HIS ASSISTANCE IN MAKING CHICOL VILLE SAFER. WE POINTED OUT THE NEED FOR ADDITIONAL KOREAN NATIONAL POLICE AND MORE LIGHTING IN THE DARK ALLEYS. SOME ADDITIONAL KNPs WERE ADDED AT THAT TIME. THESE STEPS PROVED PARTIALLY SUCCESSFUL.

IN MID-MARCH THE A-FRAME WAS PLACED ON PROBATION FOR A PERIOD OF TEN DAYS AS A RESULT OF DUCUMENTED DISCRIMINATORY PRACTICES. THEN, ON 30 MARCH WE HAD A PARTICULARLY BRUTAL ASSAULT - - A G.I. WAS BEATEN WITH A CANE. AS A CONSEQUENCE, SEVERAL ACTIONS WERE TAKEN: FIRST, SINCE THE SITUATION AT THE A-FRAME HAD NOT IMPROVED SIGNIFICANTLY, IT WAS PLACED OFF LIMITS FOR A PERIOD OF 15 DAYS. SECONDLY, WE FELT COMPELLED TO INSTITUTE A POLICY REQUIRING THE WEAR OF THE UNIFORM IN CHICOL VILLE.

I MIGHT DIGRESS A MOMENT HERE TO STATE THAT THE UNIFORM POLICY HAS BEEN WORKING VERY WELL. ALTHOUGH IT HAS UNDOUBTEDLY WORKED AN ECONOMIC HARDSHIP ON THE COMMUNITY, IT HAS LED TO NUMBER OF POSITIVE RESULTS.

7. FIRST, IT HAS DECREASED THE NUMBER OF PEOPLE IN TOWN WHICH IS OVERCROWED ALREADY AS IT IS. SECONDLY, ALL OUR PEOPLE ARE LOOKING BETTER AND BEHAVING BETTER AS A CONSEQUENCE OF THE UNIFORM POLICY. AND FINALLY, WE HAVE FOUND THAT THERE HAS BEEN A REDUCTION IN DISCRIMINATORY PRACTICES BECAUSE WHEN EVERYONE IS IN UNIFORM, THEY LOOK ALIKE AND GET EQUAL TREATMENT. I MIGHT

212

ADD THAT DUE TO THE OUTSTANDING COOPERATION OF ALL PERSONNEL IN COMPLYING WITH THE UNIFORM POLICY, A CIVILAIN CLOTHES ARE NOW PERMITTED OFF BASE BETWEEN 0400 AND 1800 DAILY.

8. TO RETURN TO THE CHRONOLOGY OF EVENTS, ON APRIL 3RD WE MET WITH GOVERNOR LEE, SENIOR SUPERINTENDENT YUN AND CAPTAIN CHOE TO EXPLAIN THE REASONS FOR PLACING THE A-FRAME OFF LIMITS AND THE UNIFORM POLICY AND TO SOLICIT THEIR COOPERATION IN MAKING CHICOL VILLE A SAFE PLACE TO VISIT.

WE ALSO MET WITH THE CLUB OWNERS LATER THAT SAME DAY. AGAIN, THEY WERE BRIEFED ON DISCRIMINATION IN THE CLUBS AND VIOLENCE IN THE VILLE, AND WERE REQUESTED TO COOPERATE IN SOLVING THESE PROBLEMS.

ON THE EVENING OF 19 APRIL, TWO AIRMEN WERE ASSAULTED, WITHOUT PROVOCATION, BY FIVE UNIDENTIFIED ASSAILANTS IN THE BIG HOUSE CLUB LOCATED IN THE AREA COMMONLY REFERRED TO AS PAPA JOE ALLEY. THIS INCIDENT LED TO SEVERAL STEPS.

FIRST, THE PAPA JOE ALLEY AREA WAS IMMEDIATELY PLACED OFF LIMITS FOR A PERIOD OF 30 DAYS BECAUSE OF THE HIGH RISK OF HARM TO THOSE ENTERING THAT SECTION. SECONDLY, GENERAL MCNEIL SENT TWO LETTERS TO SENIOR SUPERINTENDENT YUN. THE FIRST, DATED 20 APRIL 1973, ANNOUNCED THE GENERAL'S DECISION TO PLACE PAPA JOE ALLEY OFF LIMITS AND REQUESTED KNP ASSISTANCE IN PROVIDING

213

SUFFICIENT SECURITY PERSONNEL AND ADEQUATE LIGHTING FOR THE SAFETY OF ALL PERSONNEL. THE SECOND LETTER, DATED 26 APRIL 1973, REITERATED THE GENERAL'S CONCERN OVER CONDITIONS IN CHICOL VILLE AND RESTATED OUR NEED FOR INCREASED POLICE PROTECTION, BETTER LIGHTING, AND COOPERATION FROM THE BAR OWNERS IN AFFORDING BETTER PROTECTION FOR THE SAFETY OF ITS PATRONS AND, WHEN AN ASSAULT OCCURS, ASSISTANCE TO INNOCENT VICTIMS.

IN RESPONSE TO GENERAL MCNEIL'S LETTERS, SENIOR SUPERINTENDENT YUN MET WITH US ON 1 MAY. WE DISCUSSED A NUMBER OF MATTERS RELATED TO THE SAFETY OF PERSONNEL IN CHICOL VILLE, INCLUDING THE NEED FOR ADDITIONAL, UNIFORMED POLICE, MORE LIGHTING, AND THE COOPERATION OF BAR OWNERS AND PRIVATE CITIZENS IN REPORTING INCIDENTS AND ACTING AS WITNESSES.

WE HAD A SIMILAR MEETING ON MAY 3RD WITH GENERAL PARK, SUPERINTENDENT OF KYONGGI PROVINCE POLICE. AT THAT TIME WE DETAILED FOR GENERAL PARK THE MUTUAL PROBLEMS IN CHICOL VILLE AND SOLICITED HIS COOPERATION IN MAKING CHICOL VILLE SAFER. I MIGHT ADD THAT ON THE NIGHT BEFORE OUR MEETING WITH GENERAL PARK, A SERIOUS INCIDENT OCCURRED IN THE ALOHO CLUB. AN AMERICAN AIRMAN AND A ROK SOLDIER HAD A DISAGREEMENT WHICH AT FIRST WAS BROKEN UP THEN LATER RESUMED. IT RESULTED IN THE ROK SOLDIER STABBING THE AMERICAN AIRMAN IN THE ABDOMEN. AS A RESULT OF THIS INCIDENT, THE ALOHA CLUB HAS BEEN CLOSED BY THE KNP AND IS OFF LIMITS FOR A PERIOD OF

214

SEVEN DAYS.

THAT, GENTLEMEN, BRINGS YOU UP TO DATE ON THE BACKGROUND OF THE CURRENT SITUATION. AS GENERAL MCNEIL CHARACTERIZED IT IN HIS LETTER TO SENIOR SUPERINTENDENT YUN, THE SITUATION IS SERIOUS. WE ARE ESPECIALLY CONCERNED ABOUT CONDITIONS IN PAPA JOE ALLEY.

9. AS YOU KNOW, PAPA JOE ALLEY HAS BEEN A RECOGNIZED SEGREGATED AREA, FREQUENTED ONLY BY BLACKS, WHERE 85 PER CENT OF OUR PEOPLE CANNOT GO IN SAFETY. ITS A LONG, DARK ALLEY WITH A HONEYCOMBED NETWORK OF ENTRANCES AND EXITS AND MULTITUDE OF SMALL MAKLI HOUSES MAKE IT EXTREMELY PERCARIOUS FOR OUR PEOPLE. THE PAPA JOB ALLEY SITUATION IS INTOLERABLE. WE COULD, OF COURSE, DECLARE IT OFF LIMITS FOR REASONS OF SANITATION AND KEEP IT OFF INDEFINITELY, BUT WE FEEL THAT THIS IS NOT THE LONG TERM SOLUTION WE NEED.

WHAT, THEN, DO WE NEED TO ATTAIN OUR MUTUAL GOAL OF MAKING CHICOL VILLE A SAFE PLACE FOR U.S. FORCES PERSONNEL TO VISIT? I SUBMIT WE NEED THE FOLLOWING:

10. FIRST, ADDITIONAL KOREAN NATIONAL POLICE SHOULD BE ASSIGNED TO CHICOL VILLE, ESPECIALLY PAPA JOE ALLEY. AT PRESENT SOME 26 KNPs ARE ASSIGNED TO THE SONGTAN-UP SUBSTATION, INCLUDING THOSE ASSIGNED TO OUR

215

OSI AND SECURITY POLICE. WE FEEL THIS NUMBER IS INADEQUATE TO COPE WITH THE PROBLEM.

SECONDLY, WE BELIEVE THAT MORE UNIFORMED POLICE WOULD HELP REDUCE THE PROBLEM OF VIOLENCE. THE SIGHT OF A UNIFORM ACTS AS A DETERRENT TO CRIME AND IS RECOGNIZED AS A SYMBOL OF AUTHORITY BY OUR PERSONNEL.

THIRD, ADDITIONAL LIGHTING IS REQUIRED IN THE VILLE, PAPA JOB ALLEY AND THE OTHER ALLEYS LEADING TO THE NIGHTCLUBS IN PARTICULAR. THEY DON'T NECESSARILY HAVE TO BE FLOODLIGHTS. GOOD ELECTRIC LIGHTS WILL DO. AND WHILE I'M ON THE SUBJECT OF LIGHTING, I MIGHT ADD THAT THE INTERIOR OF MANY OF THE CLUBS IS MUCH TOO DIM FOR SAFETY.

FOURTH, THERE IS A DEFINITE REQUIREMENT FOR CLUB OWNERS AND PRIVATE CITIZENS TO DEMONSTRATE MORE CIVIC RESPONSIBILITY. WE WOULD LIKE TO SEE A PROGRAM DEVELOPED TO EDUCATE PEOPLE TO REPORT INCIDENTS WHEN THEY OBSERVE THEM AND TO COME FORWARD AS WITNESSES. AT THE SAME TIME WE HAVE BEEN EDUCATING OUR PEOPLE ALONG THE SAME LINES.

FIFTH, WE FEEL THAT LONG RANGE PLANS SHOULD BE DEVELOPED TO RELOCATE THE CLUBS TO THE MSR. WE REALIZE THIS WILL BE COSTLY AND THAT IT CAN'T BE ACCOMPLISHED OVERNIGHT. HOWEVER, WE BELIEVE WE SHALL ALWAYS HAVE A PROBLEM AS LONG AS MOST OF THE CLUBS ARE LOCATED DOWN BACK ALLEYS XX AWAY

216

FROM THE MAIN STREAM. FOR THIS REASON I AM VERY CONCERNED ABOUT THE VERY EXPENSIVE PROJECT TO CONSTRUCT THE WESTERN VILLAGE SO FAR FROM THE MSR.

FINALLY, AS HAS BEEN POINTED OUT TO THIS AD HOC SUBCOMMITTEE IN THE PAST, WE BELIEVE THE FACT THAT CHICOL VILLE IS NOT AN INCORPORATED CITY AND HAS NO RECOGNIZED LOCAL GOVERNING OFFICIALS SERIOUSLY HAMPERS OUR ABILITY TO MUTUALLY SOLVE THESE PROBLEMS.

I DO NOT WISH TO LEAVE YOU WITH THE IMPRESSION THAT NOTHING IS BEING DONE ABOUT THE PROBLEM EITHER BY US OR BY PYONGTAEK COUNTY OFFICIALS.

11. FOR OUR PART, I HAVE ALREADY MENTIONED THE UNIFORM POLICY, THE FREQUENT MEETINGS WITH GOVERNMENT OFFICIALS AND CLUB OWNERS, AND THE COURTESY PATROLS. IN ADDITION, AS A DETERRENT TO CRIME, WE HAVE STEPPED UP OUR EFFORTS TO PUBLICIZE WHAT HAPPENS TO THOSE WHO BREAK THE LAW BY PUBLISHING THE RESULTS OF COURT MARTIALS AND OTHER DISCIPLINARY ACTIONS IN THE DEFENDER NEWSPAPER AND ON A WEEKLY RADIO PROGRAM, OSAN IN PERSPECTIVE.

THE EFFORTS TO SOLVE THE PROBLEMS HAVE NOT BEEN ONE SIDED. WE HAVE ENJOYED WARM, HARMONIOUS RELATIONS WITH GOVERNOR LEE, SENIOR SUPERINTENDENT YUN AND CAPTAIN CHOE. WE KNOW THEY ARE WORKING THE PROBLEM AND THAT UNDER THE CAMP TOWN PURIFICATION PROGRAM, THEY HAVE MADE PROGRESS IN

217

IMPROVING CHICOL VILLE BY EXPANDING AND PAVING STREETS AND ROADS AND IN BEAUTIFYING THE CITY GENERALLY.

HOWEVER, I WOULD BE LESS THAN CANDID IF I SAID WE WERE SATISFIED WITH ALL THAT HAS BEEN DONE. AS I MENTIONED AT THE OUTSET, OUR MUTUAL GOAL IS TO MAKE CHICOL VILLE SAFE FOR ALL PERSONNEL --BOTH AMERICAN AND KOREAN. WE HOPE WE ARE MOVING IN THAT DIRECTION. THANK YOU VERY MUCH. ARE THERE ANY QUESTIONS?

248

내 무 부

관리 100 - 6185 (70. 2481) 1973. 5. 21

수신 외무부장관

참조 북미2과장

제목 기지촌 주민의 계도 요령

1. 관리 100 - 6041 (73. 5. 17)과 관련입니다.

2. 당부에서는 기지촌 대책실천 사업의 일환으로 기지촌 주민 계도 기본지침을 별첨과 같이 작성하여 각시도에 시달하고

3. 각시도지사는 본 지침을 토대로 기지촌별 지역실정에 맞는 자체 세부실천 계획을 수립 실천토록 조치하였기 통보합니다.

4. 이 사항은 군민분과위 제20차 회의 및 합동위원회에 보고하여 주시기 바랍니다.

첨부. 기지촌 주민의 계도 요령 1부 끝

내 무 부 장 관

219

General Guideline for Waging Public Campaign for Residents in Base Community Area

1. Purpose:

a. To ameliorate environmental conditions.

b. To have foreign nationals better understand Korea.

c. To maintain close ties and cooperation with foreign troops.

2. Measures:

a. Educational programs to enhance the spirit of Saemaul movement. (Movies and slides)

b. Public campaign on Government policies and measures.

c. Dissemination of Information on progress in Korea.

d. Proprieties in speech, manner, dress etc.

e. Prevention of racial discrimination.

f. Eradication of larceny, especially those involving foreigners' properties.

g. Improvement of environment for pleasant surroundings.

h. Cooperation among local authorities.

220

基地村住民의 啓導要領

內 務 部

221

基地村住民의 啓導要領

1. 目的

○ 環境淨化를 爲한 住民啓導

○ 外國人의 올바른 새 韓國觀認識

○ 基地村周辺生活環境明朗化

○ 韓·美兩國間의 紐帶增進

2. 方針

○ 基地村 새마을精神의 鼓吹

○ 國威宣揚, 國民品位維持를 위한 教養実施

○ 人種差別(黑白分糾)意識排除

○ 盜犯, 雜犯団束徹底

○ 基地村地域住民의 精神淨化

○ 地域行政官署間의 緊密한 協調

-1-

222

3. 計 劃

○ 對象地區: 全基地村

○ 對 象者:

基地村 및 周辺地域住民

観光休養業所業主

美軍相對接客業所従事者

美軍部隊従事員

淪落女性

○ 啓導內容

가. 새마을精神教育(映画 및 스라이드)

나. 政府施策의 P.R

다. 韓國의 発展相紹介

라. 言語, 行動, 服装등 올바른 礼節

-2-

223

마. 人種差別禁止 ~ 黑白紛糾未然防止

바. 對外國人關係盜犯의 根絶

사 基地村周邊 生活環境의 明朗化

아. 地域行政官署間의 紐帶强化

-3-

224

4. 細部実践要領

啓導内容	對象	期間	啓導要領	主管
1. 새마을 精神教育	· 全住民 · 觀光業主 · 接客業從事者 · 部隊從事員 · 淪落女性	月1回	1. 새마을映画上映 2. 〃 스라이드紹介 3. 새마을 成功事例 紹介 4. 새마을책자配布 5. 優秀새마을見学 6. 基地村새마을事例 研究実践	· 道 새마을課 · 道文化公報室 · 郡文化公報室 · 邑面長
2. 政府施策의 P.R 韓國의発展相紹介	〃	〃	1. 政府施策에 対한 映画 및 스라이드 2. 韓國의 発展相 紹介映画 및 스라이드 3. 道政紹介스라이드	· 道文化公報室 · 郡 〃 · 邑面長

225

指導內容	対象	期間	指導要領	主管
			4. 政府施策説明冊子 配布	
3. 言語 行動、服装의 올바른 礼節	·全住民 ·観光業主 ·接客業從事者 ·部隊從事員 ·淪落女性	随時	※ 班常会、自治会를 通한 教養実施 1. 対外國人 応待 基本会話指導 2. 粗雜한 母國語 또는 外國語使用 禁止 3. 外國人에 対한 親切한 面談要領 4. 外國人에 対한 乱暴한 行動禁止 5. 不遜外國人에 対	·道企劃管理室 ·道文化公報室 ·道社会課 ·郡内務課 ·邑面長 ·郡保健所 ※ 指導責任公務員이 指定

-5-

226

啓導內容	対 象	期間	啓 導 要 領	主 管
			한 理解 및 善導 方法 6. 地域住民의 外国軍服装着用禁止 7. 美風良俗에 阻害되는 乱雜한 衣服着用禁止 8. 接客業所勤務者의 統一된 服装着用勧奨 9. 国民儀礼에 対한 教育 및 冊子配布	
4. 人種差別(黑白紛争) 意識排除	〃	隨時	※ 班常会 또는 自治会를 通한 教養實施 1. 美國人間의 人種	· 道社会課 · 道企劃管理室 · 郡內務課 · 郡保健所

2217

啓蒙內容	対 象	期間	啓 蒙 要 領	主 管
			差別(黑白紛糾)을 間接的으로 調整할 수 있는 事例발굴 → 모든 業所에 波及 2. 住民. 業所. 從事者의 黑白人差別意識严禁 3. 人種差別業体 → 登錄取消等 行政的 措置 4. 黑白区分 專用業所의 一掃 5. 人種差別意識排除 刊行物 포스타 揭示	· 邑面長

-7-

228

啓導內容	対象	期間	啓導要領	主管
5. 外国人 関係 盜犯防止	〃	隨時	※ 防犯委員会, 自治会를 通한 教養 実施 1. 麻薬, 習慣性医薬品의 製造, 使用 및 暗去來의 徹底団束 2. 外換不法去來 및 不法所持団束 3. 窃盜品, 出處不明의 은의 또는 賣買行爲의 严禁 4. 住民의 自律的申告体制의 確立 発見者 —即時申告→ 管轄支署	· 道保健課 · 郡保健所 · 管轄警察署支派出所 · 邑面長

229

啓導內容	対象	期間	啓導要領	主管
6、基地村 周辺生活環境의 明朗化	・全地域住民 ・全地方行政官署	隨時	1. 不良業所, 基準未達業所의 是正 및 改善 2 모든 마을周辺, 業所의 청결維持 3 粗雜한 不法突出物, 不良간판의 除去 4. 住民、淪落女性의 副業場活用의 擴大 5. 住民便宜施設의 運營管理	・郡內務課 ・郡새마을課 ・郡保健所 ・管轄警察署支派出所 ・地区邑面長
7. 地域行政官署의 紐帶強化	・地区内모든 行政官署	月/回 또는 隨時	※ 基地村對策에 関한 機関長協議会 開催	・市長、郡守 ・署長支派出所長 ・保健所長

~9~

270

啓導內容	対 象	期間	啓 導 要 領	主 管
			1. 指導. 啓家、团束等 全般的 问題点 解決에 関한 討議 2. 地区内 発生事件의 解決策講究 3. 外国人建議事項의 有関機関協調 4. 啓導実績의 報告 및 分析 5. 指導方案施行要領의 統一	• 邑面長 • 住民代表

~10~E

231

SOFA 군민관계 분위의 시흥군 군자면 기지촌 현지 답사

1. 일 시 : 1973. 6. 8. (금) 0915 - 1800
2. 장 소 : 경기도 시흥군 군자면 거모 4리 미 유도탄부대 (38th ADA B Battery) 및 주변 촌락
3. 참석자 : 한국측

이상훈 외무부 북미 2과장 (군민관계분위 의장)
양세훈 외무부 서기관 (" 간사)
백세현 내무부 관리과장 (" 위원)
박희태 법무부 검사 (" ")
신창언 " (" ")
김철용 교통부 진흥과장 (" ")
황의택 치안국 수사지도과 경위
황규복 치안국 외사과 경위
정영선 시흥군수
정병모 안양경찰서장
김수근 수원 전매지청 감시과장

미국측

Capt. W. E. Sharp, USN (군민관계분위 의장)
Mr. Robert A. Kinney, USFK (" 간사)
Col. G. A. Willard, Jr., USAF (" 위원)
Ltc. John D. Granger, USA
Col. W. W. Woodside, USA

232

Maj. J. A. Hathaway, USA

Mr. Ward Thompson, US Embassy

Bg. Lynn W. Hoskins (Commander, 38th ADA)

Col. Abt (Commander, 1st Bn 2d ADA)

Ltc. J. P. Maloney (S3, 38th ADA)

Ltc. Allen R. Potter (Civil Affairs Officer 38th ADA)

Mr. Yi, S. K. (Civil Affairs, 1st Bn 2d ADA)

4. 토의내용 :

가. 해당부대 브리핑 내용 및 요망사항

(1) 미 제38 대공 유도탄 부대는 한미 합동 대공 방위임무를 맡은 특수부대로서 주로 서해안지대 18개처에 산재해 있음. (6-Hercules, 12-Hawk)

(2) 부대의 특수성으로 인한 예하부대의 산재, 한적한 산간에 위치, 부대원의 24시간 근무제, 오락시설 불비, 도로사정으로 인한 보급의 지연등이 문제점임.

(3) 기지촌주변 사정으로서 성병, 마약, 암거래등 문제가 있으나, 문제 발생시 한국측과의 적절한 협조 통로가 없고 거리관계등으로 한국 경찰당국의 즉각적인 협조를 얻기 어려움.

(4) 요망사항 :

(가) 현 한미 친선 자문위원회 (Community Relations Advisory Council)의 기능 강화

233

(나) 문제 발생시 최소한 연락 책임을 할수 있는 주재원의 상주. (반드시 경찰이나 공무원일 필요가 없음)

(다) 윤락여성들의 등록 철저 및 보건위생 점검

(라) 암거래 단속을 위한 한미 합동 정기 단속실시

나. 시흥군수 및 안양 경찰서장 발언내용

(1) 성병, 마약등 기지촌 문제해결을 위하여 보건소, 경찰등 관계기관과의 유기적 협조하에 단속을 철저히 할것이며, 기지촌의 환경개선을 위하여 노력할 것임.

(2) 5. 22.자 전매청 직원 살해사건과 관련된 문제점으로서 5. 25. 미군에게 불리한 증언을 하였다는 이유로 증인 (한장한)이 구타당하고 2회에 걸쳐 위협당하여 경찰이 동 증인을 3일간 보호 조치하였음.

(3) 동 살해사건은 미군 병사들의 욕구불만, 오락시설의 미비등에 원인이 있다고 보며, 어떤형태의 조정기구 (또는 인원)가 필요한바, 우선 지휘관 단위의 회합을 자주 갖고 한미 친선 자문위원회 활용을 적극 활용할 방침임.

다. SOFA 군민관계 분위 한국측 의장 (북미 2과장) 발언 내용

(1) SOFA 군민관계 분과위원회는 기지촌의 문제점 해결과 정화사업을 위하여 조직된 기구로서 이 지역의 문제점도 계속 다루어질 것임.

0374

(2) 여타 기지촌과는 달리 이 지역에서 폭행 치사상 사건이 발생하였음은 심히 유감스러운 일인바, 이와같은 폭력은 우선적으로 근절되어야 하며, 이는 부대장의 통솔력과 미군들의 자중으로써 근절될 수 있는 문제이므로 부대측의 적절한 행동을 촉구함.

5. 문제점 :

가. 해당 부락은 산간벽지의 빈촌으로서 주민들의 생계가 미군에 의존하는 바가 크므로 주민들은 오히려 미군측에 동정적임.

나. 행정관청 소재지와의 거리, 인원, 장비등으로 보아 능동적인 행정력이 미치지 못하고 있음.

다. 수원 전매지청 당국자에 의하면 동지역에서만 월 3,600갑의 양담배가 유출되는 것으로 추정되어 단속을 소홀히 할 수 없음.

라. 미군당국이나 주변 촌락의 오락시설이 미비하여 벽지에서 13개월간 근무하는 미군 사병들의 욕구 불만 해소책이 불비함.

6. 대 책 :

가. SOFA 군민관계 분과위에서 한미 합동으로 해결책 강구

나. 주민과 미군간의 상호 협조 및 연락기구로서의 한미 친선위원회 (Korean-American Friendship Council)활동 강화

다. 내무부가 성안한 "기지촌 주민 계도요령" 에 의한 주민 계도 철저.

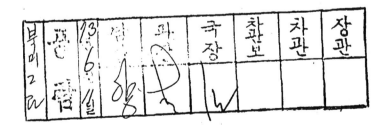

북미2과	[illegible]	73 6 11일	[illegible]	과[illegible]	국장	차관보	차관	장관

235

Schedule for ROK-US Ad Hoc Subcommittee Trip
Battery B, 38th ADA Brigade and
Saemi, Kunja-myon, Sihung-gun, Kyonggi-do
8 June 1973

0915: Depart ROK Capitol Plaza.

0930: Depart US SOFA Conference Room.

1000: Arrive at Anyang turnoff to Battery B, 38th ADA Brigade. ADA vehicle escort from Anyang turnoff to Battery B HQ.

1100: Greetings by BG Lynn W. Hoskins and introduction of Ad Hoc Subcommittee members by respective Chairmen.

1110: Briefing by LTC J. P. Maloney, S3, 38th ADA, on the mission and operations of the 38th ADA Brigade, and LTC Allen R. Potter, Civil Affairs Officer, 38th ADA, on civil-military relations problems (18 of the 42 Korean-American Friendship Councils in Korea involve ADA units).

1150: Briefings by Sihung-gun Chief, Mr. CHUNG Yong Sun; by Anyang KNP Senior Superintendent, CHONG Pyong Mo; and by the Kunja-myon Chief, WON Chong Ku.

1230-1255: Tour of nearby Saemi village.

1300: Lunch at Battery B, 38th ADA Bde.

1330-1500: Return bus trip to Seoul.

226

ITINERARY FOR BG HOSKINS FOR VISIT OF
ROK/US Ad-Hoc Sub-Committee on Civil/Military Affairs
to Battery B, 1st Bn 2d ADA
8 June 1973

TIME	EVENT	RESPONSIBLE PERSON
0950-1000	Enroute from Bde Hqs to Base Operations	Aide-de-Camp
1000-1025	Enroute from Osan to H-132	Avn
1025-1030	Enroute from H-132 to B/1/2 Admin area	CPT Wright
1030-1100	Check arrangements for visit of Sub-Committee	LTC Potter
1100	Arrival of Ad-Hoc Sub-Committee by bus	LTC Abt
1100-1215	Briefings	
	✓(1) Introductions	BG Hoskins
	✓(2) Introductions of Ad-Hoc Sub-Committee	CPTSharp/Mr. Lee, S.H.
	(3) Brigade Briefing	LTC Maloney
	(4) Brigade Civil Affairs Briefing	LTC Potter
	(5) 1st Bn 2d ADA Civil Affairs Briefing	Mr. Yi, S.K.
	(6) B/1/2 Briefing	CPT Wright
	(7) Korean Local Officials Briefings	
	✗(a) Si-Hung Gun Chief	Mr. Chang, W.S.
	(b) Anyang KNP	Sup Chang, P.M. 순사주
	✗(c) Kunja Mayon Chief	Mr. Won, Y.I.
	(8) Discussion	CPT Sharp/Mr. Lee, S.H.
1215-1245	Tour of Saemi Village	CPT Wright
1300-1330	Lunch at B/1/2	CPT Wright
1330	Ad-Hoc Sub-Committee Departs	Mr. Kinney
1330-1340	Travel to H-132	CPT Wright
1340-1400	Travel to Osan AFB Base Operations	Avn
1400-1410	Enroute to Bde Headquarters	Aide-de-Camp

Incl 1

Secluded - Scattered → Commanding control Complex
Support from many places Strategy not vulnerable to enemy attack
~~Go~~ Spare parts
Food
6 Hercules (US)
12 Hawk (US) 가해일.

23개
3 Hawk (ROK) 위박건설
4 Hercules 안하
8 Hawk
15분내 착전.

월 1 600갑 x 6

238

PRESENTATION - CIVIL-MILITARY RELATIONS 7 June 1973

It is a great previlege that I have this opportunity to deliver this presentation to you, today. I am presently working for the 1st Msl Bn, 2d ADA as Civil Affairs Specialist. I have been with this battalion for nearly 12 years out of which I stayed and worked for this Bravo battery for 2 1/2 years from the outset of the battery activation in October 1961 to April 1964. My visit here today makes me feel as though I've come back home again.

My presentation will cover 4 different areas with suggestions.

1. The Bn Civil-Military Relations from 1962 to 1970
2. Current Civil-Military Relations from 1971 to Present
3. The KAF Council Activities
4. Matters involving business entertainers (Local Prostitutes)
5. Suggestions

1. 62-70년까지의 大隊 軍民관계
2. 71년 以後의 최근의 軍民관계
3. 한미친선자문회 활동
4. 위안부 관계
5. 제안 사항

I would like to make it clear that this presentation is solely based on my personal knowledge through the years of experience gained in the performance of duty.

저의 설명 내용은 그간 근무해오는中 얻어진 경험을 통한 개인적 지식에 의한 것임을 명백히 하고저 합니다

Let's take a look at the Bn Civil-Military Relations up to 1970.

The whole battalion truly enjoyed the Korean-American Relationship with the local community and had accomplished many valuable community projects through the AFAK (Armed Forces Assistance to Korea) program. Under this program several thousand dollars were spent for the purchase of the construction materials such as cement, lumber, and steel bars.

62년에서 70년까지의 大隊 軍民 관계는 대단히 원활하였으며 AFAK 원조를 통하여 지역사회 개발에 많은 성과를 걸우었읍니다 AFAK 원조 계획에 의거하여 수천 수만의 美화가 세멘트 목재 철근 等 건축자재 구입에 투입되였읍니다

239

KAFC Council which was known as Community Relations Advisory Council discussed programs of the community needs and the battery submitted requests for materials through the AFAK program. Up to 1970 this Bn had sponsored a number of projects of which major accomplishments showed as below:

School Class Rooms	$ 5,600	Sihung, Namyang-myon Ansong-kun, Yongdungpo-ku, Seoul
Public Bridges	$ 2,050	Sihung-dong, Kwachon-myon, Ansong-kun
Orphanages	$ 3,300	Kunja-myon, Sinlim-dong, Seoul

KAFC 그당시는 "지역사회 자문회"가 지역사회 발전에 유익한 사업을 토의하여 결정되면 각 中隊에서는 자재 신청을하여 지역개발에 유용하게 기증하여드렸읍니다 그 中 몇가지 例를 들면

In addition to the above projects, various other assistance and support were rendered by the batteries of this unit to the communities as the battery projects, which included: Micro-Libraries, Potable water supplys while in droughts, Heavy equipment assistance, and transportation assistance. Much of the rural community development was a result of the US assistnce during the period prior to 1970.

위의 AFAK 業務外에도 각 中隊에서는 中隊계획下에 "마을 문고" 기증, 한해시 음료水공급 중장비 동원 차량 지원等 대민 지원을 해 드렸읍니다 따라서 지방 지역사회는 70年代以前 美軍援助에 많은 도움을받은바 있읍니다

The local populace also had strong confidence in the US Army and showed a favoralbe attitude toward local units. The full US military strength also had contributed greatly to the welfare of the villagers, who enjoyed plenty enough money circulating in a tiny village.

기지촌 주민들도 美軍들에 好意的 이였읍니다 당시의 충족된 병력은 지역 기지촌 민간의 유대 교류等을 통하여 많은 외화를 뿌렸든것도 사실입니다

240

CRAC Councils were held regularly once a month, with sponsorship alternating between the battery and the community.

지역사회 자문회도 美軍과 인촌面 사이 交代로 月 一回式 정규적으로 개최되였읍니다.

2. Now, let's take a look at the situation that developed after 1970.

Right after we opened the door of the year 1970, the US aid program through AFAK was discontinued and the AFAK was abolished. I would say that most every base community throughout the Republic of Korea was benefited by the AFAK program one way or another.

이제 1970년以後의 상황을 살펴보겠읍니다
70년에 들어서자 AFAK中断 폐지되고
사실 대한민국 전역을 통하여 기지부근지역사회가 이모저모로
AFAK의 도움을 받은것이사실

Toward the middle of the year of 1971, some unit forces of the US army stationed in Korea were rumored to be withdrowing from Korea, and it soon became a reality. A number of US vehicles were turned over to the ROK Army. Vehicle assistance for the community was limited. Villages throughout the country where US Army stationed had less activities and projects because of the reduced number of soldiers. The missile batteries did not have as many resouces available to help local villages as they used to have. CRAC Council meetings had very limited items of agenda for discussion, as they could not do much in the way of material help for the community.

71년中간에 미군철수說 곧 철수가 断행되였읍니다
얼마후 美軍部隊 차량等 장비도 한국軍에 이관되였읍니다
지역사회 존재하는 車량支援이 어려워졌읍니다 장비와 인원이
감축됨으로因하여 対民지원사업等 美軍活動이 둔화 되였읍니다
CRAC 의원회는 그다음 議題범위가 극히 한정이 되어버렸읍니다
실질적인 지역 대민활동이 어려워졌기 때문에 지은

On the other hand, however, Korean industry started to grow remarkably and the ROK government enjoyed the economic growth achieved during the 1st and 2nd five-year plan. While this nation was stepping forward to attain the established goal of the export industry, majority businessmen and city people gradually realized the possibility to achieve a "self-sustaining" economy. However, those villagers in the base communities showed very little improvements in living conditions and were still in a position to rely on the US army assistance, with the army having few if any resouces to offer.

한편 그러나 71년에 들어서면서 우리韓국은 一.二次 五개년경제계획의成功
놀라운 경제적 발전을 보게 되였읍니다 우리한국에 경제적으로
전진 발전하는데 있어 이나라 商工人과 都市民들은

241

전처- 自主自治경제 의 가능성을 깨닫게 되었읍니다
다만 이같은 발전 다변형이 이곳 기지촌 주변까지는 아직 미치지
못하고 있으며 이곳 주변 등은 아직도 美軍부대에 依存하여
生計가 마련되는 實情에 있읍니다.

In early 1972 the term " Community Relations Advisory Council " was re-designated to " Korean-American Friendship Council " and opened a new approach to Korean-American Relations.

이리하여 1972년에 "CRAC" 위원회가 "KAFC"로
명칭을 바꾸게 되었으며 이제 韓美 관계에 새로운 접근의
문을 두드리게 되었읍니다

3. Let me talk to you now about the KAFC Council activities in the rural communities. Membership -the number of Korean members ranges from 5 to 15 consisting of each different organizational head to be represented by either myon-chief or dong-chief according to each respective administrative jurisdiction. Normally 5 to 10 US members also attend with the Bn commander or battery commander acting as co-chairman. The meeting is held once a month or by monthly. As you already know the council members discuss matters of mutual interest. The primary interest of all is whether the battery or Bn could assist a community projects by furnishing transportation or materials. Generally, the assistance by US component is in the form of transportation, medical care for orphans and needy villagers, some donation of school supplies, etc.,

KAFC의 構成 會員 Korean - 5人 — 15人 面.洞長=議長
美 5人 — 10人 大隊長.中隊長"
月 一回 또는 二개月 一回
相互의 관심事에 관하여 ~~[illegible]~~ 討議 그러나 支援을 청하는 사항
이 핵심임 美軍 지원사항 = 차량, 의료진료-고아원
學生들에 學用品等 기증

The Bn Hq KAF Council conducted tours of US Tac site and the US AFB in Osan during the past seven months which attracted the interest of high Korean dignitaries as Congressman and Ku-chief of Yongdungpo, Seoul as well as other Korean members.

大隊本部 KAFC 지난 6.7개月間 미사일 기지. 및 오산
美공군기지 訪問 이러한 견학은 韓국정부 要人들(국회의원)
구청장 의 관심을 끌었음

242

Through these tours the members became better acquainted with the mission of 1/2 ADA battalion and obtained a high confidence in the Air Defense of Korea by US Army. The Bn Hq KAF Council is scheduled to visit Panmunjom on 14 June 1973.

이러한 見學을 통하여 미사일부대의 임무에 대하여 깊은 인식을 갖었음
美軍에 의한 防空임무 수행에 한국人에 깊은 신뢰를 얻음
大隊本部 — 판문점 訪問 6月14日

Through these activities Koreans and Americans will come to understand better and will realize that we pursue the same goal, that is peace, prosperity in the principle of democracy and free institution.

(9) 이러한 행사를 통하여 韓美兩국人들은 이해하고 나아가 民主主義와 自由民主制度의 원칙下에 平和와 번영의 共同목표를 추구한다는 것을 이해하게 될것입니다

As I described earlier, the KAFC activities have been somewhat restricted in the scope of its capability in accomplishing local projects. I think we have arrived in a turning point for revitalization of the council with renewed understanding that US and Koreans should equally endeavor to maintain sound relations and to promote a spirit of mutual cooperation and better understanding. The role of the Korean members for mutual relations cannot be over emphasized.

KAFC 기능이 위축되어 있음 이제 우리는 韓美兩국人이 相互의 理解와 협조정신을 앙양하여 서로가 동등하도록 공동노력을 기울인다는 새로운 인식으로 KAFC 기관에 活力을 넣어야 하는 전환점에 到達하였다고 생각합니다
韓人측의 이러한 역할이 크게 강조되어져야 하겠읍니다

The council will have to seek some cultural activities in which Korean members can take initiative in accomplishing them. Frankly, the Korean side seems to have had some problems as to how the expenses could be covered when the Korean side had to sponsor the meeting. For both Koreans and Americans it will be much discouraging if there is little fund available for the Korean-American Relations programs.

따라서 韓人측에서 솔선하여 추진시킬 方案의 하나로
KAFC 가 文化的 행사를 主催해 나아가야 할
韓人側 主催時 애로사항 (경비 문제)
KAFC 행사에 쓸 기금 조달이 필요함

243

Normally KAFC members of both components try to avoid discussion on delicate matters, as they may lead to some misunderstanding or controversial issues. Therefore, in many cases, the meeting is conducted in diplomatic and formal manner. It would be desirable for the council to discuss programs which may involve many Americans and Koreans, for example, in participation of sports events or visits to cultural sites.

KAFC 会談 — 外交的 의례적 회의
심각한 문제 기피증
보다 많은 韓美人이 참여할수 있는 行事, 운동경기
그외 관광 방문

4. Matters involving business entertainers (Prostitutes)
美大隊 위안부에 관련된 문제에 관하여

While KAFC is met with a few ranking officers and NCOs and their identical Korean counterparts from the community, a number of lower ranking Enlisted Men go off-post to meet business women or prostitutes in the village for physical relations.

KAFC는 제한된 數의 美軍장교 및 韓人기관장 사이의 모임인데 多數 졸병들은 위안부를 相対로한 관계를 맺고 있음

Throughout the battalion there are 172 such business women scattered in each different village. A breakdown figure shows: HQ -42 Alpha-33 Bravo-26 Charlie - 39 and Delta 32. The ages range from 18 to 40. Average education is graduation of elementary school. Their average monthly income is about 80 dollars in the line batteries areas and 100 dollars in the Hq area.

大隊 42 A 33 B 26 C 39 D 32
国卒 月收 80 — 100 (大隊)

A VD check is conducted at least once a week in all battery areas and twice a week in the Sihung area. VD check is conducted quite regularly by the local health officials. VD rates in the Bn are relatively high. Some unregistered girls are living in the village in an effort to evade the VD check. Living circomstances of the Korean people in the outlaying districts still remain to be traditional, same as country farmers. These women eat and live in the same environment.

성병 검진 — 정규로 주 一回 주 二回 (大隊) ~~비등록위안부~~
大隊 성병 보균율이 大体로 높은 実情임니다 → 비등록
생활실태 — 농촌의 생활 실태와 同一

244

There are no recreational facilities in the village for GIs and their girl friends. In Namyang near Charlie battery, a public bath house was built in last November for the villagers by the Hwasong-kun chief.

오락시설 — 全無 ㄷ 공동목욕탕 (화성군) 72年 11月
(美軍과 위안부를 위한) 남양七里 70万원投入

Most business women speak slang, broken English and use their hands and body to express their thought and desires. Sometimes outside investigators come to check these women, creating much noise and publicity in the village and causing arguments with the GIs. Because of the language barrier the arguments could develop into serious fights. These prostitutes could be a source of trouble of all kinds. Some sort of educational program is desirable for these women to improve their conducts and behavior.

위안부 — 은어 등 토막영어 손짓발짓도 사용
수사기관에서 [illegible] 찾아오는데 — 때때로 美軍과 시비
교양강좌 등 필요

5. Suggestions

The KAFC needs to be strengthened so that matters of mutual interest can be thoroughly handled and resolved.

KAFC 기능강화

The KAFC should not be construed as an aid organization. Cultural activities are encouraged for American servicemen by Korean authorities.

KAFC 원조기관이 않임
韓국정부 당국에 의하는 내려오 文化行事 등에 美軍을
참여시켜서 韓국文化를 소개하는 일들이
취해져야 한다는 생각도 있읍니다

245

The KAFC needs to be funded enough for cooperative program accomplishments.

KAFC에 보다 더 긴밀한 유대 강화. 운영하여 어떤 예산 준비의 [illegible] 필요로 느낍니다

A policeman or civil service official should be required to stay and work in the village on a permanent basis to serve as liason between the battery and civil organizations, and to help maintain security and order in the area. This liason officer should be used a a point of contact by Korean officials who come to check the village or for other purposes. This man will work in coordination with the battery personnel in official matters.

주기지부 保安과 질서 유지 및 외부 기관과 連絡하며
연락 기관으로 주재원(연락관) 常駐配置 必要

Unregistered business women should be apprehended for registration.

無登록娼 적발 등록시켜서 정기적인 검진을 받게 한다

It has been recognized that Yitaewon in Yongsan area and the Yongdungpo Train Station area have been pointed out as central gathering places of all kinds of prostitution and have long served as a source of VD. Continued checks are requested to eradicate the unregistered prostitutes and VD in these areas.

기지 비등록 위안부 창궐 (이태원. 영등포驛근처)
철저한 단속

Health and sanitory condition of business women should be checked regularly to maintain healthy villages and prevention of epidemics.

보건 위생 관계 건강한 마을 전염병 예방

A periodic unannounced inspection in the base villages by the Korean customs officials may help minimize the blackmarket activities. These inspectors may ask cooperation of the responsible battery officer. The battery should furnish him with a courtesy patrol.

246

기 안 용 지

분류기호 문서번호	미이 723 -	(전화번호)	전결규정 조 항 국장 전결사항
처리기간			국 장
시행일자	1973. 7. 23.		
보존년한			
보조기관	과 장		협조
기안책임자	양세훈	북미2과	
경유 수신 참조	교통부장관 관광국 진흥과장	발송	통제 1973.7.23
제목	동두천지역 군민관계에 대한 사항		

1973. 7 23 외무부

대 : 시설 1535 - 682

1. 동두천지역 군민관계에 관한 한국 관광유양업협회 건의에 대하여 73. 5. 25. SOFA 군민관계 분과위원회 한국측 관계위원들이 현지 조사를 실시한바 있으며, 6. 15. 개최된 동분과위원회에서 이 문제를 정식으로 제기, 미측의 시정을 촉구한바 있읍니다.

2. 금 7. 20. 에 개최된 SOFA 군민관계 분과위 제 21차 회의에서 미측이 그간의 조치내용을 아래와 같이 보고하여 왔음으로 알려드립니다.

가. 미군출입 간판문제 :

동두천지구 미군당국은 73. 8. 1. 을 기하여 미군출입 간판 전부를 철거할 계획임.

나. 업소에 대한 일방적 검열문제 :

지난 4월 이후 한국업소에 대한 미군의 일방적 검열을 일체 중지하였음.

정서 관인 발송

2417

공통서식1-2(갑) 1967. 4. 4. 승인 190mm×268mm(1급인쇄용지70g/m²) 조달청 (300,000매 인쇄)

다. 여성의 미군 영내 유치문제 :

여성의 미군 영내 출입은 관계 지방당국에도 통고하고 제반 신분증의 조사, 윤락행위 불허등 미군당국의 철저한 감독하에 실시하고 있음. 끝.

248

DEPARTMENT OF THE ARMY
HEADQUARTERS 2D INFANTRY DIVISION
OFFICE OF THE ASSISTANT CHIEF OF STAFF, G5
APO San Francisco 96224

미 제2보병사단 민사참모부 민사처

EAIDGC 1 August 1973

1973년 8월 1일

SUBJECT: Indianhead On Limits Signs

제 목: 미2사단 출입간판

Commissioner Min, Chung Kun 민 충 근 군수
Yangju-gun 양 주 군

Commissioner U, Kwang Son 우 광 선 군수
Paju-gun 파 주 군

Superintendant In, Kyu Kil 인 규 길 총경
Yangju-gun 양 주 군

Superintendant Kim, Son Chon 김 선 천 총경
Paju-gun 파 주 군

1. As a gesture of goodwill in a spirit of mutual cooperation and Korean-American Friendship, the Commanding General desires to remove the 400 Indianhead On Limits signs from all commercial establishments in North Kyonggi-do.

한미친선의 상호협조 정신에 의거한 친목의 상징으로서, 사단장은 경기도 북부지역에 있는 모든 영업 업소로부터 약 400장의 사단출입간판을 철거할것을 소망하고 있읍니다.

2. Accordingly, request you initiate action to have all such signs removed and returned to local Division Camps beginning 20 August 1973 and to be completed no later than 25 August 1973.

그러므로, 귀관 께서 1973년 8월 20일을 기준하여 이와같은 모든 간판을 철거하여 그 지역 지휘관에게 1973년 8월 25일 까지 완전히 반납되도록 조치를 취하도록 하여주심을 의뢰합니다.

249

EAIDGC
SUBJECT: Indianhead On Limits Signs
제 목: 미2사단 출입간판

1 August 1973
1973년 8월 1일

3. An inclosure is a list of the new Off Limits criteria of the division.
첨부물은 사단의 새로운 출입금지 기준표 입니다.

4. The elimination of these signs is not intended to signal any policy to decrease standards in off post establishments that cater to soldiers.
이 간판의 제거는 군인을 상대로 하는 영외 영업시설물에 대한 방침기준을 낮추려고 시도함은 아닙니다.

On the contrary, we look for continued improved conditions in the recurring problems of drugs, black market activities, theft, Venereal Disease, sanitation and racial discrimination.
이와 반대로 우리들은 순환하고 있는 마약관계, 암거래 행위관계, 절도, 성병, 위생 그리고 인종차별 문제등에 대하여 계속적으로 개선방안을 강구 하겠습니다.

Respectfully yours,
경 구

PETER D. BOORAS 피터 디. 보라스
LTC, GS 미 육군 중령
ACofS, G-5 민사참모부

CF: 참고서류배부:
Area Cdrs 지역 지휘관
KAFC Chairman 한미친선회장
PMO 헌병 사령관
PAO 공보부

2

250

OFF LIMITS AREAS

2D INFANTRY DIVISION

The following are off-limits areas and establishments within the 2d Infantry Division area of responsibility:

1. Bathing and swimming areas unless specifically approved by CG.

2. Gambling establishments, barber shops, beauty shops, auto body shops and vehicle paint shops.

3. All eating establishments with the exception of Freedom House Restaurant at Freedom Bridge and the Frontier House in Tongduchon.

4. All public streets, alleys, sidewalks, etc., during the hours of curfew (2400 - 0400 hours) unless personnel are on official business.

5. Vehicle wash points unless specifically approved by and under contract with the DPC.

6. Korean medical facilities, hospitals, dispensaries, clinics, pharmacies and drug stores.

*7. Any specific commercial establishments, areas or villages declared off limits by the CG.

*PRESENTLY OFF LIMITS (1 Aug 73)

1. Yonju-gol Reservoir and the area immediately adjacent thereto.

2. The area adjacent to both sides of the service road connecting Camp Casey with Hovey, except the NCO Academy compound, the ammo Storage area, Schoonover Bowl (football field) and adjacent small unit tactical training areas, and areas specifically designated for training by G-3, 2d Infantry Division.

3. Tongduchon Clubs: "Seoul," "Savoy," "New York," & "New House"

4. The area known as KATUSA Alley in Pobwon-ni.

251

미 제2보병사단

미군출입금지지역

다음의 곳은 미제2보병사단관내에 있는 미군 출입금지 및 출입금지 시설물입니다.

1. 특히 사단장이 인정하지 않은 목욕탕 및 수영장.
2. 도박시설물, 이발소, 미장원, 자수다소 및 차 빨기소.
3. 자유의 다리에 있는 자유의집 및 동두천에 있는 프론티어 집 이외의 모든 음식점.
4. 공무집행 이외의 모든 사람은 통행금지시간중에 (24—04시간) 모든국도, 공로길 기타 보행도로보행.
5. 기지사령관이 인정하고 계약체결을 하지않는 세차장.
6. 한국의료시설, 병원, 진료소 약방 및 약국.
* 7. 사단장이 출입금지 선언한 어떠한 영업중 시설물, 지역 또는 마을.

* 연제도서의 미군출입금지 지역 (1973년 8월 1일)

1. 영주관. 저수지 및 이에 근접된 지역.
2. 하사관학교 영내, 특약표지역, 수크넘분 (축구운동장) 그리고 부대에서 진행하는 훈련지역 및 미제2보병사단 작전부에서 설정한 지역을 제외한 모든 캠프 케이시와 캠프 호비간의 양쪽 전체지역.
3. 동두천에 있는 클라브모서: 서울, 사보이, 뉴스크 그리고 뉴하우스 클라브.
4. 범원리에 있는 소위 카무사 골목 (한국군 창녀촌).

252

외교문서 비밀해제: 주한미군지위협정(SOFA) 39
주한미군지위협정(SOFA) 군민관계 임시분과위원회 4

초판인쇄 2024년 03월 15일
초판발행 2024년 03월 15일

지은이 한국학술정보(주)
펴낸이 채종준
펴낸곳 한국학술정보(주)
주 소 경기도 파주시 회동길 230(문발동)
전 화 031-908-3181(대표)
팩 스 031-908-3189
홈페이지 http://ebook.kstudy.com
E-mail 출판사업부 publish@kstudy.com
등 록 제일산-115호(2000. 6. 19)

ISBN 979-11-7217-050-9 94340
979-11-7217-011-0 94340 (set)